FAULKNER'S YOKNAPATAWPHA COMEDY

FAULKNER'S YOKNAPATAWPHA COMEDY

Lyall H. Powers

Ann Arbor   The University of Michigan Press

Library of Congress Cataloging in Publication Data

Powers, Lyall Harris, 1924–
  Faulkner's Yoknapatawpha comedy.

  Includes index.
  1. Faulkner, William, 1897–1962—Criticism and
interpretation. I. Title.
PS3511.A86Z9464   813'.5'2   79–23140
ISBN 0–472–08727–4

For Loretta
and in memory of
Henrietta Holt

Acknowledgments

I want to express my gratitude to several of my colleagues who read and commented on various pieces of this study when it was in manuscript—Professors Sheridan Baker, Joseph Blotner, John Raeburn, Mary Rucker, and Earl Schulze; to numerous students of mine whose critical enquiry and observation have influenced my thinking about Faulkner, especially Judy Goble Brandon, Joanne Vanish Creighton, Karen Gulliver, John Hart, Douglas Kevorkian, Jonathan Rowe, Mary Walsh, and the late Grace Blakey; and to Mr. Toby Holzman, for his kind cordiality as Faulknerian bibliophile, and especially for providing the copy of Martin Dain's photograph of Faulkner.

I also wish to thank the staff of the Manuscript Department of the Alderman Library in the University of Virginia for their graciously allowing me access to the Faulkner collection, the Rackham Foundation of the University of Michigan for grants to help support my research and the preparation of the manuscript, and Sheryl S. Pearson for meticulously typing the manuscript and for reading it with a steady critical eye.

I owe a special debt of gratitude to the late Henrietta Holt, whose hospitality and generosity aided greatly in the final preparation of the manuscript. I am particularly grateful to my wife, Loretta, for her devotion and for her careful scrutiny and criticism of the whole manuscript. And finally, to those special people—Krysti, Christopher, Robin, Graham, and Victoria—I owe a debt of gratitude they wot not of.

Contents

Death destroys a man, but the idea of death saves him—that is the best account of it that has yet been given. Squalor and tragedy can beckon to all that is great in us; and strengthen the wings of love.

E. M. Forster, *Howards End,* XLI

Introduction

Malcolm Cowley began the recovery of Faulkner's work from its limbo of neglect and even scorn when he put together *The Portable Faulkner* for Viking Press in 1945. Five years later the award of the Nobel Prize confirmed that recovery. Books about Faulkner now outnumber the books Faulkner himself wrote, yet he remains in a somewhat more sombre light than he deserves. He is still considered by some to be merely the melancholy singer of the fall of the South, or the pessimistic recorder of the modern wasteland world that ensued. But the main thrust of his major fiction has, in truth, always been optimistic, hopeful, encouraging. Some of the most satisfactory expositions of individual works have failed to grasp Faulkner's optimistic sweep, neglecting the whole for the parts; and some of the best studies of the whole corpus have also failed of that perception. Virtually from the outset of his career Faulkner's fiction implicitly dramatized the attitude he enunciated simply and explicitly on accepting the Nobel Prize:

> I believe that man will not merely endure: he will prevail. He is immortal not merely because he alone among creatures has an inexhaustible voice, but because he has a soul, a spirit capable of compassion and sacrifice and endurance.

And he concluded that ringing affirmative by echoing Shelley on the duty and privilege of the poet, presumably including himself: "to help man endure by lifting his heart, by reminding him of the courage and honor and hope and pride and compassion and pity and sacrifice which have been the glory of his past. The poet's voice need not be merely the record of man, it can be one of the props, the pillars to help him endure and prevail."[1]

I believe we can more truly appreciate Faulkner's achievement and recognize his optimistic attitude toward mankind if we attend to a feature of his fiction largely overlooked—the regular recurrence of two dominant themes and an attendant third. One of the themes is "The Self-Destructiveness of Evil." Mr. Walter Brylowski correctly contends that Faulkner believed in the persistence of evil;[2] and it would be fatuous to suggest that Faulkner thought that evil would be destroyed, defeated before the Last Day. Yet he evidently did believe that man can not only withstand ever-present evil but even overcome it, not simply endure it but prevail over it. Moreover, Faulkner's fiction constantly shows that the human agents of evil inevitably work their own defeat and ultimate destruction. In the Yoknapatawpha Saga, the South's fall in the Civil War is the commanding metaphor for this self-destruction. We see repeatedly that the South's evil brought on its own demise, wrought its own collapse through its social organizations and its prevailing assumptions and attitudes. The South's very foundations, its exploitation of people and of the land— all this in the name of chivalry and gentility (which virtues, indeed, it is plausibly reputed to have achieved and maintained in rigid restriction)—brought about its own frustration, defeat, and ruin. That suicidal tendency of evil to destroy itself is pathetically carried in and exhibited by some of the more attractive figures of the postbellum world of Yoknapatawpha, a terrible heritage. This is Faulkner's encompassing metaphor, and it is evident not only in the individual novels but in the broad sweep of the Saga as a whole.

A second dominant theme, regularly recurrent and quite consistent, is the "Theme of the Second Chance," an opportunity to succeed morally where one has earlier failed. In a given novel this sometimes involves a repetition of characters and circumstances, sometimes with either characters or circumstances different but parallel. We might call this the "Quo Vadis Theme," for it is most evident in those novels depicting Christ-like characters (Benjy Compson in *The Sound and the Fury* and Joe Christmas in *Light in August,* for instance, and—outside the Saga—the corporal in *A Fable*). It works by giving specific individuals and sometimes society as a whole a second chance as when Christ appeared on the Appian Way before Peter, who was fleeing persecution in Rome. "Domine, quo vadis?" Peter is supposed to have asked. Replying that He was going into Rome to be crucified a second time, Christ thus gives Peter a Second Chance. Peter returns to Rome, and crucifixion, compensating for his earlier failure in thrice denying Christ, accepting the moral responsibility that love imposes, relying on the courage that love fosters and on which, reciprocally, love depends for its fruition. Faulkner gave explicit expression to the theme in his comment on the provenance of *A Fable:*

> The notion occurred to me one day in 1942 shortly after Pearl Harbor and the beginning of the last great war. Suppose—who might that unknown soldier be? Suppose that had been Christ again, under that fine big cenotaph with the eternal flame burning on it? That He would naturally have got crucified again. . . .[3]

Although few characters in Faulkner's fiction manage to rise to the Second Chance, his treatment of those who tragically fail to grasp the Second Chance nevertheless amounts to an affirmative statement about human possibilities. These depictions of the failure of love and courage, like Shakespeare's great tragedies, are neither depressing nor pessimistic: the fall of the hero is made understandable, his failure is clearly demonstrated and his weakness clearly defined. As we suffer through the very demonstration and definition of his weakness we learn what human qualities enable a man to prevail. So with the Greek tragedies, where, though the hero lies under a curse, we see him earn his fate and bring down that curse upon himself. We thus learn what man should do by seeing what he should not have done. And Faulkner's depiction of the Second Chance is finally neither depressing nor pessimistic as it defines through failure the qualities necessary for human hope and success. His fiction, like the great tragedies, is thus morally instructive and ultimately optimistic.

The attendant theme involves characters who, with varying success, confront and oppose the Self-Destructive agents of Evil, or attempt to aid those given the Second Chance, or are themselves successful in grasping it—a Faulknerian version of Matthew Arnold's "Saving Remnant":

> We have heard Plato speaking of the very small remnant which honestly sought wisdom. *The remnant!*—it is the word of the Hebrew prophets also, and especially is it the word of the greatest of them all, Isaiah. Not used with the despondency of Plato, used with far other power informing it, and with a far other future awaiting it, filled with fire,

filled with hope, filled with faith, filled with joy, this term itself, *the remnant,* is yet Isaiah's term as well as Plato's.

Arnold asks us to do homage to Isaiah's

> indestructible conviction that such a world, with its prosperities, idolatries, oppression, luxury, pleasures, drunkards, careless women, governing classes, systems of policy, strong alliances, shall come to nought and pass away; that nothing can save it. Let us do homage, also, to his indestructible conviction that States are saved by their righteous remnant. . . .

Then follows Arnold's clarification: "What is saving? . . . Plato and the sages . . . answer: 'To love righteousness, and to be convinced of the unprofitableness of iniquity.' And Isaiah and the prophets . . . answer . . . that what is saving is to 'order one's conversation aright'; to 'cease to do evil'; to 'delight in the law of the Eternal'; and to 'make one's study in it all day long.' "[4] Arnold's words are nicely applicable to Faulkner's world of Yoknapatawpha. Characters such as Dilsey, Byron Bunch, Bayard Sartoris of *The Unvanquished,* Lucas Beauchamp, Mrs. Littlejohn, V. K. Ratliff, Eckrum and Wallstreet Panic Snopes, and Charles Mallison comprise a Saving Remnant— those in whom our hope may safely reside.

These themes have, surprisingly, been overlooked. Yet, variously handled, turned this way and that, worried and examined in an anguished endeavor to understand and expose both the plight of Faulkner's South and, in those terms, the plight of the human condition generally, these themes surely comprise the fundamental informing skeletal framework of all his Yoknapatawpha novels. And their effect is to inspire in the attentive and sympathetic reader a sense of hopefulness, of encouragement, of optimism.

*

I have confined my discussion to the major Yoknapatawpha novels. With the possible exception of *A Fable,* Faulkner's greatest works are clearly those that deal with his "postage stamp of native soil," Yoknapatawpha County. Those novels, comprising a "saga," an organically whole opus, indeed belong together. I have, then, omitted the poetry and short stories and such early or digressive works as *Soldiers Pay, Mosquitoes, Pylon,* and the imposing *A Fable;* I have also omitted *The Wild Palms* and *Knight's Gambit.* The slightly Hemingwayesque *Wild*

[handwritten margin notes: "a costly limitation when measure 'incur'"
see p. 17
]

Palms is perhaps tangential to the Yoknapatawpha material. The tall convict of "Old Man" might be a distant cousin of the Bundrens of *As I Lay Dying,* or of the Gowries of *Intruder in the Dust,* or even of Byron Bunch of *Light in August,* but the couple in "Wild Palms" belongs rather to the world of *Mosquitoes.* The stories of *Knight's Gambit* are mainly peripheral. Certainly Gavin Stevens plays an important role in the Yoknapatawpha Saga, but his development in *Knight's Gambit* makes him a kind of Mississippian Perry Mason or a lightweight Rex Stout: his role there is limited, and he is only an incomplete sketch of the man who appears in the Saga proper.

I have chosen to retain *Sartoris* rather than replace it with the recently published *Flags in the Dust* (its original version) as the initial novel of the Saga. Scholars are understandably grateful for the availability of *Flags,* for it helps make explicit Faulkner's intent in his history of the Sartoris family. There the incestuous nature of the relationship between Horace and Narcissa Benbow is indelibly underlined, the relationship of Horace with the Mitchells (and especially with Belle) is more fully developed and detailed, we are given the account of Horace's affair with Belle's sister Joan and much more information about the whole Sartoris family—particularly about young Johnny and the middle generation between the old and young Bayards which is missing from *Sartoris.* Whether all this additional information makes *Flags* a superior novel is debatable, a matter of taste, as Mr. Douglas Day wisely acknowledges in his introduction to the novel. This is not the place, however, to engage in a full-scale comparison of the respective merits of the two novels; mention of one or two representative features must suffice. The nature of the Horace and Narcissa relationship as it is presented in *Sartoris* emerges clearly enough without all i's dotted and all t's crossed. Excision of Horace's affair with Belle's sister seems to me distinctly to improve the work, since involvement in an additional affair is out of character for the Horace we meet again in *Sanctuary,* as it is, indeed, for the Horace otherwise developed in both *Flags* and *Sartoris.* It may well be that Faulkner's recognition of that weakness in his original conception of Horace aided his decision to absorb Horace in the character of Gavin Stevens, who was already competing (as a more appropriate conception) for Faulkner's attention as early as *Light in August. Flags in the Dust,* then, properly belongs with its contemporary "Father Abraham" manuscript, representing the early spadework of the Saga rather than a finished piece of the Saga itself.[5]

I have also omitted *The Reivers* as falling outside the Saga proper; it is, rather, an engaging and altogether charming "Afterword." If it treats of Faulkner's familiar county, it is Yoknapatawpha by moonlight. The terms that Edmond L. Volpe uses to describe the novel— "a fairy-tale world," "a never-never land," "a fantasy world"—strike me as sufficiently apt, and they reinforce Joseph Blotner's recognition of the "mellow glow" that tinges the narrative.[6] There is a distinct difference in character and tone between *The Reivers* and the novel which properly completes the Saga even as it completes the Snopes trilogy. Faulkner had informed Random House that "with *The Mansion* he had completed the last of his planned labors."[7] And the testimony afforded by *The Mansion* itself argues (as I show in chap. 13) that in it Faulkner realized that expressed intention. He had indeed "broken the pencil" with which he had fashioned the Yoknapatawpha Saga. For in spite of its undeniable charm, *The Reivers* remains a kind of coda, a late-blooming comic sport, and thus does not fall within the purview of this study. Faulkner wrote it with a new and different pencil—one with a softer lead.

Each of the thirteen chapters which follow is devoted to a single novel; and in each I have given a reasonably full reading of the novel in question in order to indicate how it is actually informed by the pervasive themes I have mentioned. Of course I am generally indebted to the various scholars and critics familiar to students of Faulkner, but I have referred to their work only when it seemed that reference was imperative—to acknowledge specific indebtedness, to recognize analogous interpretation, to indicate crucial difference of opinion. Throughout the study I have tried to keep the sense of the polemical at a minimum; and I have made no attempt to provide a survey of Faulknerian scholarship and criticism.

Finally, the Yoknapatawpha Saga is a unified opus, very like the old traditional sagas, not simply with those three persistent themes I have defined but also with a developed *agon* between protagonist and antagonist leading to a comic resolution. The concluding chapter will offer an explanation of that facet of the Saga. My hope is thus to increase our appreciation of this rather extraordinary literary phenomenon and of its talented artificer and also to amplify in further detail Michael Millgate's just estimate of him:

> Faulkner's achievement can be adequately estimated only by our seeing him as a great novelist in the context not merely of the South, or even of the United States, but of the whole western tradition.[8]

Movement One

What shall we say who have knowledge
Carried to the heart? Shall we take the act
To the grave? Shall we, more hopeful, sct up the grave
In the house? The ravenous grave?

Allen Tate, "Ode to the Confederate Dead"

Second Chance not Taken ; War/Love
     Civil War — WWI
     Caroline Bayard — Young Bayard
     Caroline White — Narcissa

Loveless Self-Conveying community
     Bayard: creative & champion

Believing we shall be exempted
From the general condemnation
Because our self-respect is tempted
To incest not adultery . . . .

W. H. Auden, *"For the Time Being:*
A Christmas Oratorio"

I

Sartoris

Faulkner explained the source of his late novel *A Fable* by saying that
the idea occurred to him in 1942: "Suppose—who might that unknown soldier be? Suppose that had been Christ again, under that
fine big cenotaph with the eternal flame burning on it? That He
would naturally have got crucified again."[1] His association of the
Unknown Soldier— really Everyman as victim of war—with Christ is
particularly significant. The implications are, for our time, not so
much religious as humanistic: Christ is seen as the best of Man—and
hence, in Faulkner's association, the Unknown Soldier is like the best
of Man victimized by war. In Faulkner's fiction, from *Soldiers Pay* to
A Fable and beyond, war is a constant metaphor for fraternal strife.
As in T. S. Eliot's *The Waste Land,* so in Faulkner's work, all wars are
the same war, expressive not only of man's inhumanity to man but
also of brother killing brother—the legacy of Cain. And by extension, the dilemmas that are subsequent to war—and classically, of
course, the situation of the South after the American Civil War—are
shown to be consequent to that fratricide. Furthermore, by associating the particular victim with Christ (as in the quotation above),
Faulkner implicitly affirms that the fratricide destroys the best we
have: fratricide is tantamount to suicide.

In Faulkner's first major novel of the Yoknapatawpha Saga, *Sartoris* (1929), young Bayard Sartoris represents the society which has
attained the guilt of the Great War of 1914–18. The novel presents
that war as the Second Chance by establishing a series of parallels
which encourage comparison between the Civil War and World War
I. The association of the two Bayards—the old grandfather with his

memories of the war between the states, and his grandson, a freshly
returned veteran of the first Great War—is reenforced by their particular ghosts, both named John. The spirit of Colonel John Sartoris,
father of old Bayard, enters in the first line of the novel like a
latter-day Hamlet, Senior, and with the same message—"Remember
me!"—and broods thereafter over the life of his son and of the old
Negro retainer, Simon. He is "that arrogant shade which dominate[s] the house and the life that [goes] on there and the whole
scene itself."[2] That spirit represents the greatness that has gone, the
best that was and is no more—"like the creatures of that prehistoric
day that were too grandly conceived and executed either to exist
very long or to vanish utterly when dead from an earth shaped and
furnished for punier things" (p. 20). In a moment of dismay over
the way things are going, old Simon appeals to that heroic spirit,
expressing old Bayard's sentiments as well as his own:

> ". . . You jes' got ter lay down de law ter 'um, Marse John; wid all
> dese foreign wars en sich de young folks is growed away fum de
> correck behavior; dey don't know how ter conduck deyselfs in de
> gent'mun way. Whut you reckon folks gwine think when dey sees yo'
> own folks ridin' in de same kine o' rig trash rides in? You jes' got ter
> resert yo'self, Marse John. Ain't Sartorises sot de quality in dis country
> since befo' de War? And now jes' look at 'um." [Pp. 103–4]

This contrast between the epoch of the Civil War and that of World
War I is not just a red herring. It is typical of the ambiguous attitude
which exists in this novel and in much of Faulkner's early work.
Although the older war scene *was* fundamentally the same as the
later and its graces were merely superficial, they were graces nevertheless, and the later scene lacks even the superficial graces of the
"bad" old days.

The spirit of the younger John, great-grandson of the old Colonel, also enters early with the blatantly bereft young Bayard—enters
in the first words the young Bayard speaks:

> "Bayard, son?" old Bayard said. Young Bayard stood in the moon-
> light. His eyesockets were cavernous shadows.
> "I tried to keep him [brother John] from going up there on that
> goddam little popgun," he said at last with brooding savageness.
> [Pp. 50–51]

And that spirit dominates young Bayard's life. Furthermore, the
point is made frequently that John was the better of the twin

brothers—the more capable, the more attractive, the superior
hunter, etc. War has claimed both older and younger John Sartoris—
not immediately and directly, in the case of Colonel John, but definitely by extension—and, in that respect, the loss of young John in
World War I is an example of the Second Chance refused.

War is the product of the society which the Sartorises not only
represent but to a large extent lead. They make the world and the
wars go round. Horace Benbow observes: "Rotten luck they have.
Funny family. Always going to wars, and always getting killed"
(p. 143). One part of the novel's strategy is to emphasize the self-
destructiveness that war is—the classic synecdoche for man's inhumanity to man. Faulkner's preoccupation with the Civil War is, although inevitable, nevertheless most fortunate. As the American war
which pitted American against American, brother against brother, it
provided him with a useful metaphoric emblem as well as a realistic
background. The focus of *Sartoris* on young Bayard and John expresses most forcefully the effect of war: it deprives one of one's
better self, leaves one incomplete, amputated, insufficient. And the
particular bitterness here derives from the suggestion that Bayard is
in some appreciable degree responsible for John's fate. Aunt Jenny
scolds Bayard, "What did you expect, after the way you raised
him? . . . You're the oldest. . . . " (p. 52). And there is a confirming
reflection of this in Bayard's words, much later, as he frets over the
death of his grandfather (for which he is unambiguously responsible); there he scolds himself, *"You, who deliberately do things your judgment tells you may not be successful, even possible, are afraid to face the
consequences of your own acts. . . . You did it! You caused it all; you killed
Johnny"* (p. 251). Faulkner's familiar equation, fratricide is suicide, is
thus stated clearly enough in that passage: fratricidal strife destroys
man—or, at the very least, the best of man.

But of course the guilt is not Bayard's alone. It is his family's and,
as that family represents society, the guilt is all of society's. Indeed
the quotation above, in the very ambiguity of its expression, manages to convey that idea. Bayard will accept his guilt, but points to
the culpable others: *"the consequences of your own acts.* Then again
something bitter and deep and sleepless in him blazed out in vindication and justification and accusation; what, he knew not, blazing
out at what, Whom, he did not know: *You did it! . . . "* (p. 251). Thus
Bayard is victimizer, but representatively the victimizer. And as representative, he suffers most acutely.

From the outset of our acquaintance with young Bayard Sartoris, the fact is borne in upon us that his wretchedness results from the loss of Johnny, his twin brother—his other half, almost. His first speech in the novel refers to that loss; his first moment alone—in the room "which he and John had shared in the young masculine violence of their twinship"—is likewise painfully eloquent:

> He was thinking of his dead brother; the spirit of their violent *complementing* days lay like dust everywhere in the room, . . . stopping his breathing, and he went to the window and flung the sash crashing upward and leaned there, gulping air into his lungs like a man who has been submerged and who still cannot believe that he has reached the surface again. [P. 54; my italics]

Bayard's bereft, incomplete condition is responsible for most of his behavior in the novel. That behavior has all the air of a frantic and unrelenting pursuit, a violent urge to regain what has been lost. There are three facets to that behavior. First, Bayard attempts to recapture the lost youth that was once theirs—his and Johnny's; to regain the condition of innocence. He undertakes a sentimental journey through the scenes of their childhood and adolescence. The most memorable and significant part of the journey takes him to the MacCallums' place, which is described in terms that suggest a prelapsarian state: at the MacCallums' Bayard is back in the bosom of Edenic nature, the wilderness of old Ben (the remarkable and symbolic bear of *Go Down, Moses*). As though to underline the quality of life in this setting Faulkner adds a detail he will use again—a symbol to distinguish between the fallen world of time in which man is driven by his timepiece, and the world still in tune with natural cycles (and, by extension, with eternity): the MacCallums' clock is wonderfully arrested, "deriding that time whose servant it once had been" (p. 250). But there is no help here for Bayard; he discovers that this retrogressive move simply aggravates his sense of loss.

The second facet of Bayard's pursuit is his attempt to fill the void in his life through marriage. The instinct seems sound enough—it is an attempt to replace the love that has gone. Bayard woos and wins Narcissa Benbow. Again his attempt fails. Whatever love Narcissa can offer Bayard is insufficient; the fault is not hers but rather Bayard's incompleteness—the missing Johnny blights his marriage bed: "in the yellow firelight of their room she would cling to him, or lie crying quietly in the darkness beside his rigid body, with a ghost

between them" (p. 240; cf. p. 234).[3] The theme of the <u>Second</u>
<u>Chance</u> is stated here in Bayard's marriage as it is elsewhere: Narcissa is his <u>second wife</u>. And the scene just alluded to echoes a much
earlier one in the novel, where Bayard and his first wife lay in that
same bed—

> the last night of his leave, the night before he went back to England
> and out to the Front again, where John already was. . . . and she lay
> holding his arm with both hands against her breast while they talked
> quietly, soberly at last.
>   But he had not been thinking of her then. When he thought of her
> who lay rigid in the dark beside him, holding his arm tightly to her
> breast, it was only to be a little savagely ashamed of the heedless thing
> he had done to her. He was thinking of his brother whom he had not
> seen in over a year, thinking that in a month they would see one
> another again. [Pp. 53–54]

From the outset, then, the impression conveyed is that Bayard's
marriage difficulties result from his being separated from his brother; and that separation (quite clearly) is the fault of the war. The
mimetic features of this aspect of Bayard's life—their figurative, representative quality—are surely evident. The idea expressed is simply
that war sets brothers apart, deranges and frustrates young manhood, renders impossible the realization of love. And the marriage
to Narcissa marks the Second Chance for Bayard; again Bayard fails,
or rather love again fails him. (It might be added, however, that
healthy, whole men do not woo and marry *Narcissa*—more of this in
a moment.)

The <u>third</u> aspect, <u>Bayard's headlong flight from unbearable life</u>, 3,
follows naturally enough. Apparently bent on self-destruction, he
hurls himself along the road to death. In his automobile, on the
stallion, and finally in the airplane, his eagerly sought destination is
death. It is perfectly evident that that headlong career is Bayard's
attempt to rejoin Johnny in the undiscovered country of death—to
regain in that reunion the wholeness he cannot recapture on this
side of the grave. Bayard's fantasy about the relative "life" and
"death" of him and Johnny is instructive:

> Perhaps he [Bayard] was dead, and he recalled that morning, relived
> it with strained attention from the time he had seen the first tracer-
> smoke until, from his steep bank, he watched the flame burst like the
> gay flapping of an orange pennon from the nose of John's Camel and

saw his brother's familiar gesture and the sudden awkward sprawl of
his plunging body as it lost equilibrium in mid-air; relived it again as
you might run over a printed, oft-read tale, trying to remember, feel,
a bullet going into his own body or head that might have slain him at
the same instant. That would account for it, would explain so much;
*that he too was dead and this was hell, through which he moved for ever and
ever with an illusion of quickness, seeking his brother who in turn was somewhere seeking him, never the two to meet.* [P. 258; my italics]

Thus, Bayard ends his career in one sense his own victim, inasmuch as
he and the society he represents have made life loveless and intolerable. The death of Johnny, the valuable loss, is presented as the reiteration of society's folly in war. And there is an interesting association
between Johnny and the Unknown Soldier (and, hence, with Faulkner's much later comment on his seminal idea for *A Fable*). Bayard
tells Narcissa about watching Johnny bail out of his Camel—

There was a bunch of cloud right under us and he smacked on it right
on his belly. . . . But I never could pick him up below the cloud. . . . I
couldn't find him and then I thought, that maybe I hadn't gone far
enough, so I dived again. I saw the machine crash about three miles
away, but I never could pick John up again. [Pp. 206–7]

John, then, is simply missing. He "participates" in the character of
the Unknown Soldier, sharing the cenotaph in honor of that soldier
who, nameless, stands for all the lost and unrecovered.[4]

If the theme of the Second Chance is thus expressed in terms of
the comparison between the Civil War and the first Great War, the
reiteration of fratricide, it is given additional emphasis in terms of
the twin brothers, both lost as a direct result of war, John in 1918,
and Bayard in 1919. It is as though the Sartorises, and beyond them
their whole society, have been twice bereft. As the novel moves toward its close, the focus shifts to show us Bayard as the unmistakable
victim; and indeed his victimized condition is expressed in terms that
encourage us to compare him to Christ and to regard his death—as
expressly *chosen* as Christ's was—as in some way comparable to the
crucifixion. At the close of the penultimate section of the book
young Bayard rides away from the MacCallums'. It is Christmas Eve.
He rides some distance; darkness comes; he seeks shelter at the first
dwelling he comes to—and is turned away. There is not even a stable
for him. But he is sent down the road and finds shelter in a barn. "It

was already Christmas." And his hosts, the modest Negro family, share their Christmas with him:

> The Negroes drank with him, amicably, a little diffidently—two opposed concepts antipathetic by race, blood, nature and environment, touching for a moment and fused within an illusion—humankind forgetting its lust and cowardice and greed for a day. "Chris'mus," the woman murmured shyly. "Thanky, suh." [P. 277]

Bayard came to them, a stranger, like a thief in the night, and they took him in. He leaves that "illusion," however, and rides away a second time, soon to meet his death.

The Second Chance missed—the absence of a Peter-figure in whom the answer to his "Quo vadis?" rekindles love and courage—is given peculiar emphasis by the gracious action of the Negro family which accords Bayard temporary asylum on Christmas. Their acts of eloquent and genial Charity contrast sharply with the essentially loveless and lethal action of the white society, the Sartoris world, which contains them. Not only has that world left much undone by its failure of love and courage, but it has positively done what it ought not to have done: it has waged war, but worse, it has discounted the legitimacy of the love offered by figures like Bayard's Negro hosts by discounting their role in human society. Human failure and the causes of that failure are expressed emphatically.

Perhaps "causes" is not quite the word, for it is difficult to cite this or that act in the novel as specifically a cause of Bayard's end. What Faulkner has presented, however, are the symptoms of the disease which victimizes Bayard and, indeed (which is my point), the whole dominant white society: it lacks both love and courage. *Sartoris* treats the themes as complements; it is a story of love and war—of war, certainly, and the need for courage, and of love in quite the way that J. Alfred Prufrock's Love Song treats of love. There are various unions (romantic, amorous, erotic) in the novel, interestingly interrelated, which express the plight and the failure of love. The loveless union of Bayard and Narcissa Benbow finds parallels in the relationship of Narcissa and her brother, Horace; Horace has his "other" union with Belle Mitchell, and Belle hers with Harry, her husband. And there is the unrequited love of Byron Snopes (his name is worth noting) for Narcissa. Even the relationship of old Simon and Meloney serves to extend the peculiar love theme in the novel.

Horace Benbow [handwritten in left margin]

Horace Benbow is in a way the other side of the coin to Bayard Sartoris. Bayard is incomplete and incapable of love—as his painfully frustrated union with Narcissa indicates—apparently because of the loss of Johnny. Horace is unwhole in another sense. He is a split man, both halves are there but not integrated: one half of him loves Narcissa and one half loves Belle Mitchell. He has returned from the war with two noteworthy additions to his life—a glassblowing kit and a Snopes. The significance of the latter we shall consider in a moment; the significance of the former lies in the association between his glassblowing and his love of Narcissa. Put simply, both express his desire to escape the weariness, the fever, and the fret here, where men sit and hear each other groan; his hobby represents his quest for "the meaning of peace"—somewhere, all breathing human passion far above. The association in his mind between the glass vase and Narcissa is quite explicit:

> he had set up his furnace . . . and produced one almost perfect vase of clear amber, larger, more richly and *chastely serene,* which he kept always on his night table and called by his sister's name in the intervals of apostrophizing both of them impartially in his moments of rhapsody over the realization of the meaning of peace and the unblemished attainment of it, as "Thou still unravished bride of quietness." [P. 154; my italics]

To regard a vase in this way is one thing; to regard a woman so is, of course, quite another. He persists in viewing Narcissa as the changeless, ideal, serenely peaceful, unravished bride, even after her marriage to Bayard! That is, she is in his eye actually inhuman, unreal: he denies her mortality, the inevitable "wasness" (to anticipate Judith Sutpen's use of the term in *Absalom, Absalom!*) of the human condition. Narcissa represents to him the status quo safely fixed—as Caddy Compson will to her brother Quentin in *The Sound and the Fury.*

There is at the same time an unmistakably erotic quality to the relationship of Horace and Narcissa. When she comes to meet him on his return from the war, "He . . . swept her up in his arms until her feet were off the ground, and kissed her on the mouth" (p. 139). And again:

> He came and sat on the edge of the bed. But still her [Narcissa's] eyes were antagonistic and interrogatory and the shadow of her

mouth was stubbornly cold. "Narcy?" he said. She lowered her eyes to
the book, and he added: "First, I want to apologize for leaving you
alone so often at night."

"Yes?"

He laid his hand on her knee. "Look at me." She raised her face,
and the antagonism of her eyes. "I want to apologize for leaving you
alone at night," he repeated.

"Does that mean you aren't going to do it any more, or that you're
not coming in at all?"

For a while he sat brooding on the wild repose of his hand lying on
her covered knee. Then he rose and stood beside the table again,
touching the objects there; then he returned and sat on the bed. She
was reading again, and he tried to take the book from her hand. She
resisted.

. . . He laid his hand on her knee again, stroking it through the
cover. "You aren't even surprised, are you?" [P. 209][5]

Horace tells her that he is going to marry Belle Mitchell. For, of
course, in spite of the erotic quality of their relationship, theirs is a
forbidden love—Narcissa is the unravished, the perenially chaste
(like the vase); and in order that she retain that happy feature Horace must turn for full erotic satisfaction to the easy and voluptuous
Belle Mitchell. In turning from Narcissa to Belle for this purpose,
Horace is very nearly rehearsing the stereotypical pattern of the
white Southerner who "honors" the white Lady and turns for his
"pleasure" to the Negro wench. Belle is white, to be sure, and Horace will marry her, but the unhealthy division of physical love and
spiritual worship obtains in his case.

Significantly enough, furthermore, the love of Horace and Narcissa is forbidden its erotic expression because it is incestuous. To
what extent Horace and his sister have pursued their evident erotic
interest in each other—in spite of his idealistic protestations about the
serene and chaste Narcissa—is difficult to say. The interest is sufficiently strong and its nature clearly enough defined for us to recognize it as being quite as incestuous as Quentin Compson's interest in
his sister, Caddy. And here is the initial instance in the Yoknapatawpha Saga of a motif that will become familiar in Faulkner's
work—incest employed emblematically, a synecdoche functioning to
express the general attitude (as he saw it) responsible for the South's
demise, an attitude selfish, introverted, and finally self-destructive.
The emblem of incest in Faulkner's fiction serves well to represent the
attitude of strictly exclusive "love"—love kept "in the family," as who

should say—as reductive and lethal as the self-love it ultimately is. The beloved is well named *Narcissa,* and she is at the center of the network of relationships (romantic, amorous, erotic) which function in the novel. The suggestion is strongly made that healthy, whole men do not woo and marry *Narcissa*—they do not even fall in love with her.[6]

The significance of Horace's worship of Narcissa is expressed dramatically in the parallel offered by Byron Snopes's distant worship of Narcissa. Byron apparently wants Narcissa just as a man wants a woman; his attitude is not one of simple lust nor of the idealizing worship professed by Horace. Narcissa is responsible (both personally and representatively) for the seamy side of the relationship: first, the strict caste system in whose grip she willingly functions does not permit an acknowledged liaison between her kind and the likes of Byron Snopes, poor near-trash redneck creature, and thus must pervert his otherwise normal advances; and second, she clearly enough takes the notorious flirt's perverse satisfaction in provoking Byron's advances, intending to offer no normal response to them.

The novel artfully emphasizes the near parallels among the various relationships that center upon Narcissa, juxtaposing Horace and Bayard, Horace and Byron, and by extension Bayard and Byron. The relationships of Horace and Bayard with Narcissa are legitimate, but a particular quality of them is underlined in a chance observation of Miss Jenny Du Pre's on Bayard and Narcissa before their marriage—"watching the two of them . . . with their seeming obliviousness of one another. 'He treats her like a dog would treat a cut-glass pitcher, and she looks at him like a cut-glass pitcher would look at a dog,' she told herself" (p. 171). The novel thus obliges us to notice that Horace sees Narcissa as a vase, Bayard as a cut-glass pitcher; but that in Horace's case she is a vase he has himself created, while in Bayard's she is a separate and distinct objet d'art. The distinction is sharpened by Bayard's being likened to a dog— and by the picking up, thus, of the indirect echo of Narcissa's constant accusation to Bayard, *beast! beast!* (see pp. 134, 181).

The comparison of Horace and Byron is best exemplified in section eight of Part Three, where Horace's announcement of his coming marriage to Belle Mitchell is coupled with his delivery of one of Byron's anonymous letters to Narcissa. The coincidence itself is perhaps eloquent enough, but immediately following that we find Horace's erotic dream of Belle directly juxtaposed to the Snopes letter, and certain similarities stand out distinctly.

As he removed his clothes it did seem that that heavy fading odor of Belle's body clung to them, and to his hands even after he was in bed; and clinging, shaped in the darkness beside him Belle's rich voluptuousness until within that warm, not-yet-sleeping region where dwells the mother of dreams, Belle grew palpable in ratio as his own body slipped away from him. . . . Belle had freed her mouth, and for a moment, her body still against his, she held his face in her two hands and stared at him with intent questioning eyes. "Have you plenty of money, Horace?" And "Yes," he had answered immediately, "of course I have." And then Belle again, enveloping him like a rich and fatal drug, like a motionless and cloying sea in which he watched himself drown. [P. 210]

Then, three lines later, Byron's letter of fierce frustrated love to Narcissa is disclosed:

I am trying to forget you I cannot forget you Your big eyes. . . . And how you walk I am watching you a smell you give off like a flowr. Your eyes shine with mistry and how you walk makes me sick like a fevver all night thinking how you walk. . . . Your lips like cupids bow when the day comes when I press it to mine. Like I dreamed in a fevver from heaven to Hell. . . . If you unholy love a man I will kill him.
. . . I am desprate man eat up with fevver I can not sleep for. I will not hurt you but I am desprate. . . . [P. 211]

The eyes, the attractive odor, the dreams, all mark the similarity and set up the significant distinctions. Horace is fatally "enveloped" and "drowning," a desperate man (in one sense) because he *has* Belle; Byron is desperate precisely because he *has not*—and can never really hope to have—Narcissa. And then the point of Horace's dream— Belle's too practical concern with money, and the faint suggestion that carries of her prostitution—is conspicuously absent from Byron's letter. Whereas money is evidently part of the Horace-Belle arrangement, Byron robs the bank and reclaims his letters evidently as compensation for the frustrated arrangement with Narcissa. It is left us to observe that Byron's frustration is that he cannot possess Narcissa except in spirit; Bayard possesses her physically, but the spiritual component of their union is absent.

The last element in the Horace-Byron comparison—the financial—serves to connect it to the Simon and Meloney union, the last romantic union in the novel. Simon's initial gesture of approval (dropping his hand on Meloney's thigh) reminds us of the gestures of mutual approval we have seen Horace and Narcissa exchange; and that initial gesture of Simon's occurs in Belle Mitchell's kitchen, where he waits to drive Miss Jenny home. Poor Simon's sins come home to roost as the elders of his church come to collect their seventy or ninety dollars which has been in his keeping. We learn that Simon has "went and put it out"; he did get collateral, however— "Simon chuckled again, unctuously, a satyric chuckle rich with complacent innuendo. 'Yessuh, I got dat, all right. Only I never heard hit called collateral befo'. Naw, suh, not dat' " (p. 192). Meloney, of course, provided the "collateral." And as the novel draws to its close, Simon's death is reported to Miss Jenny; again the associations, the significant parallels are tacitly set out. Miss Jenny asks for details: " 'In whose house?' . . . In that of a woman named Meloney Harris, the voice told her. Meloney . . . Mel . . . Belle Mitchell's face flashed before her mind, and she remembered: the mulatto girl . . . who had quit Belle in order to set up a beauty parlor" (p. 295).

The denouement further completes the pattern and underlines the significance of the theme in question by associating finally Bayard and Harry Mitchell, Belle's ex-husband. As Bayard sits in Chicago completing his last drunk before taking off in the plane he is sure will crash, he stares fixedly at Harry, who is sitting in the same bar. " 'Brother-in-law over there,' he said, speaking slowly and carefully. 'Don't speak to family. Mad at us. Beat him out of his wife.' " Then Bayard corrects the identification with eloquent confusion and significant ambiguity: " 'Not brother-in-law,' he said, 'husband-in-law. No. Wife's brother's husband-in-law. Wife used to be wife's brother's girl. Married now. Fat woman. He's lucky' " (pp. 288–90).

Bayard's reference to Horace (wife's brother) as now associated with Belle should recall and signal the importance of Horace's earlier association with Montgomery Ward Snopes, who supplemented the YMCA canteen's offerings during the war in the role of pimp. We will come to realize with increasing conviction as the Yoknapatawpha Saga unfolds that association with Snopeses is a sure sign of corruption—Snopeses batten on human propensity for evil. And the corruption indicated is (as here, with Monty Snopes) frequently sexual corruption—the desire for illicit sexual love, both as the soldiers sought it at the canteen and as Horace has sought it with Belle. Horace, like Bayard, is unable to achieve a satisfactory love relationship, and Horace's association with Monty merely underlines the fact in his case.

Bayard:
Society

This, then, is the context in which Bayard must be understood, the society whose nature is responsible for his end; it is basically a society without love, a society whose value system makes love virtually impossible. That value system, *Sartoris* indicates (as will Faulkner's subsequent works), is false because it refuses to recognize what is real. It has idealized the past romantically and is busy idealizing the present—denying actuality in both cases. The ideals are impossible of realization and the shock of recognizing the chasm that separates the actual from the ideal is more than the characters can bear, and, indeed, more than they ought to be expected to bear. Miss Jenny perhaps best represents the idealizing of the past, the glorious Southern history and its traditions. She recalls the great J. E. B. Stuart, remembers having danced a *valse* with him, and rehearses his romantic exploits. Such memories are kept alive in the Sartoris household, which offers them a genial ambience. The office contains the library, "all Dumas was there [a lovely irony], and the steady progression of the volumes now constituted Bayard's entire reading, and one volume lay always on the night-table beside his bed" (p. 44). The very name which he shares with his desperate, bereft grandson—and indeed with preceding generations, including the Carolina Bayard, an aide-de-camp to Jeb Stuart—echoes that of the renowned Bayard, Chevalier Sans Peur at Sans Reproche, the romantic ideal of the Gentleman. And under the scolding guise of scorn for the romantic folly of Sartoris men, Miss Jenny believes profoundly in the romantic myth and persists to the very end of the novel in fostering it. The irony of her last exchange with Narcissa over the name of her son is unmistakable. Narcissa corrects Miss Jenny, "He isn't John. He's Benbow Sartoris." " 'And do you think that'll do any good?' Miss Jenny demanded. 'Do you think you can change one of 'em with a name?' " (p. 302).

Colonel John Sartoris, whose spirit dominates the book, is obviously idealized in memory—and principally by the fond old Simon, yet even to some extent by old Bayard. It is this attempt to keep alive, to perpetuate in the present time, the impossible ideals that these deluded romantics pretend existed in antebellum days that is reponsible for much of the misery and despair we witness in the novel. The overweening pride and the consequent exclusiveness it fosters—based *pride* on a belief in the greatness of the Southern heroes and in the purity of the Southern ladies—make impossible healthy human intercourse, sexual or otherwise; it is responsible for that divisive and finally reductive caste system which drives Byron Snopes to despair and which sets the Negro beyond the human pale. By perpetuating slavery's legacy, *Sartoris* poignantly demonstrates, this society has cut off its best from the human comfort and salvation that human love can offer. Young Bayard's temporary salvation cannot flourish because the master society discounts the characters who make it possible—the Negroes. Bayard can only turn to "his own"—and his own receive him not. The whole fabric is artificial, false, and fatal. This fundamental evil in the social arrangement is shown to be responsible for the loss of their "best," and the fratricide so impressively expressed in the metaphoric use of war in the novel is seen again as tantamount to suicide. The fundamental evil, then, is ultimately self-destructive. And in that we see the other dominant theme which informs the works of the Yoknapatawpha Saga.

But the beginning of hope, the road back to health, is also clearly enough expressed in *Sartoris*. It is the *natural* way, based on respect for the real which is founded in a proper attitude to man's real estate—the secrets of the soil, "primitive" knowledge of the basis of life. This countertheme to the falseness of the romantic idealization in which the Sartorises habitually indulge is sustained by Old Man Falls, the MacCallums, and the Negro peasant family. We have seen how the quasi-Edenic setting of the MacCallum place and the Christmas generosity of the humble Negro hearth offered temporary—but only temporary—sanctuary to young Bayard. Old Man Falls serves to augment the theme. He represents, in the focus of old Bayard, the voice of the past, associated as he is with the mythic Colonel John, whose pipe he bestows on old Bayard as a relic. But he is importantly associated with primitive lore by the salve he offers old Bayard to remove the wen from his cheek. He applies the salve when he feels the wen is ready and promises Bayard the wen will drop off on July ninth. Miss Jenny has been meanwhile hauling Bayard to medical men, and finally "in the second week in July" to a specialist in Memphis (p. 196) who (to serve Faulkner's intent) mistakes Miss Jenny as the patient; his attention is briefly diverted to old Bayard:

> "What's that on your face?" he demanded, jerking his hand forth and touching the blackened excrescence. When he did so the thing came off in his fingers, leaving on old Bayard's withered but unblemished cheek a round spot of skin rosy and fair as any baby's.

On the train that evening old Bayard, who had sat for a long time
in deep thought, spoke suddenly.
"Jenny, what day of the month is this?"
"The ninth," Miss Jenny answered. "Why?" [Pp. 197–98].

The salve, Will Falls had explained to old Bayard, came to his
granny "from a Choctow woman nigh a hundred and thutty year
ago. Ain't none of us never told what hit air, nor left no after-trace"
(p. 183). The recipe for the salve, like the recipe for the MacCallum
whiskey, is something of a family tradition, and one compares in a
kind of desperate amazement the traditions of the Sartoris family.
And the source in the Choctaw woman serves as an association between Will Falls and the simple Negro family, an association like that
represented later by Sam Fathers of *Go Down, Moses*. This theme will
enjoy more elaborate development in subsequent works; its significance in *Sartoris* is nevertheless perfectly apparent.

Finally, the novel manages to suggest, through its pattern of repeated names in the Sartoris family as well as the reiteration of the
Sartorises associated with war, that the Sartoris fate is a recurrent
cycle which regularly offers the chance to change, to redeem the
time, to act humanely and effect the human salvation that may just
barely be possible. The Second Chance offers itself; to grasp it requires only love and courage—the courage born of love and the love
that courage makes possible. *Sartoris* shows us the tragedy of the
Second Chance refused, of man's crucifixion of his best reenacted.
That is one face of Faulkner's "Quo vadis" motif.

And yet we trust that somehow good
Will be the final goal of ill.

. . . but what am I?
An infant crying in the night,
An infant crying for the light,
And with no language but a cry.

Tennyson, *In Memoriam*, LIV

II

The Sound and the Fury

While somewhat later in conception and composition, *The Sound and the Fury* was published in the same year as *Sartoris* (1929) and serves as an illuminating companion novel to it, offering another (and nearly contemporary) view of the continuing collapse of the South. The novel treats of the decline of the Compson family, focused in the fall and expulsion of Caddy. The signs of decay are readily apparent in the dipsomaniac Jason Compson III, in his selfish hypochondriac wife, and in his sycophantic and parasitic philandering brother-in-law Maury; and, in the next generation, in the suicidal Quentin, in the meanly mercenary Jason IV, and in the idiot Benjy—as well as in the undisciplined Caddy. Faulkner's diagnosis of the Compson disease points to its source in the general failure of love. And that general failure is given particular focus in the fall of Caddy.

Faulkner always maintained that the germ of the novel was his vision of a little girl with muddy drawers, perched in a tree. That is, of course, Caddy—his heart's darling.[1] Those drawers prove prophetic as Caddy assumes the role of the classic American-puritan sinner, descendant of Hester Prynne—the fallen woman. Yet it is clear that Caddy is the only Compson who is at all capable of expressing unselfish love; that capacity is seen in her treatment of Quentin and especially of Benjy. Her relationship with Benjy is nicely summed up and illuminated in one of Faulkner's accounts of his conception of the first part of the book (Benjy's section, as it is usually called). He explains that the thing began as a short story about some children:

> . . . the idea struck me to see how much more I could have got out
> of the idea of the blind self-centeredness of innocence, typified by

children, if one of those children had been truly innocent, that is, an idiot. So the idiot was born and then I became interested in the relationship of the idiot to the world that he was in but would never be able to cope with and just where would he get the tenderness, the help to shield him in his innocence. . . . And so the character of the sister began to emerge. . . .[2]

For it is Caddy who gives Benjy the love and tenderness and help he so desperately needs. She has the capacity to love, generously and unselfishly. Her problem, indeed, is her superabundance of love. Her fall is the result of that superabundance, uncontrolled and undirected; her "sin" is the excess of a virtue, the chiefest virtue. The lack of control and direction is the responsibility of her family. In the context of Caddy's career—the social context of twentieth-century Southern life, still strongly flavored with antebellum principles of Southern chivalry—it is the failure of appropriate care on the part of the gentlemen of the family that is to a considerable degree at fault.

The significance of Caddy's fall is defined and given its particular emphasis in the concern expressed by her three brothers, each of whom is peculiarly anguished by and almost constantly preoccupied with the loss of Caddy—none more so than the youngest and most nearly helpless, Benjy.

For Benjy, the loss of Caddy is the loss of all love, all simple joy, all meaning—whatever meaning there could be in his idiot's life. From the age of six, Caddy has supplied the tender loving care for Ben that his wretched mother is unwilling and unable to give him. Caddy has been virtually his only playmate, gamboled with him in the pasture, comforted him at bed time, and always acted quickly to right whatever wrong has prompted him to moan in unconscious moral anguish. Ben's moaning, of course, is a constant and reliable indication that things are out of joint—that some disaster is imminent, that sin threatens, that life is not as it should be. He has a nose for evil; he is the novel's moral barometer. With Caddy gone, Benjy's life is empty.

For Quentin, the loss of Caddy is quite as grievous. The source of his grief is complex. Of course he has loved his sister, loved her more than anyone else in the family, and loved her with a peculiar fraternal intensity—more, in a sense, than he really ought. And as the last Southern lady in the family, Caddy has embodied for Quentin the idea of honor: to protect her, to maintain her morally intact, to keep her unsullied in body and (if possible) in soul, would be properly to serve the demands of the Southern code and to establish her as an irreproachable representative of sturdy Compson honor. We readily recognize in the novel confirmation of Faulkner's comment that Quentin "loved not his sister's body but some concept of Compson honor precariously and (he knew well) only temporarily supported by the minute fragile membrane of her maidenhead. . . ."[3] Furthermore, her fall, her loss of virginity out of wedlock, clearly represents to Quentin the loss not only of the family honor but of the whole way of life—that of the pseudoaristocratic, antebellum South—which he has been raised to espouse. Consequently, his grief is enormously aggravated by the sense of his own failure of responsibility as a contributing cause of Caddy's fall. As for Benjy, so for Quentin, the loss of Caddy is the loss of what is most important and meaningful in his life.

For Jason, the loss of his sister means the loss of financial stability. As he sees it, Caddy has robbed him of a good job at the bank, which would have been his had she been able to remain Herbert Head's wife. Jason is significantly named: his chief interest and pursuit is a kind of debased modern equivalent of the golden fleece—money. Not only has Caddy removed easy access to this most desirable good, she has also imposed on him the burden—however he assumes it— of caring for her illegitimate daughter, Miss Quentin.

Just as much of the activity of Quentin's day (June 2, 1910) is devoted to Quentin's attempt to compensate for his failure of responsibility with Caddy (his kind though misunderstood attention to the little Italian girl and his final claim of having committed incest with Caddy), so much of Jason's activity (on April 6, and again on April 8, 1928), spent in trying desperately to control the behavior of Miss Quentin, can be seen as compensatory—although that is not quite Jason's conscious intention. He does not want the wayward daughter of an undisciplined mother to bring further trouble to the family. A final irony is that, of the three brothers, only Benjy has been able to exert moral control over the receptacle of the family honor, and that by his subrational, simply intuitive response of moaning (typically, when Caddy's behavior threatens to go "too far"—in the dark swing, in using perfume, in donning a fetching hat, etc.). It is the peculiar quality of the selfish, innocent, and "idiotic" love which Benjy expresses that makes his control possible, renders it effectively un-selfish.

The theme of love persists in the novel and is regularly wedded to the theme of time—the failure of love and the victimization by time (or, in a rare but most significant instance, the opposite of that). From the very title of the novel onward we are alerted to the role of time. The soliloquy from *Macbeth* (from which the title derives) is introduced and triggered by news of a lost loved one: Macbeth is informed of his wife's death. The scant ten lines of the mournful soliloquy are full of references to time and its ravages, from the relentless regularity of the initial iambic line to the desperate decline of the final trochee. Most of the explicit comments on time in *The Sound and the Fury* come from the cynical father, Jason III, and are directed to Quentin, to whom he has given his father's watch, "the mausoleum of all hope and desire . . . I give it to you not that you may remember time, but that you might forget it now and then for a moment and not spend all your breath trying to conquer it" (p. 93):

> Father said that. That Christ was not crucified: he was worn away by a minute clicking of little wheels. [P. 94]

> Because Father said clocks slay time. He said time is dead as long as it is being clicked off by little wheels; only when the clock stops does time come to life. [Pp. 104–5]

And then, Quentin remembers, "time is your misfortune Father said" (p. 129). These comments on time and timepieces are tested, proven throughout the course of the novel.

Benjy, of course, has no sense of time at all. He lives condemned to a perpetual *here and now*. Whatever crosses his mind (or, better, impinges on his sensibility) presents itself as happening in the present moment. And like Proust's Marcel (in *A la recherche du temps perdu*), Benjy is always moved by *present* stimuli—either to his merely sensory recognition of present events or to his "recall" of past events which are indelibly associated with those stimuli. In this sense only, Benjy is a captive of time: it is all *now* to him. *Quentin*

The highly imaginative and ratiocinative Quentin is just as firmly held in time's grasp, is inescapably time's victim. The reason for that victimization is sufficiently evident: Quentin cannot face the fact of mutability, of change; he cannot abide the Heraclitean flux. And it is in time that change occurs—most importantly the kind of change that has occurred in Caddy and, by extension, in the whole way of life she represents to his mind. Consequently, his constant desire is

instructive on Q (27–31)
but again: how does this relate to
"Faulkner's York. comedy" ? ?

to arrest the relentless flow, to fix the flux, or to escape the stream
of time altogether. Quentin's attitude to Caddy epitomizes his attitude to life generally, and it is the equivalent of Horace Benbow's
attitude to Narcissa (in *Sartoris*). He yearns to be able to call his sister
the "still unravished bride."

The complex and adroitly interwoven scheme of imagery in the
second (Quentin's) section of the novel functions admirably to express Quentin's attitude. Clocks, birds, crickets, Caddy, and of
course honeysuckle are the items which provide the several related
themes that comprise the expressive pattern in Quentin's section;
and one need not invoke Freud to substantiate the meaningful connection between timepiece and sister in Quentin's mind. His day
begins with the arresting sentence about his return to the stream of
time: "When the shadow of the sash appeared on the curtains it was
between seven and eight oclock and then I was in time again, hearing the watch" (p. 93). Then follows the reference to his father's
giving him the watch, that he forget time now and then; a paragraph
later we find him recalling his father's comment about Christ's being
worn away by the minute clicking of little wheels; the subsequent
paragraph anticipates his final "confession": "I have committed incest, Father I said." A page later we come upon this interesting
association of bird and timepiece:

> A sparrow slanted across the sunlight, onto the window ledge, and
> cocked his head at me. His eye was round and bright. First he'd watch
> me with one eye, then flick! and it would be the other one, his throat
> pumping faster than any pulse. The hour began to strike. The spar-
> row quit swapping eyes and watched me steadily with the same one
> until the chimes ceased, as if he were listening too. Then he flicked off
> the ledge and was gone. [P. 97]

The bird of time, that sparrow (we think); and we will do well to
remember that pulsating throat.

When Quentin comes upon the host of watches and clocks in the
jeweler's window (he has already removed the hands from his own
watch in a typically futile gesture), he recalls his father's comment
about clocks' slaying time and notices that on one of the chronometers in the window "The hands were extended, slightly off the
horizontal at a faint angle, like a gull tilting into the wind" (p. 105).
The gull, like the sparrow, will reappear. When Quentin enters the
jeweller's to ask, desperately hopeful, whether any of the timepieces

in the window actually registers the correct time, he notes "The place was full of ticking, like crickets in September grass" (pp. 102–3). It is patently obvious that Quentin's attempt to overcome and control the inexorable indication of his watch by turning it face down and then ripping its hands off matches his attempt to exert control over his sister, if only *ex post facto*. At several points in the crucial scene between him and Caddy at the branch—where he quizzes her about her various relationships and finally tries to force the moment to its crisis in an erotic suicide pact—the themes (Caddy, the ticking crickets, the bird of time, and the honeysuckle) are repeatedly interwoven:

> I ran down the hill in that vacuum of crickets . . . she [Caddy] was lying in the water her head on the sand spit the water flowing about her hips . . . I stood on the bank I could smell the honeysuckle on the water gap the air seemed to drizzle with honeysuckle and with the rasping of crickets. . . . [P. 186]

In response to Quentin's invitation to say she hates Dalton Ames, Caddy moves his hand "up against her throat her heart was hammering there" (p. 187). Again at the end of the scene she repeats the act as Quentin utters Dalton's name, and again he feels her pulsating throb. To emphasize the association Faulkner has introduced the bird of time specifically:

> I felt the first surge of blood there it surged in strong accelerating beats
>> say it again
> her face looked off into the trees where the sun slanted and where the bird
>> say it again
> Dalton Ames
> her blood surged steadily beating and beating against my hand.
> [P. 203]

In Quentin's view, Caddy's context is always replete with these temporal associations. Time is indeed his misfortune, and mutability his terror.

It is interesting to notice that items from the natural world—birds (both sparrow and gull), crickets, and honeysuckle—are associated in Quentin's mind with Caddy and clocks. It is as though the novel were tacitly urging recognition that Caddy's actions have been "natural"; yet, at the same time, the association itself expresses some contrast, as in Benjy's reaction to Caddy's smell—like trees or occasionally like rain, when she is "good."

Quentin cannot accept the fact of change, change that has been to a great extent the result of his own failure of responsibility, and he seems powerless to control it. One option is to escape the temporal flux—to escape into that timeless existence which Benjy seems to inhabit, where the eternal verities remain intact. Mark Spilka proposes an interesting argument to this effect:

> Benjy offers a timeless, innocent, loving, suffering perspective on the Compson family . . . a stable emotional view of family history. . . . Quentin's attraction to death is an attraction to timeless verities. He seeks the certainties of the Southern past, where Grandfather was always right, where uniformed valorous men talked with hushed dignity of established values. But if he seeks such values in death, he also seeks them in his father's world; and he is still trying to find them, in his father's world, on the day of his suicide. . . . In stopping time, apparently, Quentin has been trying to bring time and Christ to life.[4]

This is a persuasive suggestion, especially when we recall Father's observations that those clicking wheels crucified Christ and continue to slay time. One might, of course, be tempted to reply that one of Quentin's atemporal goals is hell—a fine and private hell for him and Caddy—and to ask (rhetorically) what eternal verities are to be found there. The answer, in turn, to that question is, precisely, the verity of damnation; and Quentin is indeed concerned (as T. S. Eliot was) with such a verity. Quentin's father is quite correct in his observation (if he actually made it, outside of Quentin's imagination) on Quentin's having committed incest: "you wanted to sublimate a piece of natural human folly into a horror and then exorcise it with truth" (p. 220). In the modern postbellum world (and *is* it his father's world, after all?) Quentin is certainly struck with the decay of values, the disappearance of the eternal verities. It is a world in which Caddy's act can be dismissed as a piece of natural human folly. How then can she be redeemed or her "sin" be forgiven if that act is so regarded? Eliot's remarks on Charles Baudelaire are particularly apt as commentary on Quentin's dilemma and attitude:

> . . . Baudelaire has perceived that what distinguishes the relations of men and women from the copulation of beasts is the knowledge of Good and Evil (of *moral* Good and Evil which are not natural Good

and Bad or puritan Right and Wrong). . . . he was at least able to understand that the sexual act as evil is more dignified, less boring, than as the "natural," "life-giving," cheery automatism of the modern world. . . .

So far as we are human, what we do must be either evil or good; so far as we do evil or good, we are human; and it is better, in a paradoxical way, to do evil than to do nothing: at least, we exist. It is true to say that the glory of man is his capacity for salvation; it is also true to say that his glory is his capacity for damnation. . . . Baudelaire was man enough for damnation . . . he walked secure in this high vocation, that he was capable of a damnation denied to the politicians and newspaper editors of Paris.[5]

The question remains, however, whether Quentin is actually man enough to face the damnation he ostensibly wants him and Caddy to share. The answer, of course, is that he quite definitely is not. His confession of incest is, typically, *theoretic:*

and he did you try to make her do it and i i was afraid to i was afraid she might and then it wouldnt have done any good *but if i could tell you we did it would have been so and then the others wouldnt be so.* [P. 220; my italics]

He is the typical Faulknerian Southerner: the *idea* of incest, not the actuality, concerns him. His father's comment is, as usual, apt: "you are contemplating an apotheosis in which a temporary state of mind will become symmetrical above the flesh" (p. 220). Quentin is willing to be damned *theoretically;* he cannot face the facts of actuality. There is for him, as for James's Hyacinth Robinson (*The Princess Casamassima*), really but a single option: Quentin must escape finally in suicide.

For while Father Compson is, in the terms of the novel, sufficiently correct in his metaphoric assertion that "time is dead as long as it is being clicked off by little wheels," that metaphor needs some transliteration. The point is (as the novel subsequently makes clear) that time is dead *for us* so long as *we* attend only to the measuring chronometers, the clicking wheels. Quentin's misfortune is that he is dominated by time as measured by the chronometers; the solution is not to stop the clocks, but to free oneself from commitment to them—admittedly not an easy task.

As the novel develops, we see that time is also Jason's misfortune, although he is quite oblivious of that fact. He is a different breed of cat from Quentin. The last sane Compson, Faulkner called him with

evident irony. He is at home, or thinks he is, in the modern world of
the Snopeses. Jason is by no means so preoccupied with time and
timepieces as Quentin. He is at home with the minute clicking of
little wheels, and he would be disturbed if the clicking stopped; he
would be disoriented. He is, in fact, for the most part inattentive to
time (as his employer, Earl, could well testify), but he believes implicitly in the chronometer and scorns those who do not:

> "What?" I says. He [Earl] looked at his watch. Then he went to the
> door and looked at the courthouse clock. "You ought to have a dollar
> watch," I says. "It wont cost you so much to believe it's lying each
> time." [P. 306]

For Jason is the *reducto absurdum* (in freshman Quentin's terms) of
the realist. He responds to the surface of the raw actual data of life,
the signs, the letter of the law, and will not look beyond. Furthermore, in the Poor Richard parlance of the modern world, time is
money, as Jason well knows. He regrets Caddy's fall, but his regret
expresses itself in terms of money. He might have urged her, "Then
be not coy but use your time, And while ye may, *make money.*" For he
has, as he confesses, "every respect for a good honest whore." She
makes money at it while foolish Caddy was giving it away.

Jason's evident commitment to chronometers is of a piece with his
general commitment to the superficial signs of things. He distinguishes between the various grades of hame-strings by their price
tag:

> "I didn't say it [the twenty-cent hame-string] wasn't any good," I
> says, "I said it's not as good as that other one."
> "How do you know it's not," he says. "You ever used airy one of
> them?"
> "Because they don't ask thirty-five cents for it," I says. "That's how
> I know it's not as good." [P. 242]

The same attitude appears more viciously in his adhering to the
mere letter of the law in his bargain with Caddy, who has offered
Jason <u>fifty dollars</u> if he will "fix it so I can see her [her baby] a
minute" (p. 252). He arranges, with the appropriate help of Mink
Snopes, to drive by Caddy at the appointed spot; he holds up the
baby so that Caddy can *see* her—and nothing more. Of course his
defense against Caddy's accusation that he has failed in the bargain
is a strictly literal reiteration of the *letter* of their agreement: "Didn't

I do everything I said? I said see her a minute, didn't I? Well, didn't
you?" (pp. 255–56)

Jason's commitment to the mere superficies—to the sign, the letter, the timepiece—to what his father meant by *dead* time, is at bottom very similar to the idealist Quentin's commitment to *the theoretic.*
This shared commitment receives eloquent implicit commentary
throughout the novel which identifies it ultimately with commitment
to destruction and death. That implicit commentary is given its most
effective expression through the character of Dilsey. As Quentin is
provided with his plaguey watch, so Dilsey is provided with a fascinating clock; and the reactions of these two characters to their respective chronometers provide an instructive contrast. One of the
most meaningful accounts of Dilsey's typical response to the timepiece occurs during her preparation of breakfast; there we find her

> gathering about her the raw materials of food, coordinating the meal.
> On the wall above a cupboard, invisible save at night, by lamp light
> and even then evincing an enigmatic profundity because it had but
> one hand, a cabinet clock ticked, then with a preliminary sound as if it
> had cleared its throat, struck five times.
> "Eight oclock," Dilsey said. [Pp. 341–42]

Quentin would not have to ask about this clock whether it told the
correct time. A single glance at its one-handed face would assure
him that it didn't. And the "realist" Jason would likewise know from
a single glance that Dilsey's clock is perfectly unreliable, useless. Yet
Dilsey knows the time, in spite of the clock's imperfections; she
knows *better* than the mere chronometer. The metaphoric significance is surely clear: she is by no means victimized by her timepiece,
and time is thus still alive for her—even when it is being ticked off
by her maimed clock.[6] There is further significance in the three-
hour margin of the clock's error, which I will turn to in a moment;
and that interval is reiterated when Dilsey has returned from the
Easter Sunday service and once again faces the task of gathering
together the raw materials of food and coordinating a meal:

> The stove was almost cold. While she stood there the clock above the
> cupboard struck ten times. "One oclock," she said aloud, "Jason aint
> comin home. Ise seed de first en de last," she said, looking at the cold
> stove, "I seed de first en de last." [P. 375]

Added to the reiteration of Dilsey's independence from her err-
ing clock and of its significant three-hour error is the reiteration of

the scope of her vision. Upon leaving church Dilsey has said, "I've seed de first en de last."

> "First en last whut?" Frony said.
> "Never you mind," Dilsey said. "I seed de beginnin, en now I sees de endin." [P. 371]

Certainly she is referring to the Compson family, perhaps three generations of it; but the context in which those remarks occur—that of specific scenes in which they are made, but finally that of the novel as a whole, informed as it is with persistent thematic references to time—prompts us to consider them as something broader. She seems to be saying that her vision embraces all of time. And there is even more involved than that, as I shall indicate below. Dilsey, in any case, does *see* (like the ideal Jamesian hero); she is a woman of vision. That quality of hers, we are made to feel, is somehow associated with her being a devoutly religious woman. She first made the statement about how much she has seen immediately upon leaving church, where she had just participated in the Easter Sunday service and listened to the moving sermon of the Reverend Shegog.

Dilsey is, with all this, the strongest and most appealing character in the novel. She is obviously the one who is best able to exert creative control in the novel, to assume responsibility most effectively. And she has the greatest capacity for charity, for love. Appropriately, those most in need of love are those to whom she most generously devotes her charitable care—Caddy, Miss Quentin, Benjy. They are the ones who have suffered most grievously from the failure of love in the Compson family.

Now it is true that the general collapse of the Compsons is focussed in the fall of Caddy, and the basic preoccupation of her three brothers lends emphasis to that focus; yet the principal focus of the novel as a whole is upon Benjy—as though he were the book's ultimate concern. What (it seems constantly to ask) will become of, what can be done for, this the most needy, the most innocent, the most nearly helpless creature, the last one and least one? It is apparent that Ben's welfare has been from the outset intimately involved with Caddy's welfare. As Caddy is failed—deprived of sufficient control and loving care—so Benjy is failed. Our first sense of the effect of Caddy's departure is that Ben has been bereaved; and soon enough we recognize that behind Caddy's failing Benjy is the family's having failed Caddy.

2nd Chance; Miss Q

The most anguished recognition of the failure to give Caddy the love, care, and control she needed, is, of course, Quentin's. In his eyes at least, his failure of responsibility for his sister is the most grievous, the most culpable. But an opportunity to compensate for that failure, a Second Chance for the family and specifically for the Compson brothers, is afforded by the second-generation Caddy— Miss Quentin. And as Quentin has failed Caddy, so Jason fails Miss Quentin—for much the same reason and in much the same way.

The other, and more substantial, statement of the theme of the Second Chance has to do with the more desperately needful Benjy. Initially the love and care he needs are unselfishly supplied by Caddy. When her resources are exhausted, and Ben is left desolate, bereft, moaning, someone must step in to assume the burden of responsibility. Benjy has been failed; but the opportunity to compensate for Caddy's failure remains. The Second Chance is accepted by Dilsey. Indeed, in both statements of the theme, it is Dilsey who assumes the responsibility, accepts the Second Chance. She attempts to compensate for Jason's failure with Miss Quentin, to oppose his general persecution of the girl. And of course she succeeds in her attempt to compensate for Caddy's failure to care for Benjy. Dilsey's *comic* successful assumption of the burden of this Second Chance gives the theme its comic, hopeful development, and is thus of considerable importance in contributing to the optimistic cast of the novel.

On the merely literal level of the novel, Dilsey's characterization and function are satisfactorily meaningful. Her strength obviously derives largely from the fact that she is a good church-going woman. But there is more than that to Dilsey's participation in the religious, indeed the specifically Christian, theme of the novel. The significance of her role is enormously augmented by the metaphoric expression achieved by Faulkner's manipulation of the theme of time. There is surely a distinctly Christian allusion in her clock's margin of error: it reflects the three hours of Christ's agony on the cross (as though the chronometer—with its minute clicking of little wheels— marked the beginning of the end of Christ's earthly life, and Dilsey's perception marked the end which is the beginning of His rebirth, the moment when He finally gave up the ghost). Beyond that, Dilsey's remarks about seeing the first and the last, the beginning and the ending, ought to sound in our ears another distinctly Christian echo, especially in view of the immediate context in which they are uttered, and further, in view of the general Christian tinge of

our; interested in world ; cf. 38 - 39

agud "broken tower" in effective Symmzrl24u

x12 n contexts

the whole novel. In the New Testament, in both the first and last chapters of the book of Revelation, God (in His various persons) is identified to St. John in these terms:

> I am Alpha and Omega, the beginning and the ending, saith the Lord, Which is, and which was, and which is to come, the Almighty. [1:8]

> I am Alpha and Omega, the beginning and the end, the first and the last. [22:13]

Disley's reiterated assertion carries the force of "I have seen God." And we might add that her vision is yet within this world. In terms of William Blake's distinction, Dilsey sees *through,* not *with,* her eyes.

Further illumination of the significance of Dilsey's role derives from Faulkner's development of Benjy in the novel. In answer to a question about the reference to Benjamin's being sold into Egypt ("Wasn't that Joseph in the Bible?") Faulkner explained it (a bit lamely, it seems to me) in this way:

> A—Is there anybody who knows the Bible here?
> Q—I looked it up and Benjamin was held hostage for Joseph.
> A—Yes, that's why I used them interchangeably.[8]

But his acknowledging the association is useful in reminding us of the account of Joseph and his brethren. Benjamin was indeed a hostage, a figure of potential sacrifice, like Abraham's Isaac. And that aspect of Benjy's role fits well with his ampler characterization as a Christ-like figure.

Mr. Carvel Collins first suggested some years ago that all three brothers are Christ-like, that events in the lives of all three have distinct parallels to events in the life of Christ. He argued further that "the three Compson sons . . . amalgamate at a symbolic level into one son." His conclusion was that the Christ-like parallels are in all three cases ironic in intention:

> . . . the Compson sons are in parallel with Christ but, significantly, by inversion. . . . the Compson sons pass through parallel events but go down in failure. And they do so because love, which Christ preached as an eleventh commandment, is lacking or frustrated or distorted in their family.[9]

In bringing the three sons together on the basis (in part) of superfi-cial similarities, Mr. Collins fails to take into account Faulkner's fun-

damental distinction between Benjy on the one hand and Quentin
and Jason on the other. I believe it can be shown that the parallels to
Christ are ironic only in the cases of Quentin and Jason, as my
subsequent discussion of those two brothers should make clear. Ben-Christ

The novel opens on Benjy's birthday—he is a Christ-like thirty-
three—which falls right in the middle of the Easter weekend of that
year. The figure of absolute innocence—unable to speak a word,
swaddled in darkness—becomes the family scapegoat. Ben undergoes
a three-fold sacrifice for the sake of his family. He has suffered the
loss of his pasture (where he and Caddy used to play); it is now the
golf course. He has suffered the loss of his sister; and the golfers'
repeated cry of "caddie" will not summon her back to him. He has
suffered the loss of his masculinity through castration; and all the
searching of the summoned caddies and of Luster for lost balls can
bring him no restitution. (All three of these, incidentally, are presented to us in the opening paragraphs of the novel, although they
are recognizable only in retrospect.) The first of these sacrifices that
touch Ben so intimately was made to pay for Caddy's wedding and for
Quentin's year at Harvard; the second and third for the sake of the
family honor—to remove the "shame" that Caddy caused, and to
prevent recurrence of Benjy's misunderstood attention to little girls
he anxiously mistook for his absent sister. Furthermore, while the
Christ-like Benjy is not a "savior," does not function actually to "save"
anybody in the novel, he does provide the means and opportunity of
indicating which of the characters in his world are "saved" and which
are not. Hyatt Waggoner's comment on Joe Christmas of *Light in
August* (another of Faulkner's unmistakably Christ-like characters) is
sufficiently appropriate to explain Benjy's function in *The Sound and
the Fury:* "By our attitude toward him, we ourselves, the novel implies,
are judged. . . . he sits in judgment on the world by forcing it to judge
him."[10] Ben's "judgment" is not quite tacit: he does moan and even
bellow when he senses things are wrong; and those few who have the
love and sense of responsibility to care for him hasten to attend to and
quiet him—by setting things right when that is possible, by offering
comfort and compensation when it is not.

Those few who care for Ben are those we approve of; but their
charity is rendered richer and more significant to us by the effect of
Ben's Christ-likeness. That feature of his characterization expresses
Faulkner's apparent notion that there is a spark of divinity in even
the least considerable human being. It is as though Faulkner were

"Least of these . . ." (Matt.)

* unique argument

adapting Jesus's words: "Inasmuch as ye have done it unto one of the least of these my brethren, ye have done it unto me."

That, however, is not the end of the matter and certainly not the end of the novel—as too many readers will urgently remind us. Dilsey does struggle nobly for the right against opposing forces, but (those readers will contend) she is old and, furthermore, the final triumph is evidently Jason's. What (they conclude) is the significance, in the face of that compelling evidence, of Dilsey's assuming the departed Caddy's care of Benjy, of taking up the challenge and opportunity of the Second Chance?

There are two points to be considered in responding to such readers. The first is the significance of the whole shape of the novel—beginning with the broadest strokes of its structural organization; the second is the novel's development of Faulkner's other persistent theme, the theme of the Self-Destructiveness of Evil. And these two points are intimately related.

The most obvious figure of self-destruction in the novel is, of course, Quentin; and one would not want immediately to brand that pathetic figure as evil. I will argue, however, that Quentin's crucial and pathetic failures are as much a part of the evil to be confronted in the novel as are Jason's acts of blatant villainy; and I will argue further that Jason is quite as bent upon self-destruction as is the suicide Quentin. Faulkner has given peculiar emphasis to these fundamental qualities of Quentin and Jason by insisting on superficial similarities among all three brothers, and, in his familiar mode of irony, showing us thereby the critical difference between Benjy on the one hand and Quentin and Jason on the other.

Quentin and Jason function, as we have seen, at one remove from reality. This would seem to be equally true of Benjy. The golfers' cry of "caddie" he takes as an indication of his sister's presence. The distinction is easily made between his predicament and that of his brothers, however, as we recognize that Ben's excuse is simply his idiocy. Further, Benjy seems to share with his two brothers an evidently selfish preoccupation with his sister (or, in Jason's case, with her surrogate, Miss Quentin). Benjy is again distinguished and exculpated by his idiocy, but beyond that, he alone has been able to exert some moral control on Caddy; neither Quentin nor Jason has had that success either with Caddy or with her daughter. Both Quentin and Jason are impotent in that respect as they are, in fact, in most matters.

Impotence is another quality which all three brothers eventually share. And in this novel, as so often elsewhere in his writing, Faulkner employs sexuality as a synecdoche: sexual impotence represents general powerlessness, as a rule. Once again the distinction between Ben and his brothers is clear—and arresting: (1) he is, so to speak, literally impotent, having been castrated, while his brothers are, by the same token, physically intact; and (2) his impotence was imposed on him by others (chiefly by Jason, of course), while the impotence of Quentin and Jason is self-imposed, self-willed—it represents in them a lack of courage, a fear of real commitment to life, a willful failure of love.

Finally, there is the series of parallels to Christ in each brother's life, which Mr. Carvel Collins long ago pointed out. Benjy's legitimate Christ-likeness and the nature of its function in the novel we have already considered. In the case of Quentin and Jason, the parallelism is manifestly ironic, as Mr. Collins agrees. All the details of characterization of both brothers, as we have just been examining them, strongly urge our recognition of that irony and the consequent distinction of Benjy from Quentin and Jason.

It is this shared aspect of Quentin and Jason that is most important in its contribution to the statement which the novel makes. Quentin is admittedly different from Jason in various ways: his failure is pathetic, his career nearly tragic; yet, what we might then call his "tragic flaw" is the inflexibility which renders him unable to come to terms with the modern, postbellum world. It is easy to utter the rhetorical question "Who would want to adjust to the modern world, shot through and dominated as it is with Snopesism?" But if this world is evil, to turn disgustedly away is as culpable as to join it. The necessary alternative is, of course, to confront that evil and struggle against it—to attempt to redeem this modern world. By failing to do so Quentin contributes to its perpetuation.

Quentin's "confession" of having committed incest, his attempt to assume *ex post facto* the responsibility for Caddy he had not taken earlier, is typical of his attitude to life: "if i could tell you we did it would have been so." He does not want direct, actual involvement. Paradoxically, it might have been better if he had been able to act on his incestuous desires; best of all, certainly, would have been his managing to love Caddy properly—in an acceptable fraternal way. But he has always lacked the courage. That weakness of Quentin's is established in his earliest attempt to exert some appropriate frater-

nal control over his sister's wayward tendencies. When as children
they are all playing at the branch and young Caddy gets her dress
wet, she announces that she is going to take it off; Quentin says, "I
bet you wont."

> "I bet I will." Caddy said.
> "I bet you better not." Quentin said. [P. 20]

The form of his admonition—beginning always "I bet"—gives him
away. And his peculiar weakness is reaffirmed in that most frankly
erotic scene in which Quentin is again involved with Caddy at the
branch (these two scenes are specifically associated by the reference
to the muddy drawers of the time long passed); he is proposing a
kind of mutual suicide pact:

> it wont take but a second Ill try not to hurt
> all right
> will you close your eyes
> no like this youll have to push it harder
> touch your hand to it
> but she didnt move her eyes were wide open looking past my head
> at the sky
> Caddy do you remember how Dilsey fussed at you because your
> drawers were muddy
> dont cry
> Im not crying Caddy
> push it are you going to
> do you want me to
> yes push it
> touch your hand to it
> dont cry poor Quentin
> but I couldnt stop she held my head against her damp hard breast
> I could hear her heart . . . and waves of honeysuckle coming up the
> air . . .
> what is it what are you doing
> her muscles gathered I sat up
> its my knife I dropped it [Pp. 189–90]

Quentin's pathetic impotence, his general powerlessness—especially in matters concerning Caddy—is once more manifest. Perhaps
the finishing touch to the sexual synecdoche as Faulkner fashions it to
portray Quentin's dilemma comes in Versh's little anecdote "about a
man mutilated himself . . . with a razor. A broken razor flinging them
backward over his shoulder. . . ." Quentin's response strongly implies

that his own impotence is willfully assumed: "It's not not having them. It's never to have had them" (p. 143). Never to have had the means of potency at all seems to be Quentin's devout wish.

Quentin Compson is the paradigm of the Faulknerian "good weak hero,"[11] a type which includes Isaac McCaslin of *Go Down, Moses* and the almost ubiquitous Gavin Stevens, as well as Horace Benbow (despite his Belle Mitchell). He is the nearest approach to a Faulknerian tragic hero, a type firmly glanced at in Faulkner's response to a question about Isaac McCaslin:

> Well, there are some people in any time and age that cannot face and cope with the problems [of adjusting to the modern world]. There seem to be three stages: The first says, This is rotten, I'll have no part of it, I will take death first. The second says, This is rotten, I don't like it, I can't do anything about it, but at least I will not participate in it myself, I will go off into a cave or climb a pillar to sit on. The third says, This stinks and I'm going to do something about it. McCaslin is the second.[12]

Quentin is the first, but the difference between those first two "stages" is very slight: as Faulkner's fiction makes clear, actual suicide is merely the final step of withdrawal from life, and the goal toward which both "stages" unmistakably tend.

Jason Compson, the most blatantly villainous character in the novel, is the persecutor of love in every form of its expression except the commercial. His prevailing attitude is sufficiently summarized in his initial statement, which opens the third section of the novel: "Once a bitch always a bitch, what I say." He thus expresses his hatred, and implicitly its motivation in fear, of Caddy and perhaps of her daughter and undoubtedly of life as a whole. In spite of his bluff professions to the contrary, Jason is as much intimidated by life as is his brother Quentin. One wants to call him paranoid, but he *knows* that the sun maneuvers in the sky so it can smite him on the eyeball, that poison oak treacherously lies in wait to seize on and harm his exposed limbs, that rain holds off until it gets him in the most vulnerable situation—furthest from shelter. He knows also that people will fail him in time of need: they will carefully be without an air pump to lend him to restore his flat tire—except in cases of oversight on their part—and will refuse to give him necessary information about fluctuations in the cotton market. He restricts his limited trust to mechanical contrivances (clocks and automobiles) and to the cash nexus for personal relationships.

Persistently defensive, Jason savagely protects his own most cherished and most vulnerable possessions. In our earliest glimpses of him we note a gesture that is emphatically suggestive—as here, when he is a little boy at the branch:

> He passed us and ran on up the walk. He had his hands in his pockets and he fell down. Versh went and picked him up.
> "If you keep them hands out your pockets, you could stay on your feet." Versh said. "You cant never get them out in time to catch yourself, fat as you is." [P. 27]

And again—

> "You're a knobknot." Caddy said. Jason cried. His hands were in his pockets.
> "Jason going to be rich man." Versh said. "He holding his money all the time." [Pp. 42–43]

Certainly Versh is persuasively prophetic, but more is implied than he perceives. Jason's gesture is protective, but given the full portrait of him we feel that riches other than mere money are at stake. Jason's significant association of love and money—"I've got every respect for a good honest whore" (p. 291)—is surely already anticipated in that early meaningful gesture. But what is further implied by that earliest scene is that the protective gesture itself is ultimately self-defeating: hands in pockets, Jason falls, for he "cant never get them out in time to catch" himself.

His association with Lorraine, an additional indication of Jason's defensiveness, is strictly business, controlled, and it protects him from the vulnerability that purely human associations would expose him to. Yet the control which he exerts even in this financial arrangement is illusory and deceptive, and transparently so for the reader. I can never be fully persuaded that Jason has any influence other than financial on Lorraine; my suspicion about the quality and nature of his masculine performance with her is prompted by his in effect protesting too much. Furthermore, he confuses his relationship with Lorraine and Miss Quentin in a most revealing way, illuminating the cerebral quality of his lust, the merely theoretic character of his potent manly behavior, and the evidently constant frustration both of his desire and of his performance. The scene in question is prepared for by the earlier one in which Jason

is attempting to control his niece's behavior. She has told him that
if she believed she depended on Jason for any of her clothing she
would go naked.

> "See if I wouldn't," she says. She grabbed the neck of her dress in
> both hands and made like she would tear it.
> "You tear that dress," I says, "And I'll give you *a whipping* right
> here that you'll remember all your life."
> "See if I dont," she says. Then I saw that she really was trying to
> tear it, to tear it right off of her. By the time I got the car stopped and
> *grabbed her* hands there was about a dozen people looking. It made me
> so mad for a minute it kind of blinded me. [P. 233; my italics]

Now the crucial scene shows us Jason protesting (as it seems to me)
too much; it exposes his dubious masculinity; and it indicates especially the nature of his stream-of-consciousness confusion of Lorraine and Miss Quentin:

> I'd just as soon swallow gasoline as a glass of whiskey and Lorraine
> telling them he may not drink but if you dont believe he's a man I can
> tell you how to find out she says If I catch you fooling with any of
> these whores you know what I'll do she says I'll whip her *grabbing at*
> *her* I'll *whip her* as long as I can find her she says and I says if I dont
> drink that's my business but have you ever found me short I says I'll
> buy you enough beer to take a bath in if you want it because I've got
> every respect for a good honest whore.... [Pp. 290–91; my italics]

Added to our possible doubt about his manliness in his relations
with Lorraine are the more compelling suspicions about his attitude
to his niece. We ought to recall the breakfast scene in Jason's section,
just after Miss Quentin has appeared. It is hard to avoid the constant
focus of Jason's attention on his niece's state of near undress: "She
brushed her hair back from her face, her kimono slipping from her
shoulder." A few lines later, "Her kimono came unfastened, flap-
ping about her, damn near naked.... She was fastening her kimono
up under her chin, pulling it tight around her, looking at me....
She stumbled back against the wall, holding her kimono shut"
(pp. 227–30). And this soon leads us into the scene in which Miss
Quentin threatens to tear off her dress. Later, when Jason spies her
on the street with one of the men from the fair—the man in the red
tie—once again the nature of his vision of his niece and the associations he makes are instructive:

> I stood there and watched her go on past, with her face painted up
> like a damn clown's and her hair all gummed and twisted and a dress
> that if a woman had come out doors even on Gayoso or Beale street
> when I was a young fellow with no more than that to cover her legs
> and behind, she'd been thrown in jail. I'll be damned if they dont
> dress like they were trying to make every man they passed on the
> street want to reach out and clap his hand on it. [P. 289]

(And this in turn leads us into Jason's justification of his masculinity
and his confusing of Lorraine and Miss Quentin quoted above.)

It is true that Jason's preoccupation with his niece's garb—or lack
of it—and even his association of her and Lorraine may indicate an
understandable moral concern that she is behaving like a loose
woman; but the accumulation of data—the nature of his focus on
the girl, the rhetorical framing of his observations, the flavor of his
subconscious associations involving her—renders his attitude at the
very least ambiguous, and arguably quite distinctly incestuous.

I want to urge this interpretation of the relationship of Jason and
his niece because it is a typical Faulknerian narrative theme. The
incest theme regularly involves the pseudoaristocratic Southern
white families of antebellum days or their descendants. Its most
significant function is of course metaphoric, and it gives emphatic
focus to the complex of attitudes which Faulkner encourages us to
believe characteristic of the Southern white "aristocrat." The incestuous tendency expresses an attitude of exclusion, introversion, segregation; it is an attitude of protectiveness and defensiveness against
the alien and "inferior"; and it tends therefore to be restrictive and
ultimately self-destructive. It is thus also ultimately impotent. Furthermore, the incestuous tendency virtually never leads to physical
consummation, is never realized but remains "ideal" or (better)
"theoretic"—the willing assumption of the situation of the youth on
Keats's urn, and assumed, doubtless, to fulfill the same purpose: to
maintain the beloved intact, and, by extension, to maintain the beloved status quo generally:

> She cannot fade, though thou hast not thy bliss,
> For ever wilt thou love, and she be fair!

The attitude is thus doubly impotent. And as the attitude is willfully
assumed, it is the willful assumption of a double impotence. Quentin
certainly and Jason probably embody the attitude as I describe and
explain it.

Jason's suicidal tendencies are most clearly expressed in the catastrophe which includes the theft of his savings and his consequent pursuit of Miss Quentin. That theft is poignantly ironic. He has accumulated the little nest egg through his skillful manipulation of checks which Caddy has sent for the support of Miss Quentin, which includes the lugubrious ritual of burning a bogus check each month and pocketing the cash from the valid check. Jason deceives everyone and robs Miss Quentin. By hoarding up the fruits of his thievery he renders himself in turn vulnerable to thievery; and it is of course signally appropriate that Miss Quentin be the thief who relieves him of the loot of which he has robbed her. The point to be observed is that Jason's evil itself has prepared its own frustration and defeat. That situation is typical of Jason's life.

When he discovers the robbery, he sets out in pursuit of his niece. What emerges from that headlong chase is not simply Jason's constant frustration, but the fact that he is himself responsible for most of the frustration and—most significant of all—that he perversely embraces the fact of his own frustration (actual and anticipated) with a kind of masochistic joy at his own defeat. He resorts to the aid of his cherished automobile to begin the pursuit. Not only will that wonderful piece of machinery fail him by breaking down as he pursues the fleeing lovers, but it constantly punishes him as he drives, for he has forgotten in his haste to bring along his protective camphor rag. ("When it was necessary for him to drive for any length of time he fortified himself with a handkerchief soaked in camphor," p. 383.) The final indignity is his being obliged to hire a Negro to drive him back to Jefferson.

He has begun his travels by going to enlist the aid of the sheriff, and there meets his first frustration. His reaction to the sheriff's refusal to help him is revealing:

> ". . . if I could find a law officer that gave a solitary damn about protecting the people that elected him to office, I'd be there [Mottson] too by now." He repeated his story, harshly recapitulant, *seeming to get an actual pleasure out of his outrage and impotence.* [P. 378; my italics]

Jason goes on alone, under the skies threatening rain, and stops at a gas station where the sanguine attendant opines that "hit gwine fair off after all." Again the fiercely masochistic reaction is expressed:

> "Fair off, hell," Jason said. "It'll be raining like hell by twelve oclock." He looked at the sky, thinking about rain, about the slick clay

roads, himself stalled somewhere miles from town. *He thought about it with a sort of triumph,* of the fact that he was going to miss dinner, that by starting now and so serving his compulsion of haste, he would be at the greatest possible distance from both towns when noon came. *It seemed to him that, in this, circumstance was giving him a break.* . . . [Pp. 380–81; my italics]

That, I think, is the essential Jason—"outrage and impotence" voluntarily and even eagerly embraced, "with a sort of triumph." He generally tends in all his pursuits, all his likes and dislikes, to court his own despair and disaster. All his momentary triumphs are hollow, all his victories finally Pyrrhic. His impotence is overwhelming, and his commitment to the way of self-destruction unmistakable.

This figure of mean persecution grows increasingly into the role of principal adversary and antagonist to Dilsey. The development of the novel insists more and more emphatically on that opposition as we move through the four sections, and the total narrative shape gives it significant expression.

Faulkner was given to explain that the development of the novel resulted from his making several attempts to tell the one story; each version was insufficient, so he ended up telling the same story four times (and after he added the Appendix, it was five times). The inadequacy of that jocular account is apparent to anyone who reads the novel at all seriously and attentively. There is reiteration of a kind, to be sure, but with the important difference that it is reiteration from fresh points of view; and it is the variety of views that pushes the development onward. Nor is it simply that each point of view is preoccupied with the same events. The whole movement of the novel is an extended process of gradual restriction and limitation, which might be graphically represented by the musical sign for *diminuendo:* the effect of this is to narrow our vision into a sharp focussing on the concluding episode of the novel. The span of time covered by Benjy's section of the novel—almost thirty years of family history covered there in greater or lesser detail—is by far the broadest. A good bit less is embraced by Quentin's section (and he has died some eighteen years before the present moment of the other three sections); and considerably less than that is contained in Jason's section. The final section is confined to a few hours of the present moment—the Easter Sunday of 1928—and ends with Ben's trip around the square. There is, thus, a sense of the continual narrowing of scope, of compressing the action into the parenthesis of the exactly now. In concert with this is the gradual simplification and clarification of the narrative surface: Benjy's narration, initially almost incomprehensible, gives way to the more manageable stream-of-consciousness narrative of Quentin's section; Jason's section is mainly first-person narrative, although augmented with occasional internal monologue and the occasional stream-of-consciousness passage. The final section offers us the comparative relief of the clarity of traditional third-person, omniscient-author narration. The steady progression in simple narrative clarity matches, thus, the other progress I mention; and together the increasing clarity and the steady narrowing in on the strictly present produce the focussing effect. Added to that is Faulkner's contribution of a touch that suggests that the wheel is coming full circle. The concluding scene is almost immediately preceded by a reiteration of the novel's opening scene—Ben and Luster are again at the edge of the old pasture and Ben is again upset by the golfers' tantalizing cry, "Caddie."

The other contributive element I would mention in this connection is the Christian motif in the novel, especially the use of the dates of the three days of the Easter weekend of 1928, as a device of broad, general control. Even Quentin's section, dated 1910, has features which would qualify it as a kind of Maundy Thursday.[13] The disrupted chronology of the weekend effectively serves two purposes: it permits the novel to begin by reflecting, in Ben's confused and grief-stricken rehearsal of bereavement, the confusion and emptiness appropriate to Holy Saturday. The tale of the original Holy Saturday must indeed have seemed to the disciples to be "told by an idiot." Then the adjusted chronology throws Good Friday and Easter Sunday into immediate juxtaposition, with the advantageous dramatic effect of heightening the contrast between those two days. The appropriateness of imposing the narrative burden of the Holy Saturday section on Benjy is matched by giving Jason the narrative authority for the Good Friday section. Simple neatness would require, then, that the final section, if not narrated by Dilsey, ought to focus on her as the most appropriate representative of the spirit of Easter Sunday. And that is almost the case, but not quite. The effective juxtaposition of Good Friday and Easter Sunday is extended metaphorically into the final section, where the focus is shared by Dilsey and Jason—by Dilsey's taking Ben to church and Jason's frantic and frustrated pursuit of Miss Quentin. The felt contrast between those two figures and between the dominant attitudes they embody and represent is thus carried through the final section and into the concluding episode, on which (as I have argued) the whole shape of the novel has bent its sharpest focus. And to what end?

Fully to appreciate the significance of the concluding episode we must have attended sensitively to the concerns of the novel in passing, and have retained our impressions intact. We must recognize that the ultimate concern of the story has been, both literally and figuratively, that Benjy receive the loving care he needs. We recall that he expresses that need most strikingly at his moments of severest anguish by moaning or even bellowing. The admirable characters in the story have been those who most effectively pacify and quiet Benjy. And we might reflect again on the extra dimension of significance added to the situation by Faulkner's creating Ben as a Christ-like figure. It would seem monstrously ironic, at first glance, that the final gesture in the novel be given to Jason—especially since the final gesture of this familiar figure of persecution and selfish meanness achieves precisely the effect of the repeated gestures of the charitable and generous characters in the novel, Caddy and Dilsey. Certainly his motivation is fiercely opposite to theirs, yet the effect is the same.

We might be tempted to conclude that the novel shows us that Jason's is the ultimate triumph. But a moment's reflection leads us aright. This is, after all, the same Jason we have always known—not only the Pyrrhic persecutor but the figure of constant outrage and impotence. He is, after all, the novel's Good Friday figure. There are a couple of passages of realistic dialogue which are at the same time redolent with reflective significance. They are simply temporal references to Easter. Here is the most instructive; Jason's mother explains,

> . . . "The darkies are having a special Easter service. I promised Dilsey two weeks ago that they could get off."
> "Which means we'll eat cold dinner," Jason said, "or none at all."
> "I know it's my fault," Mrs. Compson said. "I know you blame me."
> "For what?" Jason said. "You never resurrected Christ, did you?"
> They heard Dilsey mount the final stair. . . . [P. 348]

The point is that the characterization of Jason—the figure of constant frustration which he embraces with masochistic glee—is thus colored by the Christian motif in the novel. And his place in the novel's pattern is that of the self-destructive figure of evil. According to the significance of that pattern, Jason's ultimate frustration is the empty and self-defeating triumph of the spirit of Good Friday. This is glimpsed, indeed, in one of Jason's extremely rare moments of epiphany. He stands staring at the automobile he cannot abide without his protective camphor, the machine which has failed him in his pursuit of Miss Quentin. He looks vainly for his camphor rag, "He looked beneath both seats and stood again for a while, cursing, seeing himself *mocked by his own triumphing*" (p. 383; my italics). And this is the Jason who reenacts the novel's basic concern with persecution and charity in the brilliant focus of the final episode. That scene is surely an eloquent emblem of the self-destructiveness of evil.[14]

The sense of resolution and peace that rises inevitably from the gently cadenced final sentence—"his eyes were empty and blue and serene again as cornice and facade flowed smoothly once more from left to right; post and tree, window and doorway, and signpost, each in its ordered place"—must not be rejected. It is Faulkner's even more hopeful equivalent of Eliot's "Shantih, shantih, shantih" that closed *The Waste Land*. *The Sound and the Fury* is, after all, neither a history nor a family biography, but an artistic structure. That concluding sentence is the final musical phrase, the last brush stroke, the terminal couplet of a literary work of art; it makes a complementary twofold statement about the self-destructiveness of the agents of evil and about the recognizable existence of the Saving Remnant, who can be relied upon to assume successfully the burden and opportunity of the Second Chance. That statement is boldly and affirmatively hopeful.

Yes: Men die, Mankind prevails

but argument re "comedy" strained here

but, here, not Powers'— madness

> Much Madness is divinest Sense—
> To a discerning Eye—
> Much Sense—the starkest Madness—
>   Emily Dickinson, no. 435*

III

As I Lay Dying

It is in some ways surprising that in later years Faulkner would seem to dismiss this novel of 1930 as something rather eccentric and inferior. During his visit at the University of Virginia (1957–58) he repeatedly referred to *As I Lay Dying* as a *tour de force,* something he had dashed off in six weeks and revised less than any other of his novels.[1] For this novel is initially interesting as a technical achievement, like *The Sound and the Fury* (and perhaps is most familiar to readers in the single Modern Library volume which the two novels share). It is the story of the Bundren family's preparations for and enactment of the funeral journey to Jefferson to bury Mrs. Addie Bundren in compliance with her request that she be buried there with her own blood kin. The story is told in fifty-nine sections, each controlled by a single narrator; there are fifteen narrators (members of the family, neighbors, a couple of strangers), and the number of sections narrated by each varies from the nineteen given to Darl Bundren to single performances by seven of the narrators, including Addie. The technique is Jamesian, of course, like that used in "A Bundle of Letters" (1879) and in the novel *The Awkward Age* (1899) and like that of the first three sections of *The Sound and the Fury.* Each narrator, necessarily confined to his own point of view, will contribute his peculiar coloring and interpretation casting the central object or event in a variety of lights, which increases the complexity and richness of our experience. At the same time each narrator thus exposes himself—his telling of the story becomes a kind of

*Numbers of Emily Dickinson's poems appearing in this volume refer to Thomas A. Johnson, *The Poems of Emily Dickinson* (Cambridge, Mass.: Harvard University Press, 1951).

reflexive characterization, willy-nilly. The narrative technique of *As I Lay Dying* is by no means so stunning as that of *The Sound and the Fury*, but it has its own interest and certainly deserves better than Faulkner's faintly pejorative dismissal of it would seem to allow. And while it is in some important ways distinct from the other Yoknapatawpha novels, it is certainly not inferior to all of them. *As I Lay Dying* has no concern with the descendants of the pseudoaristocratic Southern families of antebellum days like the Sartorises and Compsons of its immediate predecessors, but rather with the simple poor whites. Further, it seems at first glance to have nothing to do with those dominant themes which I am suggesting animate and inform the whole Yoknapatawpha Saga; a second glance, however, may correct that impression.

The novel unmistakably belongs in the Saga, if only because of its attention to the simple Bundrens; for Faulkner's sympathetic treatment of them is truly prophetic. The Bundren family members are part of that larger group of "the poor sons of bitches" for whom the Reverend Goodyhay will pray much later in the Saga;[2] they quite clearly inhabit the world of the "Father Abraham" story. The society in which the Bundrens perform in *As I Lay Dying* includes not only Cora and Vernon Tull and Armstid as actual narrators, but also Quick (old Lon's son), Littlejohn, the MacCallum twins, Eustace Grimm, and the less penurious Houston, Billy Varner and son Jody, and the itinerant V. K. Suratt. And also the Snopeses. The horse Jewel Bundren buys—a "durned spotted critter," his father calls it[3]—likewise derives from the "Father Abraham" material: it descends from the animals in Flem Snopes's great pony auction. The pathetic Bundrens are of the same sort as the ubiquitous Snopeses and the Gowries (whom we will meet later, in *Intruder in the Dust*); the general similarity among these three families serves to emphasize the crucial distinction between Bundrens and Gowries on the one hand, and the main run of Snopeses on the other. If the Snopeses will emerge with increasing clarity as a threatening blemish on Yoknapatawpha County, the other two families exhibit the naked human goodness—however overlaid with its rough and thick veneer—that Faulkner evidently cherished in the simple folk. If the Snopeses come to represent the threat posed by the rising redneck, the Bundrens and Gowries are the innocent or at least naive and unthreatening poor whites. Faulkner's compassionate treatment of Bundrens and Gowries encourages the nascent hope that out of the mass of these lowly creatures can come the qualities of endurance and even redemption that may ultimately include even the Snopeses, what you might call "an accepted type of Snopes." In this respect Faulkner's depiction of the family in *As I Lay Dying* seems prophetic.

For the Bundrens are really not evil but just naively foolish.⁴ One might call them their own worst enemy. They are that, to be sure, but the conditions under which they are obliged to live are also to blame for their wretched folly. Anse, father of the family, grievingly observes,

> It's a hard country on man. . . . Nowhere in this sinful world can a honest, hardworking man profit. It takes them that runs the stores in the towns, doing no sweating, living off of them that sweats. It ain't the hardworking man, the farmer. Sometimes I wonder why we keep at it. It's because there is a reward for us above. . . . Every man will be equal there and it will be taken from them that have and give to them that have not by the Lord.
>
> But it's a long wait, seems like. . . . I am the chosen of the Lord, for who He loveth, so doeth He chastiseth. But I be durn if He dont take some curious ways to show it, seems like. [Pp. 104–5]

We easily recognize the dramatic irony in those words, of course, for poor feckless Anse is anything but hard-working. Yet the druggist Moseley echoes Anse's observation on the lot of folks like the Bundrens, and even reflects a similar religious persuasion: "But it's a hard life they have; sometimes a man . . . if there can ever be any excuse for sin, which it cant be. And then, life wasn't made to be easy on folks: they wouldn't ever had any reason to be good and die" (p. 192; Faulkner's ellipsis). And the novel otherwise offers ample evidence to support Anse's complaint and Moseley's observation: life *is* hard for the Bundrens. Faulkner clearly sympathizes with them—though he by no means overlooks their folly. His treatment of them is complex and just, and his comment thus on the human condition generally is profound and profoundly moving.

Mr. Allen Tate has reported⁵ that the germ of *As I Lay Dying* was an anecdote Faulkner heard about a poor white's explanation of the significance of life's organization according to vertical and horizontal planes. It is to be found specifically in Anse's bitter comment (at the beginning of his first narrative) on the road that runs by his house— and a highly significant comment it is. "Durn that road," he says,

> A-laying there, right up to my door. . . . I told Addie it want any luck living on a road when it come by here, and she said, for the world

like a woman, "Get up and move, then." But I told her it want no luck
in it, because the Lord put roads for travelling: why He laid them
down flat on the earth. When He aims for something to be always
a-moving, He makes it longways, like a road or a horse or a wagon,
but when He aims for something to stay put, He makes it up-and-
down ways, like a tree or a man. . . . Because if He'd a aimed for man
to be always a-moving and going somewheres else, wouldn't He a put
him longways on his belly, like a snake? It stands to reason he would.
[Pp. 34–35]

This not only further characterizes Anse as lazy and opposed to the
necessity of movement but also clearly enunciates one of the most
important informing patterns of the novel—the opposition of vertical and horizontal.[6] Reinforcing Anse's observation and emphasizing
the informing pattern is the plump Doc Peabody's dilemma as he
faces the prospect of being hauled up the path to the Bundrens' to
pay his last professional visit to the dying Addie. Appropriately
enough, the path is almost vertical: "The path looks like a crooked
limb blown against the bluff. Anse has not been in town in twelve
years. And how his mother ever got up there to bear him, he being
his mother's son." His view of Anse, waiting at the top, is especially
pertinent, employing as it does the very terms of Anse's complaint
quoted above:

> He stands there beside a tree. Too bad the Lord made the mistake of
> giving trees roots and giving the Anse Bundrens He makes feet and
> legs. If He'd just swapped them, there wouldn't ever be a worry about
> this country being deforested some day. Or any other country. [P. 41]

In her single narrative soliloquy, Addie gives the fullest and most
articulate presentation of this pattern and its significance. To the
specified opposition of stasis and movement (i.e., of vertical and
horizontal) which poor Anse has developed, Addie's narrative adds
the associated opposition of the abstract and the concrete, of the
representative word and the actual deed, which to her is the opposition between the false and the true. The insight Addie offers resulted (she informs us) from her initial pregnancy, "when I knew
that I had Cash." One might say that for her Cash is the word made
flesh—an idea realized, the abstract made concrete and actual:

> That was when I learned that words are no good; that words don't
> ever fit even what they are trying to say at. When he was born I knew
> that motherhood was invented by someone who had to have a word

for it because the ones that had the children didn't care whether there was a word for it or not. I knew . . . that we had had to use one another by words like spiders dangling by their mouths from a beam, swinging and twisting and never touching, and that only through the blows of the switch could my blood and their [the schoolchildren's] blood flow as one stream. I knew that it had been, not that my aloneness had to be violated over and over each day, but that it had never been violated until Cash came. Not even by Anse in the nights. [Pp. 163–64]

And so when Cora Tull would tell me I was not a true mother, I would think how words go straight up in a thin line, quick and harmless, and how terribly doing goes along the earth, clinging to it, so that after a while the two lines are too far apart for the same person to straddle from one to the other; and that sin and love and fear are just sounds that people who never sinned nor loved nor feared have for what they never had and cannot have until they forget the words. [Pp. 165–66]

To a considerable extent, the whole action of the novel dramatizes, fleshes out, and tests the dualism which Addie enunciated—as she lay dying. And what is made manifest, discursively in Addie's narrative and dramatically in the novel's action, is a typically Faulknerian response to the question of how to live. It is no simple irony, furthermore, that the question of how to live is here confronted in the story of Addie's dying and death: those two crucial phenomena—living and dying—are of necessity inextricably combined, as they are in the brief exchange between the vital Dilsey and her husband, Roskus, on this subject in *The Sound and the Fury*. Roskus has rehearsed all the signs of an imminent death, including the magic number three: "They been two, now. . . . Going to be one more. I seen the sign, and you is too." Dilsey's simple reply reveals a recognition that is an important source of the strength of her vital being: " 'Going to be more than one more.' Dilsey said. 'Show me the man what aint going to die, bless Jesus.' "[7] If one is to be truly alive, the fact of mortality as an inescapable feature of human existence is not to be blinked. One must recognize death as the inevitable *terminus ad quem* of the process called life. The importance of that truth lies at the core of this as of every other novel of the Yoknapatawpha Saga. And it is Addie who utters that truth in her quaint way as she recalls her father's saying "that the reason for living was to get ready to stay dead a long time" (p. 161).

As I Lay Dying, then, might well be called Addie Bundren's novel.

At the center of the action, her dying motivates the journey to Jefferson, and causes all the living which the novel rehearses—at least
of the Bundren family and of those members of the community
immediately associated with them. The Bundrens undertake the
journey to gratify Addie's wish to be taken to Jefferson and buried
with her kin, and they are beset by virtually all the plagues that can
be visited upon man in the course of his life; it is, as numerous critics
have observed, the typical metaphoric expression of the journey of
life. Death causes the journey and the burial of the dead is its goal.
Addie's dying commits the whole family, with whatever degree of
reluctance, to the road that leads to Jefferson—the horizontal weft
of the novel's fabric that represents movement, action, vitality.

Ironically, Anse, a bundle of contradictions, the vertical man (in
the novel's terms), obliges the family to undertake the journey after
Addie's death. A further irony lurks in his explanation of why they
must set out in spite of the threatening weather; his reason seems
merely honorable—he must adhere to his promise to Addie:

> ". . . I wouldn't upset her for the living world. With that family
> burying-ground in Jefferson and them of her blood waiting for her
> there, she'll be impatient. I *promised my word* me and the boys would
> get her there quick as mules could walk it, so she could rest quiet.
> [P. 18; my italics]

But what emerges, with the helpful prompting of the context, is
Anse's reluctance to face the fact of death. He speaks of Addie's
impatience and of her being able to "rest quiet" as though she will
remain alive (as he has spoken of her kin "waiting for her"). Furthermore, the vertical-horizontal pattern which the novel has established adds a different coloring to Anse's claim of having "promised
my word." This, like other special words in the novel, can only
belong to that vertical string of words which Addie claims "go
straight up in a thin line, quick and harmless." The static Anse, then,
seems to be opposing his own deepest feelings in committing himself
and his family to the active journey along the earth. The occasion
thus seems a singular exception.

Other members of the family are like Anse in their refusal to
admit Addie's mortality and actual death.[8] Cash, the oldest son,
seems an exception since he is busily preparing Addie's coffin; but
two features of his industry cast it in a different light. At the outset
he is preparing the coffin for the benefit of the *living* Addie, work-

ing directly outside her window so that she may be aware of his industry and so that he can actually hold up the various finished pieces for her approval. Furthermore, the carpentering itself is an activity in which Cash can immerse himself sufficiently to insulate himself from the harsh reality of his mother's imminent death. That aspect of Cash's activity is underscored for us by Jewel's reaction; he opposes, severely and virulently, anything that seems to suggest his mother's death. The first words of Jewel's single narrative address themselves to Cash's display, "right under the window . . . where she can see him saying See. See what a good one I am making for you" (p. 14). And in the subsequent narrative (Darl's), in which they discuss whether to haul the load of wood, Darl suggests that Anse could borrow Tull's team and wagon "If she didn't wait for us." Jewel's abrupt retort is "Aw, shut your goddam mouth." Then he adds his brief aborted comment on the scene, and Darl supplies a significant explanation.

> "It's laying there, watching Cash whittle on that damn . . ." Jewel says. He says it harshly, savagely, but he does not say the word. Like a little boy in the dark to flail his courage and suddenly aghast into silence by his own noise. [P. 18]

Like Anse, Jewel believes in the power of the word; he will not say "coffin," for he does not want to confirm its actuality and, by association, the actuality of its purpose.

Dewey Dell is not so clearly disturbed by her mother's death, yet her activity with the fan at Addie's bedside may be seen as similar in protective function to Cash's carpentry—Jewel, at least, makes that specific association. Indeed, Dewey Dell, terribly preoccupied by the bud of life within herself—the result of going to the woods, the "secret shade," with Lafe—can scarcely attend to Addie's death (or to anything else). Little Vardaman, however, is the most pathetic in his frantic attempts to deny Addie's death, to come to terms with the lifeless figure lying in his mother's bed. His sadly grotesque action of boring holes in the coffin lid after Addie's remains have been enclosed is striking evidence of his confused dismay. And then Darl. But Darl in this, as in most of the family's affairs, is another matter.

All of the family (Darl excepted) seem unwilling to face the fact of death, to recognize mortality and mutability as necessary features of the human condition—the potential "wasness," as Judith Sutpen will call it (in *Absalom, Absalom!*) in Faulkner's most explicit expression of

this basic idea.[9] If Cash and Dewey Dell find distraction from the
momentous fact in carpentry and fanning, respectively, others turn to
actual surrogates for the departing Addie. Virtually from the outset
of the whole funereal action, Anse simply anticipates continued union
(or association) with his Mrs. Bundren—a second Mrs. Bundren, to be
sure, but Anse seems not to be overly troubled with nice distinctions.
We appreciate the somewhat acid prediction on Anse's widowerhood
made by Kate Tull: " . . . if it ain't her [Addie], he'll get another one
before cotton-picking" (p. 32). And we are strongly urged to recognize that Jewel's spotted horse functions for him (and to some extent
for Vardaman) as a mother surrogate, and that the huge fish functions similarly for Vardaman.[10] These diversions and surrogates,
then, are all means of evading the central synecdochic fact of Addie
Bundren's death. To resort to such evasions is to be associated with
the vertical plane, the warp of the novel's pattern (as established by
Anse and especially by Addie), to embrace that line that rises upward
(like words) away from the horizontal, the line of reality, true action,
concrete actuality, and thus to turn aside from the business of life's
journey and blink the journey's end. Such evasiveness simply denies
the truth of life, so Faulkner would urge us to believe; and in its way is
suicidal—like Horace Benbow's devotion to his blown vase and its
equivalent, the still unravished bride Narcissa, and like Quentin
Compson's devotion to his *idea* of Caddy, of her virginity, and of the
value embodied therein.

As denying Addie's death virtually denies her life, so it also denies
that familial or maternal relationship she makes possible—and that is
apparently so necessary to most of her children and even to Anse. It
is clear enough that one of the concerns of the novel is the problem
of individual self-identification. Darl's observations most effectively
explain the problem. Not all of the Bundrens, certainly, confront it,
but that (Darl strongly suggests) is so much the worse for them. So
denial of Addie—of her death and hence of her life—deprives the
Bundrens to some considerable extent of the awareness of communion with her that would aid in their identification of themselves;
that is especially true for Jewel and for Vardaman and even for
Anse, less so for Cash and for Dewey Dell, and of course for Darl
not at all. These several themes—identity, communion, actuality—
are drawn together in a memorable scene narrated by Vardaman,
the most anguished by his dilemma. Anse announces they will all
ride together "in the wagon with ma . . .":

> But my mother is a fish. Vernon seen it. He was there.
> "Jewel's mother is a horse," Darl said.
> "Then mine can be a fish, can't it, Darl?" I said.
> Jewel is my brother.
> "Then mine will have to be a horse, too," I said.
> "Why?" Darl said. "If pa is your pa, why does your ma have to be a horse just because Jewel's is?"
> "Why does it?" I said. "Why does it, Darl?"
> Darl is my brother.
> "Then what is your ma, Darl?" I said.
> "I haven't got ere a one," Darl said. "Because if I had one it *was*. And if it is was, it can't be *is*. Can it?"
> "No," I said.
> "Then I am not," Darl said. "Am I?"
> "No," I said.
> I am. Darl is my brother.
> "But you *are*, Darl," I said.
> "I know it," Darl said. "That's why I am not *is*. *Are* is too many for one woman to foal." [Pp. 94–95]

The general problem is focussed here in the anguish of little Vardaman as he attempts to understand the absence of Addie, to get a grip on "reality" and a sense of his own being, and to establish his identity. Significantly, he turns to Darl for aid. In his most important response to Vardaman, Darl simply confesses he has no mother and gives the attendant explanation "if I had one it *was*. And if it is was, it can't be *is*." (He will press the importance of this recognition again on Vardaman, a little later in the novel.) His continuation with the wordplay on the verb "to be" is half jocular and obliges Vardaman to recognize that Darl can exist *without* a mother; and then in his last sentence he turns to another but related subject that preoccupies him—Jewel's paternity—and mystifies his little brother, who then gives up the colloquy.

Associated with the theme of identification by relationships we find the complementary theme of identification by palpable, physical association; it is the attempted confirmation of being through touch (something like a Faulknerian equivalent of D. H. Lawrence's "blood consciousness"). Jewel's spotted horse (and surrogates in general) figures prominently in the development of this theme, and most obviously at the moment of Vardaman's frantic flight into the barn to establish close physical communion with the horse. Bereft of both mother and fish, he feels doubly deprived: "I can feel where the fish was in the dust. It is cut up into pieces of not-fish now, not-blood on my hands and overalls." He runs to the barn—

Then I can breathe again, in the warm smelling. I enter the stall, trying to touch him, and then I can cry then I vomit the crying. . . .

The life in him runs under the skin, under my hand, running through the splotches, smelling up into my nose where the sickness is beginning to cry, vomiting the crying, and then I can breathe, vomiting it. It makes a lot of noise. I can smell the life running up from under my hands, up my arms, and then I can leave the stall. [Pp. 52–53]

Little Vardaman gets some relief from this experience, even moves a step toward the hoped-for self-identification Darl was helping to guide him toward, as the horse seems to dissolve in the darkness and leave the boy to himself:

It is as though the dark were resolving him out of his integrity, into an unrelated scattering of components . . . an illusion of a co-ordinated whole of splotched hide and strong bones within which, detached and secret and familiar, an *is* different from my *is*. I see him dissolve . . . and float upon the dark in fading solution; all one yet neither; all either yet none. I can see hearing coil toward him, caressing, shaping his hard shape . . . smell and sound. I am not afraid.

"Cooked and et. Cooked and et." [P. 55]

Dewey Dell's narrative follows immediately, and the sequence helps confirm her involvement in the same necessity. She is looking for Vardaman and goes into the barn. There she too confronts the animal essence that her little brother has just been experiencing. First the cow: "She nuzzles at me, snuffing, blowing her breath in a sweet, hot blast, through my dress, against my hot nakedness, moaning." Further contact there is postponed,

Then I pass the stall. I have almost passed it. I listen to it saying for a long time before it can say the word and the listening part is afraid that there may not be time to say it. I feel my body, my bones and flesh beginning to part and open upon the alone, and the process of coming unalone is terrible. Lafe. Lafe. "Lafe" Lafe. Lafe. I lean a little forward, one foot advanced with dead walking. I feel the darkness rushing past my breast, past the cow; I begin to rush upon the darkness but the cow stops me and the darkness rushes on upon the sweet blast of her moaning breath, filled with wood and with silence. [P. 59][11]

The most meaningful blood contact for Dewey Dell has been that with Lafe in the woods at the end of the row of cotton, and as a result she is pregnant.

She and Vardaman are indeed their mother's children. Addie, too, has known the desperate need of blood consciousness. As Addie tells us, she had to establish palpable contact with her pupils—"especially in the early spring, for it was worst then."

> . . . my father used to say that the reason for living was to get ready to stay dead a long time. And when I would have to look at them day after day, each with his or her secret and selfish thought, and blood strange to each other blood and strange to mine, and think that this seemed to be the only way I could get ready to stay dead, I would hate my father for having ever planted me. I would look forward to the times when they faulted, so I could whip them. When the switch fell I could feel it upon my flesh; when it welted and ridged it was my blood that ran, and I would think with each blow of the switch: Now you are aware of me! Now I am something in your secret and selfish life, who have marked your blood with my own for ever and ever. [Pp. 161–62]

And she tells us further that the same thirst for blood knowledge, blood consciousness, obliged her to take Anse as husband. The same need that drove Dewey Dell into the woods with Lafe, that drove Jewel to buy his horse, and little Vardaman to anguish over his big fish and seek solace of Jewel's horse in the barn. The need for brute blood contact appears finally as destructive as the need for abstract symbols to replace the sane accommodation to actual life—the ability to refrain from denying life.

In view of all this it would seem monstrously ironic that the whole family agree to undertake the perilous journey to Jefferson to help Anse keep his *word* to Addie. None of them (Darl, always, excepted) seems really to want to admit she is dead, yet all seem agreeable to undertake the journey, ostensibly for Addie. Yet we soon enough realize that Addie has provided only the occasion for the journey: each of the Bundrens has an ulterior and compensatory reason to embark in the face of clearly threatening odds. Anse obviously wants the chance to "get them teeth" and to marry a new Mrs. Bundren. Vardaman early observed that "Pa shaves every day now because my mother is a fish" (p. 95). Little Vardaman himself welcomes the opportunity to get to Jefferson so he will be able to see the marvels of the toyshop, and especially the mechanical train. Dewey Dell sees the chance to get to a drugstore and buy some abortion medicine. Darl has said to her, knowingly, "You want her to die so you can get to town: is that it?" (p. 38). For Jewel the journey provides the opportunity to confirm Addie's faith in him, as she expressed it to

Cora Tull: "He is my cross and he will be my salvation. He will save me from the water and from the fire" (p. 160). The case is perhaps less clear for Cash; but it seems that at last his expertise as carpenter will be put to the test (coffins for the ladies, not shingles for the Lord), and perhaps the reward of a machine to make music to soothe the savage breast. As for Darl, the constant exception, the journey is a continual nuisance, and he wants only to see his mother—distinctly dead—buried and out of the way. It is no wonder that in our last view of him, Darl is demented and laughing madly at the prospect of his family's folly.

Vernon Tull, a balanced and objective and sardonic commentator on the folly of the Bundrens as motivated by Anse (as it appears to him), has clearly observed on the preparations for the journey, "They would risk the fire and the earth and the water and all just to eat a sack of bananas" (p. 133). And as we rehearse the consequences of the undertaking we can readily see how *As I Lay Dying* utters its peculiar statement of Faulkner's persistent theme of Self-Destruction. One cannot claim that here it is the Self-Destructiveness of Evil, for the Bundrens are too feckless, too innocent to be capable of actual evil. Rather their collective folly threatens them with destruction. They are, as we say, their own worst enemy. But as we review the effects of their journey we can see that they are dire enough. Anse has lost a span of mules. Cash has got a seriously broken leg and fierce complications from the inept attention given to it by his family, and he has furthermore been relieved of his small cache of money intended for a phonograph. Jewel has had to sacrifice his cherished spotted horse and has in addition been severely burned. Dewey Dell has been thwarted in her attempt to get the abortion medicine she hoped to find in Jefferson, and has in her turn been relieved of the little financial stake that was to make the purchase. Vardaman's great hope of achieving a par with the town boys by getting to see the fabulous toy train has been dashed. Even the well-intentioned Darl seems finally frustrated as he is taken into custody as a madman. But one can only believe that his final burst of uncontrolled laughter is a bizarrely sane commentary on the arrant folly of his family sitting in their stationary wagon, hugging their compensations in the midst of their fond futility.

For each of the Bundrens has achieved some compensatory reward for suffering the ardors of the journey. Anse has his new wife and his teeth. Cash has the comfort which the music of the phonograph will bring. Jewel can enjoy the peace that follows from finally having placed his mother with her own blood kin. And Dewey Dell and Vardaman are at least feasting on that sack of bananas which Tull foresaw as the pot at the end of their rainbow. But Darl, mad Darl, has his compensatory reward in institutionalization. And yet he laughs.

But what has he to laugh at?

If the novel is, in one sense, really Addie's, it is in another quite as much Darl's. It is he who focusses most sharply and intelligently on her dying and most persuasively analyzes and comments upon the behavior of the Bundrens. One almost feels at the end of *As I Lay Dying* that it has all been Darl's story, that just as what Tiresias sees is the substance of Eliot's *The Waste Land* so what Darl sees is the substance of this novel. He is given almost a third of the total number of narrative sections (there are fifty-nine, Darl has nineteen) and almost twice as many sections as the next busiest narrator (Vardaman with ten). But his function in the novel—his character and his behavior—encourages us to regard him as the predominant focussing agent. He is indeed mad; yet he is also the healthiest and most realistic of all the Bundrens. He shares with the idiot Benjy Compson the strange ability to *sense* what is going on where he is not—especially the descent of death—and to *sense* relationships of which he has little factual knowledge. In terms of the novel's vertical-horizontal pattern, he seems the sanest of the family. He relies neither on the empty symbols nor on the surrogates that the others employ in an attempt to manage their existence. He has the ability to communicate effectively without resorting to words—at least with one who is similarly attuned; and he is sane enough not to attempt it with those who are not. Dewey Dell shares the ability with Darl. After going into the "secret shade" with Lafe, Dewey Dell realizes that Darl *knows* what she has done:

> I saw Darl and he knew. He said he knew without the words like he told me that ma is going to die without words, and I knew he knew because if he had said he knew with the words I would not have believed that he had been there and saw us. . . . And that's why I can talk to him with knowing with hating because he knows. [P. 26]

Unlike Darl, however, Dewey Dell tries desperately to communicate silently with those who are not so attuned; her attempt to let Doc Peabody know of her pregnant condition and so enlist his aid pathetically exemplifies her futile effort at wordless communication.

If Darl thus escapes the condition of those who foolishly rely on words—that "go straight up, quick and harmless," and that "don't ever fit even what they are trying to say at"—he can speak aloud meaningfully enough when the situation demands it. His curt commands during the barn burning episode provide one example of his effective oral ability; and his brief dialogue with Vardaman about what their dead mother most wants is such another. He is, then, not to be confused with the static and ineffectual *vertical* members of the family: he is much more the active and effective *horizontal* figure who is realistic, capable of meaningful movement, sure of his own identity. His wistful poetic observations upon the road help us recognize his healthy commitment to the horizontal way: "tunnelled between the two sets of bobbing mule ears, the road vanishes beneath the wagon as though it were a ribbon and the front axle were a spool" (p. 38). The significance of that rather poetic image is implied by the association set up through the immediately subsequent question to his brother, "Do you know she is going to die, Jewel?" Much later a rehearsal and elaboration of the ribbon image (he is again in the wagon) confirms the association: "How do our lives ravel out into the no-wind, no-sound, the weary gestures wearily recapitulant: echoes of old compulsions with no-hand on no-strings: in sunset we fall into furious attitudes, dead gestures of dolls. Cash broke his leg and now the sawdust is running out. He is bleeding to death is Cash" (pp. 196–97). And before the end of that narrative section he adds another facet to the image: "If you could just ravel out into time. . . . It would be nice if you could just ravel out into time" (p. 198). Darl's observation at the ford where they try to cross with the coffin prepares for that facet of the image. Vernon Tull, Dewey Dell, and Vardaman are on one side of the river with Anse, the others have remained with the wagon; Darl looks across:

> It is as though the space between us were time: an irrevocable quality. It is as though time, no longer running straight before us in a diminishing line, now rises parallel between us like a looping string, the distance being the doubling accretion of the thread and not the interval between. [P. 139][12]

Precisely such passages as this encourage readers to understand the Bundrens' journey as synecdoche, as representing generally man's journey through life. Darl not only associates the road with time and sees it as being like a diminishing ribbon but also sees

clearly the goal toward which the road of life inevitably leads. Well
aware of the twin features of mutability and mortality as defining
characteristics of the human condition, he, unlike the other members of the family, can confront and accept those features. Darl
alone understands the importance of the concept of "wasness" and
the distinction between *was* and *is* generally; and Darl alone can
confront and accept Addie's death—both when it is imminent and
after it has occurred. And the peculiarly Faulknerian paradox is
here again eloquently effective, that in confirming Addie's death
Darl also confirms her life: in his willingness to speak of her as *was*
he implicitly recognizes she has been *is*. *but see AILD 204-205*

However unwilling to run counter to the manifest intentions of
his whole family, Darl cannot go against his knowledge of the demands of the human condition and must therefore attempt to confirm his mother's death by definite action. In the moving scene with
little Vardaman he tries to explain the situation in a way that the boy
will understand. (Appropriately, Vardaman's narrative contains the
scene.)

> . . . we can hear her inside the wood.
> "Hear?" Darl says. "Put your ear close."
> I put my ear close and I can hear her. Only I cant tell what she is
> saying.
> "What is she saying, Darl?" I say. "Who is she talking to?"
> "She's talking to God," Darl says. "She is calling on Him to help
> her."
> "What does she want Him to do?" I say.
> "She wants Him to hide her away from the sight of man," Darl says.
> "Why does she want to hide her away from the sight of man, Darl?"
> "So she can lay down her life," Darl says. [Pp. 204–5]

Darl attempts to cremate her by burning the Gillespies' barn while
her coffin is in it. When his attempt is frustrated he lies upon her
coffin and weeps in near desperation (see pp. 214–15).

Darl's sound attitude to death is complemented by his sense of
self-identity, clearest in the family; he need not depend on others to
help define his own being.[13] In fact, his affirmation of Addie's death
makes his relationship to her more meaningful than the others' ostensible attempt to prolong the relationship through their lugubrious journey and their resorting to surrogates like the fish and the
horse. Darl exhibits those virtues which Addie associates with the
horizontal way: he is realistic and active and life-affirming; he does

not need to rely on empty abstractions or on static representations of life. Darl is in contact with the real thing. Both Vernon Tull and Cash, in his best moments, encourage our view that the mad Darl is perhaps sanest of all. Tull muses, "I have said and I say again, that's ever living thing the matter with Darl: he just thinks by himself too much" (p. 68). And at the end of the journey Cash ponders the barn-burning and the evident need to send Darl to the asylum:

> Sometimes I aint so sho who's got ere a right to say when a man is crazy and when he aint. Sometimes I think it aint none of us pure crazy and aint none of us pure sane until the balance of us talks him that-a-away. It's like it aint so much what a fellow does, but it's the way the majority of folks is looking at him when he does it.
> Because Jewel is too hard on him. Of course it was Jewel's horse was traded to get her that nigh to town, and in a sense it was the value of his horse Darl tried to burn up. But I thought more than once before we crossed the river and after, how it would be God's blessing if He did take her outen our hands and get shut of her in some clean way, and it seemed to me that when Jewel worked so to get her outen the river, he was going against God in a way, and then when Darl seen that it looked like one of us would have to do something, I can almost believe he done right in a way. But I dont reckon nothing excuses setting fire to a man's barn and endangering his stock and destroying his property. That's how I reckon a man is crazy. That's how he cant see eye to eye with other folks. And I reckon they aint nothing else to do with him but what the most folks says is right.
> But it's a shame, in a way. [Pp. 223–24]

Having settled the problem so "reasonably," the careful Cash immediately escapes into his useful realm of controlled concern—bevels, trimmed edges, and rightly driven nails.

So the mad Darl is sent away. He leaves the scene laughing madly but crying out his affirmation, "Yes yes yes yes yes yes." What he has to laugh at is the final scene of his family in the stationary wagon, and the accumulated folly that scene represents; as though he were thinking of Tull's sardonic summation, "They would risk the fire and the earth and the water and all just to eat a sack of bananas"— and so much more. Darl, the Tiresias of *As I Lay Dying*, sees the Self-Destructive folly of his family and can only laugh. Not just the general or collective folly, but especially the specific folly that engulfs Dewey Dell as it had engulfed her mother years before. Two features in particular of the novel's closing movement direct us to that interpretation. The first is the sequence of narratives that im-

mediately precedes Darl's departure. MacGowan's narrative recounts
the seduction of Dewey Dell, who expects him to give her a "cure"
for her pregnancy. ("It wont hurt you. You've had the same opera-
tion before. Ever hear about the hair of the dog?" [p. 237].) Then
Vardaman, waiting for his sister, muses on Darl's being sent away to
the asylum at Jackson, and on his own disappointment over the toy
train—and the compensatory bananas. "Dewey Dell comes out. She
looks at me. . . . 'It aint going to work,' she says. 'That son of a
bitch' " (p. 241). And then Darl: " 'Why do you laugh?' I said." But
the terms he uses to recount his experience on the train with his two
guards make quite clear what is foremost in his thoughts:

> One of them had to ride backward because the state's money has a
> face to each backside and a backside to each face, and they are riding
> on the state's money which is incest. A nickel has a woman on one side
> and a buffalo on the other; two faces and no back. I dont know what
> that is. Darl had a little spy-glass he got in France at the war. In it it
> had a woman and a pig with two backs and no face. I know what that
> is. "Is that why you are laughing, Darl?"
> "Yes yes yes yes yes yes." [P. 244]

The focus upon the familiar image of the two-backed beast[14] is associated in Darl's intuiting mind with Dewey Dell's experiences first
with Lafe and consequently with MacGowan, and beyond that with
the experience of the young Addie. The association is made specific
in Darl's narrative concerning Jewel's purchase of the spotted horse,
"when he was fifteen." He recalls Addie's special protection of the
fatigued Jewel and expresses his intuitive perception of its meaning:

> That night I found ma sitting beside the bed where he was sleep-
> ing, in the dark. She cried hard, maybe because she had to cry so
> quiet; maybe because she felt the same way about tears she did about
> deceit, hating herself for doing it, hating him because she had to. And
> then I knew that I knew. I knew that as plain on that day as I knew
> about Dewey Dell on that day. [P. 129]

Darl alone of the Bundrens has adhered willingly enough to the
horizontal way, the life-affirming weft of the novel's fabric. He alone
seems intuitively to have recognized and been able to act upon the
truth that Addie utters. He seems also to have intuited the weakness
in Addie's life—that what she *did* denied the truth of what she *said*.
A significant feature of Addie's commentary on life is the mem-

orable image of the spider and its part in the warp and weft pattern of the novel: "I knew . . . that we had had to use one another by words like spiders dangling by their mouths from a beam, swinging and twisting and *never touching,* and that only through the blows of the switch could my blood and their blood flow as one stream" (p. 164; my italics). The blood she speaks of fits the pattern as weft, as the horizontal, just as the spiders and the line of words fit it as warp, as the vertical. Addie speaks of "the alive, . . . the terrible blood, the red bitter flood boiling through the land" (p. 166), and "of the wild blood boiling along the earth, of me and of all that *lived*" (p. 167; my italics). The blood, obviously, is the stream of life, and its course reminds Addie and us of "how terribly doing goes along the earth." We have been encouraged to see the horizontal as the vital way, the life-affirming way; yet Addie describes it repeatedly with the adverb "terribly." What is terrible in Addie's eyes, it seems to me, is the compulsion toward physical communion, toward blood-consciousness—it is the awful need to *touch.* That compulsion is seen also in Jewel's and Vardaman's and even Dewey Dell's association with the spotted horse, and Dewey Dell's carnal coupling with Lafe. It is seen quite clearly in Addie's terrible need to whip her pupils, to take Anse as husband—because he was there—and to take Whitfield later as lover. "In the early spring it was worst," she understandably confesses (p. 162).

It would seem, indeed, that yielding to that terrible compulsion to touch, as a further means of communion to aid self-definition and to confirm one's being, is finally as destructive as relying on symbolic abstraction—on words, quick and harmless. That equation is dramatized particularly in Addie's taking the Reverend Whitfield as lover. Addie's awareness of the futility of words was awakened, she tells us, by the birth of Cash. He was a palpable fact, a word made flesh, and he had "violated" her loneliness and made her really *mother,* with no need then for the word. But her desperate need is to have other abstractions made concrete and palpable; to have the important words "sin and love and fear" incarnate within her grasp. Hence the usefulness of Whitfield:

> I would think of sin as I would think of the clothes we both wore in the world's face, of the circumspection necessary because he was he and I was I; the sin the more utter and terrible since he was the instrument ordained by God who created the sin, to sanctify that sin He had created. While I waited for him in the woods, waiting for him

before he saw me, I would think of him as dressed in sin. I would
think of him as thinking of me as dressed also in sin, he the more
beautiful since the garment which he had exchanged for sin was sanc-
tified. I would think of the sin as garments which we would remove in
order to shape and coerce the terrible blood to the forlorn echo of the
dead word high in the air. [Pp. 166–67]

Having doffed the abstraction, she could grasp the thing itself. Whitfield is also for Addie the word made flesh. But it finally brings her
no more satisfaction than the empty word itself—even though it has
given her Jewel.

All this Darl must have sensed—not Whitfield specifically, perhaps, but someone who fulfilled his role with Addie. There is ample
evidence in the novel that Darl, like Tiresias in *The Waste Land,* has
indeed seen. He has gathered that Jewel is illegitimate and therefore
Addie's favorite, and often enough plagues Jewel with his question
"Who is your father?" And the mad Darl, furthermore, has seen the
awful but understandable folly of yielding to either compulsion—
both the resorting to abstractions and symbols and the rushing to
carnal touch—as a means of coming to terms with life and with
oneself. He himself resorts to neither, but is able to "straddle" both
lines. But then Darl is mad—mad as any sensitive soul hurt into
poetry by mad Ireland or mad Yoknapatawpha or the Bundrens.

Two responses Faulkner made to questions posed at the University of Virginia cast a good deal of light on Darl's situation. In explaining little Vardaman's dilemma Faulkner said, "He was a child
trying to cope with this adult's world which to him was, *and to any
sane person,* completely mad. That these people would want to drag
that body over the country and go to all that trouble, and he was
baffled and puzzled."[15] Then, explaining the special relationship of
Darl and Dewey Dell, Faulkner said, "She knows without being able
to phrase it that he is different somehow from the others through
his madness. That maybe he is more perceptive . . . that Darl is capable of a sympathy, a sensitivity, that won't react in violence to
serve an empty and to a woman foolish and silly code. . . ." And on
that peculiar sensitivity Faulkner added this:

Who can say how much of the good poetry in the world has come
out of madness, and who can say just how much of super-perceptivity
the—a mad person might not have? It may not be so, but it's nice to
think that there is some compensation for madness. That maybe the
madman does see more than the sane man. That the world is more

moving to him. That he is more perceptive. He has something of clairvoyance, maybe, a capacity for telepathy.[16]

It is Darl, principally, who has made poetry of the bizarre meanderings of the Bundren family. He is mad indeed, but perhaps the most sane. It is a further paradox, then, that so many of the *words* in *As I Lay Dying* are Darl's—he is the busiest narrator. But it must be recognized that for Darl (as for Faulkner behind him) real life is the abstraction which as poet he tries to make concrete and actual in his art, and words are the poet's poor means of rendering that abstraction concrete and actual.[17] But for Darl there is no confusion between his own actions and his "poetic" representation of those and his family's actions; and that saving health aids in his refusal to succumb to the general Bundren folly. Cash's observation at the close of the novel reveals a profound truth, after all:

> I would think what a shame Darl couldn't be to enjoy it [the phonograph music] too. But it is better so for him. This world is not his world; this life his life. [P. 250]

The justice of that observation, particularly the final sentence, has prompted readers to discern a kind of suicidal tendency in Darl and to compare him readily to Horace Benbow and Quentin Compson and others of that ilk yet to appear in the Saga—characters who feel, with some justification, that this world is not theirs. Panthea Reid Broughton may be allowed to speak for such readers (although in this instance she compares Darl and Quentin's father):

> ... even characters so astutely conscious of human motive and human error as Mr. Compson and Darl Bundren have performed a magical exaggeration of the world's difficulties. They have allowed awareness to defeat and debilitate them because they too wish to retreat from human responsibility. ... [*As I Lay Dying*] establishes that Darl's problem remains his inability to bear absurdity.[18]

Professor Broughton adds the very sound observation that "awareness of absurdity need not obviate commitment, as it does with Darl. Faulkner's heroic characters are always those who have seen how ultimately inaccessible to reason is existence; yet they are not paralyzed by the sight."[19]

Yet in spite of Darl's seeking escape in madness, he seems to me to appeal more fully to the reader's sympathy than do Faulkner's other suicidal characters (actual or potential). There is also a distinct and significant difference in social class between the poor-white Darl and the pseudoaristocratic Horace and Quentin and (later) Isaac McCaslin and Gavin Stevens. It is the arrant folly of "this world" that plagues Darl; those other characters regret the loss of the good old days and are plagued by mutability and mortality, which features of human existence Darl can confront with a contrastingly healthy attitude.

With Darl providing the critical focus on the activity which Addie's dying has prompted, the novel makes its interesting commentary on how to live. Not quite the *tour de force* Faulkner rather pejoratively claimed, it is yet something of an anomaly in the Yoknapatawpha Saga. To be sure, the familiar Faulknerian truths are there, especially the importance of facing those basic facts of the human condition— mutability and mortality. But the persistent informing themes which shape the whole development of the Saga, that of the Self-Destruc- tiveness of Evil and the theme of the Second Chance, by no means appear so clearly as important structural features in *As I Lay Dying* as they do in other pieces of the Saga. They are discernible here, cer- tainly, but seem somewhat skewed, as though Faulkner were not quite so sure—with whatever degree of consciousness—of how they ought to function in this novel. We have seen (with Darl's help) that in certain ways the Bundrens are their own worst enemies, that their determination to undertake the journey to Jefferson has led severally to a broken leg, severe burns, the loss of a span of mules and a horse and some money, and so on. But none of this is the result of what can seriously be called evil. The theme has become, then, the Self- Destructiveness of Folly—and even at that the self-destruction is per- haps merely threatened, not fully achieved. The novel is hardly tragic, pathetic much rather, as it exhibits the pathos of the Bundrens ("my people humble people") as they fondly seek compensation for life's wretchedness and misery. What tragedy there is derives from our sense of the real reason for the Bundrens' journey—a kind of poor-white hubris; and if that is their "tragic flaw" it is one that has largely been imposed upon them by the very social arrangement that has them in thrall and is responsible for their wretchedness.

Yet *As I Lay Dying* seems as close to being comic as it is tragic. Some faint sense of hope is there in its expression of the right attitude to life, its implicit indication of how to live. That regenera- tive attitude involves and fosters the right view of oneself, the prop- er means of achieving self-knowledge and individual identification

Second Chance

and of engaging in human intercourse. Beyond that there is the
novel's development of the theme of the Second Chance. For it is
there clearly enough, even though this novel develops it rather dif-
ferently than do the other novels of the Saga. At the conclusion of *As
I Lay Dying* one has the distinct sense that the remaining "free"
Bundrens—that is, all except Darl—are about to embark generally
on a Second Chance, that another cycle of Bundren activity is about
to begin. And that cycle is to begin with the compensatory reward
that most of them have realized.

But what is one to make of this implied new cycle, this Second
Chance for the Bundrens? Either the implication is ironic, that they
will merely repeat their folly, that things will go onward the same
though dynasties pass; or the implication is that these tough simple
folk will persevere, will endure—and perhaps not only endure but
prevail. Dewey Dell is something of a second-chance Addie, and
carries within her something like a second-chance Cash. But we are
not made to see that her coupling with Lafe was really prompted by
the same fierce compulsion that drove Addie to Anse and to Whitfield. Dewey Dell's union with Lafe is much rather like the innocent,
"natural" coupling that we shall see caused the pregnancy of the
delightful Lena Grove in *Light in August.* Dewey Dell seems, too, to
have learned even from her mean experience with the opportunistic
MacGowan—"That son of a bitch." And little Vardaman. He has
been to town and had his share of bananas and has at last seen
where the wonderful toy train performs its marvels; but more than
that, he has had the experience of the kind Darl's comments—and
who knows how much of that tender commentary will stay with him
and help guide him in his future?

Robert Hemenway's observations on the novel confirm this reading. He admits that the Bundrens' journey is in part an absurd
comedy, yet contends it is also at last a triumph:

> Faulkner was apparently using the Bundrens to exhibit two different
> attitudes toward time. As a promise to the past, their trip is ultimately
> absurd. As a commitment to the present, their trip may be justified.
> ... The Bundrens are foolishly motivated in an absurd journey,
> but they do not perpetuate the past (i.e., their foolish commitment to
> the past) beyond the point of burial.[20]

There is, after all, the possibility that the next go-round for the
Bundrens will be easier and more fruitful. And that possibility is
enhanced by what I have called the prophetic quality of Faulkner's

indulgent treatment of these simple folk. As we move from *As I Lay Dying* on toward the end of the Saga we shall see that increasingly Faulkner came to feel that the real hope for the future—not only for the fallen South but for mankind generally—was to be sought in the simple human creatures like the Bundrens, the Gowries of *Intruder in the Dust,* and finally even among the swarming Snopeses. Can they only endure, they may indeed prevail; and among them may finally be found the Saving Remnant.

> The Heart asks Pleasure first—
> And then—Excuse from Pain;
> And then—those little Anodynes
> That deaden suffering. . . .
>
> Emily Dickinson, no. 536

IV

Sanctuary

This powerful but often maligned novel of 1931 is Faulkner's most blatant presentation of the raw horror of evil. The evil is sharply defined by terms which Faulkner will use regularly thereafter to give it definition—terms which are effective, dramatically impressive, and generally compelling. Evil is presented as a gross perversion both of the natural and of human love; and of course the two are shown to be closely related.[1] *Sanctuary* tells the story of young Temple Drake who, fascinated by the forbidden, ventures like a female Young Goodman Brown into the dark labyrinth, and finds there more than she had bargained for. A human freak, Popeye, eagerly guides Temple into the depths of that labyrinth, and Horace Benbow, a lawyer and "intellectual," vainly attempts to combat some of the evil effects thrown up by Temple's venture.

This pair of characters, Temple and Popeye, dramatically focusses the evil; they are the center of action in the novel—the eye of the evil hurricane. Their union gives horrible expression to the perverse, unnatural lust, to human "love" gone sickeningly awry. Because of his impotence, Popeye must resort to substitutes in his intercourse with Temple—first a corncob, then the young man called "Red"; more generally, his pistol may be taken as Popeye's surrogate means of potency. That phallic surrogate is a nicely ironic symbol: its ejaculation carries the force of death rather than of life. Popeye's characterization from the very outset depicts him as unnatural and bizarre, opposed to natural life and willfully destructive of it. His face looks "bloodless"; his eyes are "two knobs of soft black rubber"; his whole figure has "that vicious depthless quality of stamped tin."[2] He spits into the spring at which he first meets Horace Benbow, on

73

the Old Frenchman's Place; he shoots nature's creatures simply because they impinge too closely on his living space. These features prepare us—if anything can—for Popeye's indulging in sex by remote control.

Partnership with Popeye is the goal toward which Temple's sick curiosity leads her. The fool Gowan Stevens, a burlesque of the Virginia Gentleman, can be held, in part, responsible for getting Temple into that mess, since he drove her to Goodwin's and wrecked his car, preventing their easy departure. But his responsibility is minimal: after all, Temple's brief history makes it quite clear that if not Gowan, another would have served as the convenient conveyance. The direction of her tendencies is plain enough, as her provocative behavior at Goodwin's makes clear. She is frightened there, to be sure, but fascinated by the situation—and the opportunities. Ruby Goodwin makes the correct diagnosis of Temple, recognizing her type as the most vicious kind of flirt. Temple wants the involvement to which Popeye is condemned—that of intimate observer. "You poor little gutless fool," Ruby chides. "Playing at it" (p. 58). And then, more seriously, "Afraid? You haven't the guts to be really afraid, any more than you have to be in love" (p. 59). A profoundly moral judgment of Temple, it touches the question not only of the perverse nature of her sexual fascination but also of any human sexual involvement of hers at all.

Confirmation of Ruby's interpretation seems to come from Temple herself, some time later, when she has agreed to tell Lawyer Benbow what went on at the Goodwins'. As she unfolds her tale of Van's attempt at her and of Popeye's eerie tactile explorations of her—and her anticipating his steady progress—which culminates in her rape, "suddenly Horace realised that she was recounting the experience with actual pride, a sort of naive and impersonal vanity, as though she were making it up, looking from him to Miss Reba with quick, darting glances like a dog driving two cattle along a lane" (p. 209). We recall Ruby's taunt: "You'll have something to tell them now, when you get back. Won't you?" (p. 58).

Faulkner gains a good deal by placing the perverse Temple-Popeye union in the setting of the Goodwins' common-law contract. Lee Goodwin, although innocent of the murder for which he is tried and of the rape for which he is lynched, is not altogether admirable. But Ruby gives him the single undeviating devotion and willingness to sacrifice that we like to believe are characteristic of true love.

Furthermore, the healthy physical aspect of that love—its "animal" side—is favorably presented: it is "natural." (This aspect of Ruby's love needs such favorable emphasis to help the reader later evaluate Horace Benbow's derogatory judgment of her as "mammalian"; perhaps it is not too much to anticipate that judgment a little by suggesting that it is the "nature" of mammals to be mammalian.)

The other principal setting in which Temple and Popeye are placed is the Memphis brothel of Miss Reba Rivers. Here man's "animal needs" are frankly admitted and catered to. The wheezy Miss Reba, salty, earthy, and humane, disapproves of Popeye's perverse carryings-on with Temple, once Minnie has enlightened Miss Reba about them.

> " . . . Minnie said the two of them [Temple and "Red"] would be nekkid as two snakes, and Popeye hanging over the foot of the bed without even his hat off, making a kind of whinnying sound." [P. 251]

Miss Reba indignantly claims that the reputation of her house has been threatened by Popeye. After she had run a respectable "shooting gallery" for twenty years, he tries to "turn it into a peep-show." The Temple-Popeye arrangement is here more explicitly contrasted with straight "normal," "healthy" sex.

Added to the perverse aspect of the union of Temple and Popeye is the vicious fact that Popeye's lethal influence produces, directly or indirectly, a series of victims. First is the simple Tommy, who tries unselfishly to protect Temple from being molested by the men at Lee's; Popeye shoots him. Second is Lee Goodwin, who, though innocent of Tommy's murder, for which he is tried and convicted and later lynched, will not contribute to his own defense lest he invite a slug from Popeye's unerring pistol. The third is Red, the stud whom Popeye has employed for vicarious fornication with Temple; Popeye kills him when Temple shows preference for Red as the real thing. Temple herself has been driven to a living death as a result of her association with Popeye. Miss Reba's prognosis— "She'll be dead, or in the asylum in a year, way him and her go on up there in that room" (p. 213)—is all the more convincing after we have Temple's almost zombielike perjury at Goodwin's trial. And again, at the close of the novel, when we have our last glimpse of Temple in the Luxembourg Gardens, seeming "to dissolve into the dying brasses, across the pool and the opposite semicircle of trees

where at sombre intervals the dead tranquil queens in stained
marble mused, and on into the sky lying prone and vanquished in
the embrace of the season of rain and death." Finally, of course,
Popeye himself is dead, and while it is not strictly a case of suicide,
he showed himself stubbornly unwilling to do anything on his own
behalf or even to allow the Memphis lawyer to undertake his defense, although he is, ironically, innocent of the murder for which
he is hanged.

In spite of this, its terrifying dramatic focus, the novel seems
finally to be the story of Horace Benbow, whose main concern is to
combat the evil that is and results from the Temple-Popeye union.
Specifically, Horace's attempts to defend Lee Goodwin against the
unjust charge of murder directly pit him against the antagonist evil
represented by that pair. At first glance he seems to have the necessary qualifications. He is an educated man trained in the law, a man
of some position in the community, and from an established family.
Furthermore, he is advantageously contrasted with Popeye in the
opening scenes of the novel as one who is evidently as much at home
with the natural world as Popeye is alien from it. Horace Benbow
sees quite clearly the difference between Good and Evil, and would
champion the former as he would oppose the latter.

It is easy to sympathize with Horace's dilemma as he attempts to
prepare a defense of the innocent Lee Goodwin, charged with a
murder Popeye committed. To begin with, Lee's refusal to do anything in his own defense frustrates Horace's attempts. Thanks to
Ruby's better sense, Horace learns that Temple had been at the Old
Frenchman's Place, is able to trace her to Miss Reba's brothel, and
there gets the story he needs. He loses track of this important witness; and then, with supreme irony, Temple appears at the trial like
a wound-up automaton to give perjured testimony which not only
convicts Goodwin but leads to his lynching. Poor Horace.

Well, perhaps; but before we take a second look at Goodwin's trial
and Horace's role in it, we might consider whether Horace's fate
there comes as a surprise or whether we have been at all conditioned
to expect something like that to occur. We may have understood and
appreciated his efforts to look after Ruby Goodwin, but the image of
Horace with which we are left is that of an incompetent. In getting
the Benbow house in shape he discovers he has "no more skill with a
mop . . . than he had with the lost [notice] hammer with which he
nailed the windows down and the shutters to ten years ago" (p. 115).

He adds the information that he couldn't even learn to drive a car, and begins his observation, "Sometimes, when I think of all the time I have spent not learning to do things. . ." (p. 118). There is something much more to this mildly charming stereotype of the intellectual for whom the practical matters of life are just too much—or too little: life's practicalities intimidate Horace; he wants to escape and rest from them; and in short, he is afraid. In the opening scenes of the novel, when the garrulous Horace is accounting for his presence at the Old Frenchman's Place, telling the men he had left home because he needed rest, Ruby hears him explaining over and over again that he just wanted a hill to lie on. He denies that spring was the mischief in him and adds, oddly, that Little Belle (his daughter) had set him off: he just wanted a hill to lie on for a while. "You see," he offers as an illuminating bolt of lightning, "I lack courage: that was left out of me. The machinery is all here, but it won't run" (p. 16). Poor Horace, indeed. Since his machinery won't run, Horace is "run" by the gaggle of women in his life, as we gradually discover. His wife, Belle, and his stepdaughter, Little Belle; his old aunt, Miss Jenny Du Pre, and his sister, Narcissa; all of these do with Horace just about what they want, and (with the possible exception of Miss Jenny) they almost "run" him to death. Worst of all, surely, is that Horace knows this about himself and his situation and can or will do nothing but yield—in spite of his protestations. The truth of the matter glimmers out when, for example, Horace assures Ruby that he will not be bossed around by the women of the town who want her moved out of respectable Jefferson dwellings; as Horace helps move Ruby out of a respectable Jefferson dwelling and into the ramshackle house of "an old half-crazed white woman" who "manufactured spells," he asserts himself to Ruby: " 'I've already let too many women run my affairs for me as it is, and if these uxorious. . .' But he knew he was just talking. He knew that she knew it too, out of that feminine reserve of unflagging suspicion . . . which is in reality practical wisdom" (p. 194).

It is hard to escape the truth that with all his professed good intentions, in spite of his evident ability to distinguish quite plainly between Good and Evil and his certain knowledge that one ought to espouse the former and eschew the latter, yet Horace Benbow is not man enough (as we say) to do what he ought and to realize his theoretic pretensions. He is simply not man enough.

Although Horace is initially set in opposition to Popeye, and may be considered to maintain that role throughout much of the plot, the novel expresses by that very juxtaposition a tacit comparison between the two. Horace's fundamental tendency toward resignation makes him, in effect, as impotent as Popeye. Furthermore, certain marked features of Horace's proclivities suggest that he and Popeye are equally out of tune with nature. These two aspects of Horace's character are most markedly sketched by his attitude to Little Belle, his stepdaughter. The first substantial indication of that attitude occurs in the opening scenes at the Old Frenchman's Place. It deserves full quotation. Horace recounts—

> "From my window I could see the grape arbor, and in the winter I could see the hammock too . . . That's why we know nature is a she; because of that conspiracy between female flesh and female season. So each spring I would watch the reaffirmation of the old ferment hiding the hammock; the green-snared promise of unease. What blossoms grapes have, that is. It's not much: a wild and waxlike bleeding less of bloom than leaf, hiding and hiding the hammock, until along in late May, in the twilight, her—Little Belle's—voice would be like the murmur of the wild grape itself. She never would say, 'Horace, this is Louis or Paul or Whoever' but 'It's just Horace.' Just, you see; in a little white dress in the twilight, the two of them all demure and quite alert and a little impatient." [P. 13]

We are familiar enough with Faulkner's hammocks and swings, having read *The Sound and the Fury,* and we might almost expect Horace's head to be plagued with the bewitching and poignantly suggestive scent of honeysuckle (as poor Quentin Compson's head too often was); and we know what happens in spring to a young man's fancy—and to a young woman's too. Horace is fascinated by the scene in spite of himself—fascinated, attracted, and repelled. He later scolds Little Belle mildly for having picked up a strange young man on a train. She responds hotly, taunting him about what he picks up on trains (shrimp, for her mother), and cries at him "Shrimp! Shrimp!" She apologizes immediately and hurls herself into his arms, "I didn't mean that! Horace! Horace!" And he gratefully accepts her embrace and apparent contrition. Then he sees her face, over his shoulder, reflected in one of two opposing mirrors, of which Little Belle is unaware: "she was watching herself in the one behind me, forgetting about the other one in which I could see her face, see her watching the back of my head with pure dissimulation. That's why nature is 'she' and Progress is 'he'; nature made the

grape arbor, but Progress invented the mirror" (pp. 14–15). That
little wretch (or bitch), we say. Poor Horace.

But poor Horace is hooked, fascinated by the girl. Subsequent
references to Horace's attitude toward her as he looks at the photograph of Little Belle (not of her mother, his wife) which he keeps
with him, develop the theme of Horace's perverse attraction. Following his conversation with Miss Jenny, who tells him of Narcissa's
"heartless" refusal of Gowan Stevens' proposal of marriage (the sequence is significant), Horace returns home and looks at the photograph of Little Belle:

> . . . the photograph had shifted, slipping a little from its precarious
> balancing against the book. The image blurred into the highlight . . .
> he looked at the familiar image with a kind of quiet horror and de-
> spair, at a face suddenly older in sin than he would ever be, a face
> more blurred than sweet, at eyes more secret than soft. In reaching
> for it, he knocked it flat; whereupon once more the face mused ten-
> derly behind the rigid travesty of the painted mouth, contemplating
> something beyond his shoulder. [Pp. 162–63]

The last phrase pointedly echoes the earlier scene in which Little
Belle contemplates in the mirror her performance with poor Horace.

A third reference to his disturbed attitude to the girl seems quite
explicit enough to settle the matter. Horace returns home after
hearing Temple's shocking relation of her experiences at Goodwin's
(and again the sequence is significant); he turns on the light and
picks up the photograph:

> Little Belle's face dreamed with that quality of sweet chiaroscuro. . . .
> the face appeared to breathe in his palms in a shallow bath of high-
> light, beneath the slow, smokelike tongues of invisible honeysuckle
> [and there it is—Quentin Compson's legacy]. Almost palpable enough
> to be seen, the scent filled the room and the small face seemed to
> swoon in a voluptuous languor, blurring still more, fading, leaving
> upon his eye a soft and fading aftermath of invitation and voluptuous
> promise and secret affirmation like a scent itself. [Pp. 215–16]

Horace's attraction to Little Belle appears to be of the kind and
strength of Quentin's attraction to his sister, Caddy, or of Horace's
earlier attraction to his own sister, Narcissa. Not only is it patently
erotic and indeed lustful, it has been granted full recognition after
Horace has seen the marks of sure corruption in that sweet little
face—a face older in sin than he would ever be, as he had earlier

phrased it to himself. The context in which this steamy passage is set requires for its completion the subsequent and final paragraph of the chapter (chap. 23). It may seem ambiguous at first. Some shock of recognition drives Horace to the bathroom where he succumbs to a fit of nausea following his association of Little Belle with Temple Drake which gives way to a nightmarish hallucination in which Little Belle/Temple is bound naked on her back on a flatcar roaring through a tunnel and then on outward and upward "toward a crescendo" (p. 216)—not at all unlike the rocket that shoots up and bursts over Leopold Bloom as he finishes spying on the little lame Gertie McDowell on the beach (in *Ulysses*).

Critics have suggested that Horace is overcome by the thought that Little Belle might well fall prey to the evil which seized Temple Drake; it seems likelier, however, in view of the total characterization of Horace Benbow, that he is overcome by the recognition of his own attitude to his stepdaughter—a kind of cerebral lust. At best, the passage and its context remain ambiguous—there may well be something of both; but to rule out the second is, I think, to miss much of what the novel is expressing about Horace Benbow. And again the parallel with Popeye is striking: Horace's impotent desire for Little Belle—the cerebral lust, as I have called it—matches Popeye's impotent lust for Temple Drake.[3]

Nor is this the first example of impotent desire in Horace's life, as readers of *Sartoris* will remember. In that novel Belle Mitchell served to answer Horace's physical needs, as glassblowing and his sister partly satisfied his spiritual. In *Sanctuary*, Little Belle has largely replaced Narcissa, who has emerged as far less sympathetic than she was as the unhappy wife of young Bayard Sartoris some ten years earlier. Yet something remains of the old Horace-Narcissa relationship. She dominates him rather cruelly, yet it is to her he turns at his moment of severest disappointment—weeping like a child, as he suffers her to take him home. As usual, Horace is much more than half aware of his situation as it involves him with Narcissa.

An interesting association between Narcissa and Little Belle is briefly but sharply set up for us, as it perhaps exists in Horace's mind, by a couple of images used to depict Narcissa when we first see her and Horace together. He has entered his sister's home unexpectedly, yet she greets him "without outward surprise, with that serene and stupid impregnability of heroic statuary; she was in white." (She has apparently "lived into" the role Horace had created

for her a dozen years before, that of the still unravished bride of
quietness whom he would address as "O Serene," as we recall from
Sartoris.) "She had never been given to talking, living a life of serene
vegetation like perpetual corn or wheat in a sheltered garden instead
of a field . . :" (p. 103). The association of Narcissa with nature in
this simile reminds us of Horace's association of Little Belle and the
grape arbor (and the useful hammock). The latter association appeals to one side of Horace's desires—the lusty, animal, natural appeal of sap-rife spring, yet touched by the piquant aroma of the
already corrupt; the former appeals to his other side—the controlled, fenced-in, exclusive and private, the retiring and secret even,
where nature is tamed and formalized and her products not even
intended for their usual and proper use but only as decoration. In
both cases the "nature" is somewhat unnatural, and that is at least
partly due to the eye of the beholder. Horace is fascinated, both
attracted and repelled, by the exciting and dangerous, the corrupt
and forbidden Little Belle; he is mildly repelled but yet feels at
home with the calm, serene, domesticated Narcissa, who no longer
really extends her seductive appeal. This aspect of the garden variety Narcissa is only reinforced by the earlier image of her as the
serene and stupid—and impregnable, notice—piece of heroic statuary. It is with that object that Horace doubtless belongs. He will
certainly belong to some woman; certainly no woman will belong to
him. His impotence, his inability to cope with the actual world,
makes that impossible.

Again the parallel between Horace and Popeye emerges. Faulkner
has arranged further expression of that instructive association by the
juxtaposition of two otherwise barely related scenes. Chapter 25
ends with Miss Reba and friends lamenting the late Red, and Miss
Reba telling them of Popeye's impotent, vicarious intercourse with
Temple. Chapter 26 begins with Horace finishing a letter to Belle,
asking for a divorce, which of course he never gets, and dreaming of
escape into peace. The striking impotence of both men is expressed
here, appropriately in terms of their relations with women—the two
cases benefiting from tacit mutual commentary. The intervening
transitional paragraph makes this particular juxtaposition effective,
providing excellent cohesion by the illumination obliquely reflected
from its superficial narrative. The paragraph tells of the boy, Uncle
Bud, drinking himself sick on beer stolen from Miss Reba and her
guests and from the house's icebox. Yet because of the context and

the moment of the scene, the realistic items seem heightened to metaphoric eloquence. We have just had Miss Reba's account of Popeye, watching Red and Temple copulate, "hanging over the foot of the bed without even his hat off, making a kind of whinnying sound." Of course that recalls other accounts of Popeye's performance, his facial expression, and so on. The next chapter begins its reference to Horace with the information that "he had not been to bed, nor even undressed"; it reminds us of his relations with the two Belles in his family and also of the scene, just two chapters earlier, in which thinking of Little Belle and Temple simultaneously had sent him retching to his bathroom. The intervening paragraph reflects eloquently and with innocent unconcern on the two wretched men in their limp impotence and incapacity for life:

> Feet came up the hall; they could hear Minnie's voice lifted in adjuration. The door opened. She entered, holding Uncle Bud erect by one hand. Limp-kneed he dangled, his face fixed in an expression of glassy idiocy. "Miss Reba," Minnie said, "this boy done broke in the icebox and drunk a whole bottle of beer. You, boy!" she said, shaking him, "stan' up!" Limply he dangled, his face rigid in a slobbering grin. Then upon it came an expression of concern, consternation; Minnie swung him sharply away from her as he began to vomit. [P. 252]

A brilliantly effective passage, which one hates to maim with commentary; it is so exactly right and so exemplary a piece of dramatic expressiveness that one wants to borrow a line from Henry James's appreciation of a similar example in Turgenev's fiction: "We close the book for a moment and pause, with a sense of personal excitement."[4]

Finally, the insistent comparison of Horace and Popeye as two characters out of tune with nature, perversely involved in the realm of human love as observers (not to say voyeurs), and impotent, leads us to the recognition of a profoundly important distinction between them. Popeye cannot help being impotent; Horace can (in the usual sense of the word) help it, but chooses to be so. From most of what we learn about Horace, we are obliged to conclude that he fears and hates most of actual life—its reality, its animality, its truth. Horace's refusal of Ruby's offer to pay him for his legal services in the only way she knows is interesting not because of the refusal, but because of the terms in which it is couched. "O tempora! O mores! O hell! Can you stupid mammals never believe that any man, every man— You thought that was what I was coming for?" (p. 267). "Mammals" gives it away. Not principally the prostitution, but the resorting to the fundamental nature of the human animal strikes Horace. One can easily make too much of this, certainly; but we have the evidence of the whole novel, with all its preoccupation with the basically animal—but "natural"—in man and the perversion of that natural aspect. Another guide to our understanding of Horace and of his most representative failing—as it will appear in the continued development of the Yoknapatawpha Saga—is given by his concluding remark to Ruby in this conversation. He counsels courage and optimism and trust in the Lord: "God is foolish at times, but at least He's a gentleman. Don't you know that?" Ruby's reply speaks volumes: "I always thought of Him as a man" (p. 273).[5] That distinction, of which Faulkner would think well enough to repeat it in the sequel, *Requiem for a Nun,* adds a fitting final touch to Horace's distaste for the physical, actual reality of life. He would not involve Him in it—or himself either.

Horace fervently wishes to resign from life. We remember his response to Miss Reba's sage comment on Temple—that she will soon be dead or in the asylum; Horace thinks it would be better if she were dead now, better if they were all dead: "her, Popeye, the woman [Ruby], the child, Goodwin, all put into a single chamber, bare, lethal, immediate and profound. . . ." Then he adds the understandable and significant inclusion of himself.

> And I too; thinking how that were the only solution. Removed, cauterized out of the old and tragic flank of the world. And I, too, now that we're all isolated; thinking of a gentle dark wind blowing in the long corridors of sleep; of lying beneath a low cozy roof under the long sound of the rain: the evil, the injustice, the tears. [Pp. 213–14]

How very like Quentin Compson's is his desire to be isolated out of the loud world. Seldom so explicit in his thoughts as he is here, Horace has revealed what we nevertheless recognize as his habitual attitude of mind—not just a momentary fit of depression and yearning for total escape, like that of the speaker in Frost's "Stopping by Woods" who has promises to keep and will keep them. Thus we catch fully the heavy yearning behind the comparatively mild expression of his desire to get away to Europe. Having finished the letter to Belle asking for a divorce, Horace thinks, "I'll finish this business [the trial] and then I'll go to Europe. I am sick. I am too old for this [Horace is forty-three]. I was born too old for it, and so I am sick to death for quiet" (p. 253).

Horace, then, is amply characterized as a man fitted for failure—
not simply one to whom success will be denied but who will not want
to involve himself in any real struggle for success. He is an incompetent in matters small and large; his interests are perverse and unnatural, especially his interest in the opposite sex. Horace is impotent
generally and willfully. This is the man who failed to defend Lee
Goodwin effectively. Should that failure come as a surprise and
should we consider Horace a victim of ill luck? I would suggest that
Horace's conduct of his defense perfectly coincides with his characterization, even including Temple's perjured testimony—although
that is a vexed matter and will need an additional word.

An apparently simple matter reveals that Horace is not quite what
one would hope for in a lawyer. Narcissa has, of course, been objecting strenuously to his trying to care for Ruby Goodwin and her
baby—putting them up in the old Benbow home, and so on. Miss
Jenny adds her voice to the objection, but on quite a different basis.
She asks Horace whether the attention he has given Ruby doesn't
amount to collusion, connivance: "It seems to me you've already had
a little more to do with these folks than the lawyer in the case should
have" (p. 114). In his jocular response, Horace calls Miss Jenny
"Mrs. Blackstone," but seems to agree with her point of view: "sometimes I have wondered why I haven't got rich at the law. Maybe I
will, when I get old enough to attend the same law school you did"
(p. 114). Then, when confronted with Temple's testimony during
the trial itself, Horace quite collapses, gives up, resigns. He simply
lets the District Attorney have his way with an apparently objectionable line of questioning. The judge himself virtually chides Horace
for failing of his responsibility by neglecting to object to the questioning. Thus, even though he knows a good deal of what Temple is
hiding, Horace asks her not a single question as defense attorney.
Furthermore, he knows that Gowan Stevens was at the Old Frenchman's Place for at least some of the time, but he has made no effort
to find him and bring him to testify. Horace simply gives up; he is
not only less than competent, but unwilling even to try. His last
posture is one of willed impotence. Of course, Goodwin might well
have been convicted in spite of all Horace's efforts; but the point is
that, once seriously challenged, Horace made almost none. I find it
very difficult indeed to see Horace as anything but culpable in his
misconduct of Goodwin's defense; it is difficult even to see that his
intentions were good. The novel finally alters its dramatic focus to

portray this concluding failure of the impotent Horace Benbow, as though that were its ultimate concern. The very last scene, Popeye's brief trial and execution, seems calculated to serve as terminal commentary on Horace's miserable defense of Goodwin. The slight but pointed parallel between the two juries' deliberations—"The jury was out eight minutes" (pp. 284, 304)—compels us to think of the two trials and verdicts as closely related. We can speculate on the significance of that connection in a moment.

First, Temple's testimony. It is admittedly a bit of a puzzle, but it does seem clear that Eustace Graham and the Memphis lawyer are in some important way responsible for Temple's appearance at the trial and also for the nature of her testimony. The behavior of the lounging Memphis lawyer suggests that he is the power there, that Eustace is acting on his advice and instructions. It would appear that that Memphis lawyer and the Memphis lawyer who shows up at the last minute offering to intervene in Popeye's case are one and the same. From that probable association has come the suggestion that Popeye sent him to see that Temple duly appeared at the trial to give evidence against Goodwin. The assumption that Popeye instructed the lawyer in what to do may rest on Popeye's remark when he refuses the lawyer's aid in his own case: "I didn't send for you. Keep your nose out" (p. 306). The implication is that he could have sent for him in this instance if he had wanted, and hence might well have sent for him to act in Goodwin's trial. It seems to me quite as likely, however, that someone other than Popeye sent for the lawyer in *both* cases, and that the someone sent the lawyer to look after Temple's testimony not only to protect Popeye but also as a means of getting at, gaining control of, Judge Drake, Temple's father. Certainly Judge Drake would not have hired this sort of lawyer; and anyway it is evident that Judge Drake has only recently been informed that Temple would appear in court and that he could "recover" her there. (His spurning Temple's flashy purse as he leads her away indicates that he had not been present to check her dress and accessories before her appearance in court.) Clarence Snopes's unsavory and clearly frustrated role in all this finagling seems to have been an attempt to play both sides—that is both Judge Drake and Horace—in his information peddling scheme, and finally to do business with the Memphis lawyer. I think it most likely that he ran into something much too big for him when he approached the Memphis lawyer (if he did), and that some associated thugs—not Temple's brothers—roughed Clarence up.

I am working toward the implication that, hovering around the edges of the novel, filling those puzzling spaces into which we cannot see, rebuffing our unanswered questions, and threatening our speculations, is an opaque, all-embracing system of evil—a system (or syndicate or organization) which includes the Memphis lawyer and Popeye and the thugs present on the occasion of Temple's abortive attempt to escape with Red, and which brushes with its wings almost all the characters of the novel. We never know the source of Popeye's money; we know that he is very handy with his pistol. We wonder why the Memphis lawyer charges Popeye, "Are you so tired of dragging down jack that . . . You the smartest—" (p. 306).[6] The implicit suggestion here that Popeye is a valuable contract man, a professional killer, in that system or syndicate would explain his money and his associations—even perhaps his unexplained presence at the Old Frenchman's Place: he may have been hiding out there for a while, and Goodwin's bootlegging industry may be part of the syndicate's interests. The appropriate response, however, is not an attempt to fill in the blanks (an attempt doomed to failure, anyway), but our dim awareness of some organized system of evil looming just beyond our range of vision—the more frightening as it remains vague and unspecified.

I think that Aubrey Williams's general observation on the novel is quite sound and extremely helpful:

> The true and ultimate shock in the novel is not to be found in the single grotesque episode in which a young girl is raped with a corncob. It is to be found in the larger pattern of evil and injustice of which this episode is one mere instance. It is a pattern of evil and a vision of the world which is hardly comparable with anything else Faulkner has written, though it does have important unexplored connections with the rest of his work. In this novel at least, Faulkner presents us with a bleak assertion that the human body is not a temple of the holy spirit, and with an equally bleak assertion that, for man, there is no sanctuary.[7]

(We will attempt to determine the justice of that final comment on Faulkner's "bleak assertions" as we continue to consider the whole shape of the novel.)

Horace Benbow's discovery of such a system of organized evil "out there" is the significant anagnorisis of the novel. (*Sanctuary* is surely not concerned with Horace's simple discovery of evil or with his discovery that evil exists in the nature of things.) Associated with

Horace's discovery is his recognition that he himself participates in that system of evil, (1) because certain aspects of it so nearly match the evil in himself, and (2) because in his unwillingness to confront that evil and attempt to combat it, he himself contributes to its continuance. I take it that something like this—a semiconscious recognition of it, perhaps—is behind Horace's thought that "it is upon the instant that we realize, admit, that there is a logical pattern to evil, that we die . . ." (p. 214). Included in that recognition may be Horace's realization of the parallel between himself and Popeye—in all those terms in which we have seen the novel express that parallel. Popeye may almost appear to Horace (as he surely does to us) as something like the emblem of Horace's own failures—his impotence, his rather perverse fascination with Little Belle, and so on—an externalization, a symbol of his own evil.[8] We must be aware, however, that the words last quoted above belong to Horace, i.e., that they do not represent Faulkner's thoughts on the matter. When *Horace* realizes and admits that there is a logical pattern to evil, *he* thinks *he* is dead—or knows he is as good as dead because of his participation in it. But Horace has long been committed to death, or its "other kingdom." That is the "tragedy" of *Sanctuary*. Toward the very end of his career in the novel, Horace plaintively notices nature's persistence, and utters his revealing observation upon that phenomenon, mixing memory and what little remains to him of desire: " 'It does last,' Horace said. 'Spring does. You'd almost think there was some purpose to it' " (p. 285). Horace reveals himself as the modern wasteland man who lacks the courage and vital love that would enable him to share in the rites of spring. In Horace's eye alone, then, is vernal promise fraudulent and meaningless; April is the cruelest month, not because its promise is purposeless, but precisely because it demands positive, creative action.[9]

I have suggested that *Sanctuary* presents the tragedy of Horace Benbow; "tragedy" is certainly too ponderous a term for his career, as Horace never shows us much at all of tragic stature. Yet that term comes closest to giving the sense of what the novel is about. He is, by various standards, the best man on the scene. He is intelligent and has been "well educated," he knows the difference between Good and Evil, and he is the obvious champion of the Good, of Truth and Justice—at least professedly. But, unable to act on his knowledge, he disappoints our legitimate expectations. That inability, in turn, seems to rest upon his antipathy to the gross reality of life—Horace's equivalent of a tragic flaw. His hubris is the feeling that he is "above all that." He cannot love actual nature—human nature especially—and therefore fails of courage. That is the pity of his case, and from that derives much of the terror of his involvement.

Yet the end of this tragic spectacle produces an effect closer to depression than tragedy is usually found to produce. There seems little enough to put our hope in. The one saving shred derives from the influence upon us of the theme of the Self-Destructiveness of Evil. To be sure, the forces of Evil commit enough mayhem, and one feels that there is more where those came from. The evil is focussed, to a considerable extent, in the figure of Popeye, however, and all of his characterization expresses the idea that Evil's principal agent is not only incapable of perpetuating itself but is finally destructive of itself. Evil's agents, we infer, will work their will for a while, but being impotent and self-destructive, they can not endure and ultimately will not prevail—even in the absence of a strong and courageous antagonist and champion of the Good. Since the virtually impotent Horace, bent as he is on finding peace (like Quentin Compson) outside of actual life, is finally as destructive of himself as is Popeye, one can grasp at the hope that someone—some courageous man of good will—can step into the void he leaves and lend a hand to speed the self-destructiveness of the agents of Evil.

Sanctuary leaves us fully conscious of the awful possibilities of Evil's ravages and disappointed in the failure of one who clearly sees the better way but sags into the path of escape. For all that, its effect is not devastating despair, and we may be allowed to wait patiently for the first notes of a requiem that would reaffirm our hope for sanctuary.

> I wonder where I'm gonna die,
>   Being neither white nor black?
>   Langston Hughes, "Cross"

V

Light in August

This popular novel, published in 1932, is the *locus classicus* of the principal themes with which I am concerned. Insofar as it treats of the career of Joe Christmas it is something of a *Bildungsroman* which traces the education Joe receives at the hands of various mentors who represent the dominant elements of his society and its guiding values. Principal among those values are the ethical teachings of their religious persuasion—Protestant Christianity of a sternly "Puritan," Calvinist cast. Joe emerges finally, after his slaying of Joanna Burden, as a kind of scapegoat; and the novel makes clear that Joe is exactly the product of his education, that his society has prepared him to be precisely what he has become, and that in their vengeful punishment of him they punish not only their own sinfulness but in very fact strike against themselves—all unwittingly: their evil doings are reflexive. The education of Joe Christmas thus develops the theme of the Self-Destructiveness of Evil. The explicit condemnation, however, prominently excludes two major characters who comprise a Saving Remnant in the novel—the good man Byron Bunch and the regenerate Gail Hightower. (Conditional exculpation may finally be extended much more broadly by the implicit expression of the novel as a whole, as we shall consider below.) Those two major characters, coincidentally, also provide important links connecting the novel's two main "stories"—that of Joe Christmas and that of Lena Grove. The two-part structure of the novel as defined by those two "stories" permits the effective expression of the theme of the Second Chance, underlined by the pair of characters named Joe— Christmas and Lena's baby, never officially named, but never called anything but "Joey."

The interesting two-part structure might be described as the tragic story of Joe Christmas held in the bracketing embrace of the comic story of Lena Grove; the latter frames the former, as the novel begins and ends with depictions of Lena's odyssey. And one might add that, in those terms, the novel is a two-part love story—in its comic mode as far as Lena and Byron Bunch are concerned, and in its tragic mode (like the tragic love song of J. Alfred Prufrock) as far as Joe Christmas is concerned.

The bulk of the novel, of course, is devoted to the career of Joe Christmas. In depicting Joe, Faulkner creates initially a strongly antipathetic impression of the character, and later provides the explanatory influences and experiences that make the reader reassess his early reaction to Joe and perhaps overcompensate for that with a comparably strong sympathetic response, a strategy he will use again, most obviously in the depiction of Thomas Sutpen in *Absalom, Absalom!* The *Bildungsroman* aspect of the novel soon begins to unfold, enabling us to follow the process of perverse education responsible for producing the gruff, repulsive creature we first met at the mill and for driving him to the murder of Joanna Burden—the crucial episode in Joe's tragic career.

Joe's education, the moulding of his character, is punctuated by his experiences with a series of women (or at least females): the maternal little Alice at the orphanage, the orphanage dietician, Mrs. McEachern, the Negro girl, Bobbie Allen, and finally Joanna Burden. Those experiences, furthermore, colored by the pervasive Calvinist influence of his Grandfather Hines, of his foster-father McEachern, and again finally of Joanna, teach him that womankind, love, and what it means to be Negro are three related features of Evil. Joe learns to associate woman with evil in two ways. First, he learns that she is devious, surreptitious, and unreliable, and (what is more) deceptively kind or generous or even gentle, inviting reliance, openness, and hence vulnerability; in this she is the distinct opposite of the frank and direct hardness of Calvinist Christian authority, usually represented by men. Second, as the female of the species (the *she*, the *ewig Weibliche*), woman represents all Joe can know of love, that is, sex—the Puritan abomination. And in addition, Joe learns the indelible lesson that "Negro" is synonymous with "evil."

What Joe's education does not teach him unequivocally is whether or not he is himself Negro. It is of crucial importance for a proper understanding of the novel to recognize (as too many critics have failed to do) that no one knows Joe's racial identity. Joe's mentors have taught him unequivocally the signal importance, for their society, of knowing whether one is "white" or "black." The suspicion that he may be black, once planted in Joe's mind, prevents him forever from accepting for himself the simple identity of a human being. What further complicates Joe's "identity crisis" is the conviction, indelibly impressed upon him by his education, that to be black is to be evil. The novel gives emphasis to that equation at the moment when Joe's "identity" is established by Brown's disclosure that Joe is a "nigger" and by the acrid irony of the marshall's response:

> " 'Nigger?' the sheriff said. 'Nigger?'
> ". . . 'The folks in this town is so smart [Brown says] . . . I knew before he even told me himself.' . . .
> " 'You better be careful what you are saying, if it is a white man you are talking about,' the marshall says. 'I dont care if he is a murderer or not.' "[1]

The marshall has reasserted the society's ranking of values. And part of the tragic bitterness of Joe's ultimate return to Jefferson, where he faces capture and "crucifixion," is that he apparently prefers accepting the identity society has at last definitely imposed on him to having no identity at all. He has finally given up the struggle against the education his experience has given him.

Almost every one of Joe's formative experiences contains all three features of the triple-faceted structure of evil as he is taught to understand it. At the orphanage, under the smoldering eye of his mad grandfather and amidst the children who had "been calling him Nigger for years" (p. 125), Joe is befriended by the girl, Alice. But one morning he awakes to find that she has deserted him: "Vanished, no trace of her left, not even a garment. . . . He never did know where she went to" (pp. 127–28), and he has no memory of her taking leave of him. A minor episode, but as one in an undeviating list it makes its impression. The first major episode in the education of Joe Christmas follows a couple of years later, his being caught *in flagrante delicto* by the orphanage dietician: he is eating her toothpaste in her closet while she is making love with the young interne named Charley. Little Joe is, of course, not playing voyeur and is not consciously aware of what the dietician has been doing with Charley. He is sure, however, that he has been doing wrong (stealing toothpaste), and that particular wrongdoing is for him asso-

ciated—if only subconsciously—with "the soft womansmelling garments" and the "rife, pinkwomansmelling obscurity behind the cur-
tain" (pp. 113, 114). And when he is caught, his evilness is characterized for him distinctly by the dietician: "you little rat! . . . You little
nigger bastard!" (p. 114). Then follows his puzzlement over the apparent inversion of values and his discovery of the secretive and
devious nature of woman: the dietician asks him not to tell and
offers to bribe him with a dollar. "It never occurred to her that he
believed that he was the one who had been taken in sin . . ." (p. 115).
When he refuses the bribe to keep quiet about his evil (as he understands it), the strange woman curses him again: "Tell, then! You
little nigger bastard! You nigger bastard!" (p. 117). He has thus
learned: (1) to be evil is to merit the identity of "nigger," and (2)
woman is devious and secretive and on evil's side (she has offered to
bribe him to conceal his evil). He has also associated those two, at
some level of his consciousness, with sex, with woman as *she*, not
simply by the association with the "womansmelling garments" but,
retrospectively, by the association he makes between this experience
with the dietician and his later one with the Negro girl (and he will
make further such associations among his various experiences of this
kind—i.e., with the several women).

At age fourteen, now residing with the McEacherns, he is introduced to sexual experience by four of his chums and the willing
Negro girl. The crucial moment connects this encounter with his
experience with the dietician, and quite specifically enough characterizes the three-fold nature of evil as it has been impressed on him:

> His turn came. He entered the shed. It was dark. At once he was
> overcome by a terrible haste. There was something in him trying to
> get out, *like when he had used to think of toothpaste.* But he could not move
> at once, standing there, *smelling the woman,* smelling the negro all at
> once; enclosed by the womanshenegro and the haste, driven, having to
> wait until she spoke. . . . He kicked her hard. . . . She began to scream,
> he jerking her up, clutching her by the arm, hitting at her with wide,
> wild blows, striking at the voice perhaps, feeling her flesh anyway,
> enclosed by the womanshenegro and the haste. [Pp. 146–47; my ital-
> ics]

The portmanteau "womanshenegro" captures the essence of the
three-fold evil, Joe's Unholy Trinity: *woman,* the devious, secretive
female; *she,* the potential sexual partner; *negro,* bluntly evil.

The context of this scene associates it in turn with the McEacherns and specifically with Mr. McEachern. The scene begins with Joe's realization that he would be whipped when he reached home: "he would receive the same whipping though he had committed no sin as he would receive if McEachern had seen him commit it." Then, as he awaits his turn with the Negro girl, "Perhaps he did not even think of it as a sin until he thought of the man who would be waiting for him at home . . ." (p. 146). For McEachern represents Christian teaching, stern rectitude, authority; and in his eyes, Joe is clearly a sinner. (Joe vis-à-vis McEachern is comparable to Huck Finn vis-à-vis society: whenever Joe does what he wants, he tacitly echoes, in effect, Huck Finn's crucial "All right, then, I'll *go* to hell." This is not to equate Joe's fornication with Huck's aiding the fleeing Jim, but to equate generally McEachern's prohibition against Love in its broadest sense with the similar prohibition of Huck's society.)

Consequently, Joe suspects and resents Mrs. McEachern, whose acts of generosity and maternal affection he interprets as evil: she acts thus against her husband's wishes—secretly, deviously, and even blatantly—and her appeal to Joe (like the dietician's proffered bribe) he can only fear because he cannot understand it, and further because it is the appeal of gentleness and hence an invitation to vulnerability. When she brings him a tray of supper after his day-long ordeal with McEachern and the catechism, Joe cannot accept it, but must dump the tray and its contents unceremoniously onto the floor. For the hardness of McEachern is unambiguous if hateful, and Joe knows where he stands with him. When, finally, Joe takes Mrs. McEachern's secret savings, he roughly assures her, "I didn't ask, because I was afraid you would give it to me. I just took it" (p. 196). He wants things clear and uncomplicated.

Joe's experience with Bobbie Allen furthers his education. With Bobbie lay the possibility of straightening out his inverted values—as, indeed, there had lain with Mrs. McEachern. But again the rude, punitive intrusion of McEachern breathing the wrath of Jehovah prevents any good corrective result. Bobbie is kind and generous and protective in her treatment of Joe. After his initial shock at the discovery of her menstrual "sickness," Joe can accept Bobbie as a woman and subsequently as the sexual *she*. He is then moved to test the third part of the "unholy" trinity: after telling her "about the negro girl in the mill shed on that afternoon three years ago," he adds "I think I got some nigger blood in me" (p. 184). Her refusal to accept that bit of information seems to Joe to confirm her complete acceptance of him, and promises to lead him to some salvation from the corrupting effects of McEachern's diabolism. But as Joe attempts to commit himself to his new-found good, McEachern comes storming in crying abomination and bitchery (echoing Hines's language) to persecute Joe's pursuit of love outside his home as he successfully did within it. In so doing, the evil force of McEachern provokes its own destruction: Joe kills him.

Yet the Calvinist intrusion has upset Joe's attempt at love and seriously frightened Bobbie; the well-intentioned but simple girl can see only trouble ahead—trouble brought by Joe. Her response to the situation is a reversion to the dictates of her society, for she has "discovered"—as Joe had and would again—that "nigger" means evil. She had accepted him and in a sense loved him, but in the moment of crisis the current prejudice of her society and specifically the scornful attitude of Mame and Max prevail. She damns Joe: "Bastard! Son of a bitch! Getting me into a jam, that always treated you like you were a white man" (p. 204). And then the familiar curse: "He told me himself he was a nigger! The son of a bitch!" (p. 204).

Poor Joe had come offering marriage to Bobbie. The evil in her which springs forth and repulses Joe, the "nigger," deprives Bobbie, in turn, of what may well be her own last chance for love. The act of hateful rejection thus defeats Bobbie's better self. Her act is self-destructive.

And so Joe begins his fifteen-year flight, testing his lesson about the three-fold evil of the world with a series of prostitutes—woman and *she*—and adding always his own component, Negro. That repeated act is certainly an attempt at confirming self-knowledge, but at the same time it is an act of self-condemnation. Significantly, Joe beats up the one prostitute who has nonchalantly refused to be revolted at his telling her he is a Negro. The irony persists. And when finally he encounters Joanna Burden, it is to learn yet again all the lessons about womanshenegro and Calvinist Christianity that he has already been taught.

At first, Joanna is, for Joe, the secret and devious woman he had found Mrs. McEachern to be. He enters her house at night "like a thief, a robber" (p. 221); and Joanna assumes her role as *she*, the sexual partner. Their love-making is at first like combat (the inversion of love), and Joe's attitude to his conquest of her is punitive: " 'I'll show her,' he said aloud. . . . 'At least I have made a woman of her at

last,' he thought. 'Now she hates me. I have taught her that, at least' "
(pp. 222–23). But things threaten to right themselves, albeit suspiciously. Joanna's apparent generosity in setting out food for him reminds him of Mrs. McEachern's suspicious bringing of food (rewarding him after he has done wrong), and Joe's reaction is the same—he
dumps the food onto the floor. Yet Joanna's generosity is apparently
like Bobbie's, and Joe relents, yields to the kindness. But again he
must test, with the nearly acceptable woman, the not-revolting *she,* the
third term of his trinity: "one of [my parents] was part nigger"
(p. 240). Joanna's rather noncommittal "How do you know that?"
seems as good as acceptance—as good as Bobbie's acceptance.

Joanna has prompted this "confession" from Joe by telling him her
own life story. At first she seems to offer a tale parallel to Joe's, but at
last it proves to be rather the negative inversion. Joe's has tended to
relieve him of the sense of evil attached to womanshenegro (as it had,
temporarily, with Bobbie) and thus to permit redemption, while Joanna's is a preparation to plunge with abandon into the recognized
evil of that trinity—and again with that peculiar, inverted Christian
authority. Her autobiography proves her to be a true descendent of
Calvin, and the irony of her surname appears in the rehearsal of the
paternal teaching about the white man's burden: "the curse of the
white race is the black man . . . God's chosen own because He once
cursed Him" (p. 240). Thus is prepared the second phase of their
relationship; it was "as though he had fallen into a sewer" (p. 242).

> At first it shocked him: the abject fury of the New England glacier
> exposed suddenly to the fire of the New England biblical hell. . . . she
> appeared to attempt to compensate each night as if she believed that it
> would be the last night on earth by damning herself forever to the hell
> of her forefathers, by living not alone in sin but in filth. [P. 244]

She plunges with a vengeance into the role Joe has learned to recognize—of the devious, secretive woman ("hidden in closets, in
empty rooms, waiting") and the eternal *she* ("in the wild throes of
nymphomania"); and she leaves Joe in no doubt that she revels in his
contribution of the third part of the Unholy Trinity. "She would be
wild then, in the close, breathing halfdark without walls, with her
wild hair . . . and her wild hands and her breathing: 'Negro! Negro!
Negro!' " (p. 245). That terminal exclamation of lustful ecstacy
strikes Joe's ears with the force of "Sin! Sin! Sin!" He knows; he has
been well taught.

The third phase begins as it must with Joanna's ceasing her bath in sin and deciding to save herself and Joe—to shoulder her white man's burden. Joe leaves her alone, begins bootlegging on the side; and, as he thinks of this decision, he recalls something of his history, thus drawing together his experiences and underlining for us the similarities among them:

> Very likely she would not have objected [to the bootleg whiskey]. But neither would Mrs McEachern have objected to the hidden rope; perhaps he did not tell her for the same reason that he did not tell Mrs McEachern. Thinking of Mrs McEachern and the rope, and of the waitress whom he had never told where the money came from which he gave to her, and now of his present mistress and the whiskey, he could almost believe that it was not to make money that he sold the whiskey but because he was doomed to conceal always something from the women who surrounded him. [P. 247]

The third phase and the whole relationship also end as they must, with Joanna's explicitly impressing on Joe his role as a figure of evil: she wants to pray for him and wants him to pray for himself. She had taken Joe, accepted him, apparently as Bobbie Allen had, but in fact in quite the reverse way—as complete evil. Joanna's offer to aid Joe in going to college is contingent upon his agreeing to identify himself unequivocally as Negro, as the figure she had exulted over in her depths of lustful ecstacy—the very act and association for which her prayers (and his) are to ask forgiveness. Her praying expresses Joanna's wish to reject him exactly as she had originally accepted him and as she had obliged and encouraged him to be. The irony is again sharp and double-edged. Joanna's rejection of Joe provokes her own destruction, as her last act and the result it produces dramatically express. Once again Joe has been hated and taught the lesson of hate when he might have expected love. And once again the hatred proves self-destructive.

The killing of Joanna and the subsequent pursuit of Joe leads us to the novel's most explicit expression of its theme of the Self-Destructiveness of Evil. As the pursuit reaches its climax, the Reverend Gail Hightower focusses our attention sharply on that theme. He does so in two steps, the one in general terms, the other in specific. Joe has been caught and incarcerated; Hightower sits musing and listening to the music from the church that once was his:

> . . . the music has still a quality stern and implacable, deliberate and without passion so much as immolation, pleading, asking, for not love,

not life, forbidding it to others, demanding in sonorous tones death as though death were the boon, like all Protestant music. . . . he seems to hear within it the apotheosis of his own history, his own land, his own environed blood. . . . Pleasure, ecstacy, they cannot seem to bear: their escape from it is in violence, in drinking and fighting and praying; catastrophe too, the violence identical and apparently inescapable. *And so why should not their religion drive them to crucifixion of themselves and one another?* he thinks. It seems to him that he can hear within the music the declaration and dedication of that which they know that on the morrow they will have to do . . . to the doomed man in the barred cell within hearing of them and of the two other churches, and in whose crucifixion they too will raise a cross. [Pp. 347–48; Faulkner's italics]

Their religion, the religion of Hines and McEachern and the Burdens, drives them to crucify themselves and one another. Their persecution and destruction of Joe amounts to persecution and destruction of themselves. (Here again Faulkner's fiction makes the equation of fratricide and suicide.) Hightower explains that for them to pity Joe "would be to admit selfdoubt and to hope for and need pity themselves" (p. 348)—most obviously Mrs. McEachern's dilemma—and they dare not admit it. So the crucifixion will take place.

The crucifixion of Joe Christmas is accomplished by the enthusiast Percy Grimm, the efficient and heartless neonazi who tracks down Joe, pursues him into Hightower's home, and kills and mutilates him. Later, Hightower again sits musing on all that has occurred and the various actors in the tragedy; his musing (the second step) envisions a kind of wheel of history surrounded by a halo full of the faces of the actors:

They are peaceful, as though they have escaped into an apotheosis; his own is among them. In fact, they all look a little alike, composite of all the faces which he has ever seen. But he can distinguish them one from another: his wife's; townspeople [etc.] . . . and that of the man called Christmas. This face alone is not clear. It is confused more than any other, as though in the now peaceful throes of a more recent, a more inextricable, compositeness. Then he can see that it is two faces which seem to strive . . . in turn to free themselves one from the other, then fade and blend again. But he has seen now, the other face, the one that is not Christmas, "Why, it's . . . , " he thinks. "I have seen it, recently. . . . Why, it's that . . . boy. With that black pistol [i.e., Percy Grimm]. . . ." [Pp. 465–66]

These two quoted passages together suggest very strongly that the action of the society as a whole and of Percy Grimm individually is suicidal, self-destructive, reflecting the old Abolitionist argument that the slaveholders are themselves enslaved, that the evil they do turns back upon themselves. That is also an adaptation of a principal message of Christ; and here we recognize clearly the function of the Christ-likeness of Joe Christmas—his name, the foot-washing, his betrayal for cash by a disciple, his final mutilation by a soldier, etc.[2]

The characters in the novel are tested and judged according to their treatment of Joe Christmas as are the characters of *The Sound and the Fury* according to their treatment of Benjy Compson; and to lend particular value to that judgment, Faulkner has so character-ized Joe as to oblige us to think of Christ as we read of him. Both Benjy and Joe suffer through lack of Charity; while Benjy responds favorably to the love of Caddy and then of Dilsey, Joe has been so conditioned that his reaction to love is perverse rejection. Thus Joe suffers on the one hand from uncharitable treatment, and on the other from his *learned* inability to respond to Charity, to gestures of love. As most critics agree, the dominant mode of *Light in August*—or at least of that part of the story which has specifically to do with Joe's career—is irony. For not only is the Christ-like figure a character who hates and murders, but the whole theme of religion in Joe's story expresses Christ's teachings ironically. Love has become hatred and Joe's religious training is, like the practice of his teachers, bla-tantly inverted. The explanation of Joe's "inversion" lies with those who have educated him: his Christ-likeness serves to emphasize the evil of those inverted "Christians" responsible for driving him into the evil he does. And insofar as that evil harms those who have instilled it in him, those original evil sources (the inverted Christians) are hoist on their own petard—they are themselves victim of the evil they have done.

It is as though the novel were finally paraphrasing, in the focal scenes quoted above (Hightower's musings), the admonition of Christ: "Inasmuch as ye have done it unto one of the least of these my brethren ye have done it unto me." Or, of the persecutors collectively, that in hounding and slaying a fellow man they are in effect destroy-ing the best that is within them, that they are in their evil self-destruc-tive. In his depiction of Joe Christmas's career, Faulkner seems intent on expressing that to harm one's neighbor is to harm oneself. It is Faulkner's adjusted expression of the second great commandment.

Yet the novel does not end on this note, but moves to its comple-tion by resuming the story of Lena Grove, and thereby giving final emphasis to its second principal theme—the theme of the Second Chance. And *Light in August* offers one of the clearest statements of that theme in its optimistic mode. Its obvious manner of development is (to use a favorite term of Faulkner's) recapitulant. The novel began by leading the reader into the scene of action as he watches Lena's terrifically slow approach; Lena and the reader, both outsiders, are drawn into the scene which is to be dominated by the fierce figure of Joe Christmas—himself quite expressly an outsider also. And when we learn the motive for Lena's journey, we come to recognize the main question which the novel poses: "Who will care for Lena's baby?"

The novel closes with Lena and her baby leaving that scene of action (and of course drawing the reader's eye away also, with something of the sense of "tomorrow, to fresh woods, and pastures new") but taking with them the best representative of that society's virtue, its capacity for charity—Byron Bunch. Thus the novel's main question is largely answered. Byron has earned his place finally at the side of Lena and her baby through his courageous and truly charitable concern for them. And the same is true for all those characters who have functioned in both "stories" of the novel—especially Gail Hightower and the Hineses but really all the various minor characters of the whole society who rose to the occasion (however reluctantly in some instances) presented by the advent of Lena and the birth of her baby. Lena Grove and her "Joey" have given these people the chance to demonstrate their capacity for love. Indeed, they are really thus given their Second Chance, for it is a chance to compensate for their collective failure to accord true charity to Joe Christmas and hence the chance to gain something very like redemption for themselves.

The theme of the Second Chance has been consistently developed in the novel. The Hineses, Joe Christmas's maternal grandparents, began the persecution that hounded Joe to the murder of Joanna Burden and finally to his death. In particular, the crazed Doc Hines relentlessly pursued Joe as the product of "bitchery and abomination"; for him the additional horror is that Joe's father was (Hines believes) a Negro. But when finally they are thrown together with Byron and Hightower and Lena and "Joey," Mrs. Hines lavishes on the baby all the compensatory love she had been unable to bestow on her Milly's Joe. Significantly, it is Mrs. Hines who, in her distraction, gives Lena's baby the only name it bears in the novel, "Joey," confusing Lena with her own daughter, the present with the past. And her persistence in using the name has a marvellous influence on Lena, who says, "She keeps on calling him Joey. When his name aint Joey. . . . She is mixed up someway. And sometimes I get mixed up too. . . ." Then Lena confesses to an additional confusion which contributes an interesting dimension to the relationship that the novel establishes between Christmas and the baby: "She keeps on talking about him like his pa was that . . . the one in jail, that Mr Christmas. She keeps on, and then I get mixed up and it's like sometimes I cant—like I am mixed up too and I think that his pa is that Mr—Mr Christmas too—" (pp. 378–88). Willy-nilly, however, Mrs. Hines has faced her Second Chance and done so with a display of courage and conviction.

The Reverend Gail Hightower represents an evil that is auxiliary to those chiefly active in the novel (the evils of racism and of the fanaticism of inverted Christians)—the nostalgic idealization of the Southern past as chivalric romance. In the case of Doc Hines, fierce racial hatred and bizarre religious fanaticism blocked any capacity to love and contributed to the perversion of Joe's tendency to love; in the case of Hightower, a foolish fascination with the romantic myth concerning his forebears—those galloping horses and waving plumes that surge between him and reality—has blocked his capacity to love, has spoiled him in his role as husband and so frustrated his wife's need for love as to drive her directly to her wretched death, and finally has deprived him of his church. Hightower has virtually cut himself off from society; Byron Bunch sustains his last, fragile social link. But as the capture and imminent punishment of Joe Christmas press in upon his consciousness, Hightower finds that he cannot continue to escape involvement altogether. And the process of Hightower's reclamation and redemption begins as that involvement increases—whether he will or no. His redemption depends upon his own self-discovery, the recognition of his own weakness and culpability.

His first stage in that journey is his musing realization of the weakness and guilt of his former parishioners and of the people of Jefferson in general. He recognizes their shared guilt, their participation in the suicidal, reflexive evil, focussed in their persecution and crucifixion of Joe Christmas. As he listens to the church organ and the voices singing hymns, he thinks of Joe, of "the doomed man in the barred cell within hearing of them and of the other two

churches, and in whose crucifixion they too will raise a cross. 'And
they will do it gladly,' he says. . . . 'Since to pity him would be to
admit self-doubt and to hope for and need pity themselves . . .' "
(p. 348). But he cannot yet admit his own involvement with them; he
does catch a glimpse of that important truth as he hears in the music
"the apotheosis of *his own* history, *his own* land, *his own* environed
blood" (my italics), but he cannot yet accept it. Like Hemingway's
Nick Adams (in *In Our Time*) and Frederick Henry, Hightower believes he has made "a separate peace." When Byron asks him to
intervene and provide an alibi for Joe, Hightower refuses fiercely: "I
wont! I wont! do you hear?" (p. 370).

Gail Hightower is offered his Second Chance, specifically the
same as that offered to the people of Jefferson generally, by Lena
Grove and the coming Joey. Byron gives him the opportunity to
become involved in the affairs of Lena as her time of labor is imminent. And that opportunity is itself presented in two parts—a Second Chance within a Second Chance, so to speak. At first he refuses
Byron's invitation, dismisses him, and takes refuge in his study;
there he selects a book—

> He turns from the window. One wall of the study is lined with books.
> He pauses before them, seeking, until he finds the one which he
> wants. It is Tennyson. It is dogeared. He has had it ever since the
> seminary. He sits beneath the lamp and opens it. It does not take long.
> Soon the fine galloping language, the gutless swooning full of sapless
> trees and dehydrated lusts begins to swim smooth and swift and peace-
> ful. It is better than praying without having to bother to think aloud.
> It is like listening in a cathedral to a eunuch chanting in a language
> which he does not even need to not understand. [P. 301]

Tennyson's language is the equivalent of Hightower's obsessive, nostalgic dream; and it is, of course, lifeless and emasculate. When
Byron returns later to offer the opportunity again, he employs a
shrewd psychology, making no explicit request this time, but simply
announcing "She says it's about due now" and asks about Hightower's midwifery book—"I just wanted to remind you in case you
would need to take it with you" (p. 373). Having made no request,
Byron has given Hightower no occasion to refuse. So when Byron
and the doctor arrive at Lena's bedside, they find that Hightower
has preceded them and indeed has functioned as midwife in the
birth of Joey. The significance of Hightower's reinvolvement, his
thus accepting the Second Chance, especially its revitalizing and per-

haps redemptive effect, is emphasized by his subsequent reaction on returning home. " 'I showed them!' he thinks. 'Life comes to the old man yet, while they get there too late. . . .' He moves like a man with a purpose now, who for twentyfive years has been doing nothing at all between the time to wake and the time to sleep again. Neither is the book which he now chooses the Tennyson: this time also he chooses food for a man. It is *Henry IV . . .*" (pp. 382–83).

An additional result of his having accepted the Second Chance is his willingness now to respond to Byron's request that he intercede on Joe's behalf with an alibi. It is, of course, too late, for the matter is well beyond Hightower's control, rendering futile his belated attempt to provide an alibi for Joe. Yet the attempt in itself indicates the progress Hightower has made in his reengagement, his resumption of moral responsibility. Furthermore, that reengagement vouchsafes him a clearer understanding of himself and of his social involvement. He can now recognize other responsibilities: his failure in his church, the fond vanity of his nostalgic dream (responsible for his failure as pastor), and his guilt in the death of his wife (for which that fond dream was also responsible).

> He seems to watch himself among faces, always among, enclosed and surrounded by, faces . . . the faces seem to be mirrors in which he watches himself. . . . He seems to see reflected in them a figure antic as a showman, a little wild: a charlatan preaching worse than heresy, in utter disregard of that whose very stage he preempted, offering instead of the crucified shape of pity and love, a swaggering and unchastened bravo killed with a shotgun in a peaceful henhouse, in a temporary hiatus of his own avocation of killing. [P. 462]

The foolish, nostalgic idealization of his grandfather and his actual attempt to recapture that identity himself is oddly fused in Hightower's mind with his new sense of guilt in his wife's death:

> . . . if I am the instrument of her despair and death, then I am in turn instrument of someone outside myself. And I know that for fifty years I have not even been clay: I have been a single instant of darkness in which a horse galloped and a gun crashed. And if I am my dead grandfather on the instant of his death, then my wife, his grandson's wife . . . the debaucher and murderer of my grandson's wife, since I could neither let my grandson live or die. . . . [P. 465]

This stage completes Hightower's *anagnorisis*, his final recognition of his own inevitable involvement and participation in his society's shared guilt—the inescapable reciprocity and mutuality. And he is thus led to that final musing vision of the wheel of history surrounded by the halo of faces—"his own is among them" (p. 465). His perception that no man is an island, that fratricide is suicide, that Percy Grimm and Joe Christmas (crucifier and crucified) are one and the same—his perception, in a word, that every man is his brother's keeper and that one must indeed love one's neighbor as oneself—has resulted from his successful acceptance of the Second Chance. And we cannot avoid here the signal effectiveness of Faulkner's depiction of Joe as a Christlike figure and his careful association of Joe and Joey (Joe I and Joe II, we think) as a means of augmenting the significance of Hightower's choice.

Certainly our last glimpse of the Reverend Gail Hightower, again musing at his window, would seem to suggest that he has suffered a relapse, a regression, for again his thoughts are full of the plumes and sabres and galloping horses. But we have been prepared to reject that easy and superficial interpretation, prepared by all that has preceded this closing scene: we have seen Hightower recognize and admit his own moral involvement in society's total responsibility—the significance of "his own environed blood"; and while Faulkner's depiction of the new Hightower hardly bears comparison with Dickens's depiction of the new Ebenezer Scrooge, we realize that the Reverend Gail Hightower now knows those wild bugles, clashing sabres, and thundering hooves for the fond, empty dream they truly are. He has been revitalized, regenerated, and indeed virtually redeemed. The end of his career is comic; he is become one of the Saving Remnant.

Hightower's ultimate courage and brotherly love place him, then, quite properly at the side of the good man Byron Bunch. Before turning finally to Byron, however, we must briefly consider one minor actor in this drama and his gesture of apparent kindness toward Joe Christmas—or at least a posthumous kindness to Joe's remains. I refer to Gavin Stevens. There is, incidentally, something vaguely familiar about him, although the name is new to us. His credentials—lawyer, Harvard man, Phi Beta Kappa—and his family's long association with the Sartoris family make him strongly reminiscent of Horace Benbow of *Sartoris* and *Sanctuary*. Gavin promises the Hineses that he will see that Joe's body is put on the train and sent home. It is a gesture, condescending and avuncular, with which we will become familiar. He undertakes this act of palliative charity—the kind that

William Blake so fiercely castigated—because he, like most of his society, assumes that Joe is black and therefore part of the "responsible" white man's burden. (And Gavin's act of spurious charity here quite specifically anticipates his behavior in the concluding section of *Go Down, Moses,* the occasion of his next appearance in the Yoknapatawpha Saga.)

Gavin Stevens seems to represent in his attitude the worst of that society as Byron Bunch can reasonably be said to represent its best. From the outset Byron has been a kind of standard of virtue, and we feel that he merits the reward that seems to be just within his reach as the novel closes—winning the woman he loves. His role has been in some sense representative, as though his society's rallying to Lena's aid merely focusses in him as representative of their better selves. In any case, he emerges unmistakably as one of the Saving Remnant. He himself has escaped the need to choose whether or not to accept the Second Chance that the rest of his society is given in the novel, since, from the first, he has been ready to give what aid is possible to the persecuted Joe Christmas; yet Byron does function as part of the novel's means of expressing the theme of the Second Chance. Byron Bunch is tacitly paired with Lucas Burch; the very similarity of their names (necessary, of course, to permit the confusion which brings Lena to the former as she seeks the latter) emphasizes the pairing, and that simple parallel sharpens our sense of the difference between them. Burch and Bunch are, in the novel's patterning, the First and Second Chance at the responsibility of paternity for Lena's baby. In simple terms, Burch has refused the responsibility through failure of love and courage while Bunch has accepted the role, thanks to his possession of the necessary love and courage.

The novel, then, offers us a happy ending; the tragic story of the first Joe is held in the embrace of the comic story of the second Joe, Lena's baby. And as he brings the latter story to its conclusion, Faulkner employs an additional narrator to tell us the last of Lena and Byron and the baby. He is the man who gave them a lift, and is telling of them to his wife, with whom he is in bed making love—a singularly appropriate note on which to conclude the novel. And as we contemplate that final vignette of "Faulkner's version of the holy family,"[3] we are moved to ask ourselves whether this Joey will indeed be obliged to face another "crucifixion." In one important sense we must feel the question's illegitimacy, since the novel's pattern has been completed with the successful acceptance of the Second Chance. And thus the novel's main question—"Who will care for Lena's baby?"—has been given its full and optimistic answer: "Those very souls who persecuted and crucified Joe Christmas will—provided they are given the chance to make amends." To that, moreover, may be added that, at the very least, *Light in August* has given a careful and cogent definition of goodness and demonstrated the successful action of characters in whom enlightened hope for the redemption and salvation of mankind may confidently rest. Byron Bunch and probably Gail Hightower—or the spirit which animates them—can triumph in this life, can endure and even prevail.

Thus saith the Lord, Behold, I will raise up
evil against thee out of thine own house.

2 Samuel 12:11

VI

Absalom, Absalom!

In *Absalom, Absalom!* (1936) Faulkner returns to the character who
perhaps most nearly embodied his own anguished view of the South's
decline, Quentin Compson.[1] The novel is a flashback to a moment
some few months before Quentin's suicide in June, 1910, as recorded
in the second section of *The Sound and the Fury,* while he is still a
student at Harvard. As though to explain more fully the motivation
for that suicide, Faulkner here presents Quentin's discovery of his
own history in full detail, his inherited legacy as contained in the
career of Thomas Sutpen. Relying on the reports of Miss Rosa Coldfield and of his father, on his own brief encounter at the ruins of
Sutpen's Hundred, and on his creative imagination as it is prodded
and challenged by Shreve McCannon, Quentin pieces together
Sutpen's life. Whether or not his recreation is truly accurate, or factu-
ally verifiable, is beside the point. It is sufficiently true and convincing
for Quentin—and that is what matters finally. It is, in the full sense of
the phrase, Quentin's story, terrifically meaningful for him and for
us, since, through Quentin's recreation of Thomas Sutpen's career,
we gain Faulkner's most searing penetration into the evil at the heart
of the antebellum South's social organization, his most revealing ex-
posure of the rot at the base of the Southern edifice.

The narrative strategy of disturbing regular chronology in the
rehearsal of Sutpen's career contributes significantly to the novel's
verisimilitude, as it reflects the way in which one might actually learn
someone's life story—as does Ford Madox Ford's similar technique
in *The Good Soldier.* But much more important is the way in which
the narrative arrangement carefully manipulates our responses.
Sutpen emerges for us and for Quentin as a somewhat ambiguous

106

and equivocal creature—part hero, part demon—and the narrative
is thus also aptly designed to prepare for and anticipate Quentin's
ambivalent concluding response to Shreve's question, "Why do you
hate the South?"

> "I dont hate it," Quentin said quickly, at once, immediately; "I dont
> hate it," he said. *I dont hate it* he thought, panting in the cold air, the
> iron New England dark; *I dont. I dont! I dont hate it! I dont hate it!*[2]

Our introduction to Thomas Sutpen comes from the amazed and
still outraged Miss Rosa, who, while she does some justice to Sutpen
by admitting to certain of his virtues, nevertheless paints a portrait
of him as a rather horrific demon. He seems to be a frantic version
of the American ideal of the self-made man fiercely obsessed with
the design of founding an endless future. He has vigor, creative
energy, and undeviating determination as he both leads and drives
the creatures he has brought suddenly into Mississippi—from no
one knows where—to establish his estate. But he is, if not malevo-
lent, then certainly maleficent as he rigorously uses (or abuses) anyone who can serve his ends—the band of unrecognizable Negroes,
the evidently kidnapped French architect, the Coldfields, et al. His
past is a murky mystery. We do not know the source of the trickle of
cash that sustained him and his during the building of his edifice,
but we are told that it was from old Ikkemotubbe he got the land—
"A matter between his conscience and Uncle Sam and God" (p. 44).
He drives the French architect to the limit of his endurance, hunting
him down like a beast when he tries to run off, and virtually discard-
ing him when he has finally served out his usefulness. He uses his
Negroes not only as laborers and hunting dogs and the means of
entertainment, but also for his personal male pleasure. Clytie stands
as living testimony to that pleasure, the imposed miscegenation that
is Faulkner's constant synecdoche for slavery. Sutpen uses Coldfield's economic vulnerability to obtain his daughter Ellen as his
wife, and she serves as his means to begin the dynasty he dreams of.
He is unscrupulous and fiercely proud, pontific and indeed hubristic. Miss Rosa's account prompts Quentin to visualize him "creating
the Sutpen's Hundred, the *Be Sutpen's Hundred* like the oldentime *Be
Light*" (p. 9).

Mr. Compson's account, on the whole gentler and more understanding, initially does little to alter the impression of Sutpen as a

man in the grip of an *idée fixe* who has been guilty of those abuses—
of snatching the land from its rightful caretakers, of the disregard of
human integrity as seen most blatantly in black slavery (and imposed
miscegenation, which is part of it), and of overweening pride—that
seem to characterize many of Faulkner's pseudoaristocrats. Consequently, while the suffering he undergoes during the Civil War—the
virtual destruction of Sutpen's Hundred and especially the loss of his
son (not to mention his son's cultivated college friend who is also
evidently Judith's fiancé)—is pathetic, it seems almost to be his just
desert.

But later, halfway through the novel, a chronological shift affords us Mr. Compson's account of Sutpen's childhood and early
life, modifying rather considerably Miss Rosa's depiction of her
demon, and raising in us some feelings of guilt for having judged
Sutpen prematurely and perhaps too harshly. For Sutpen's trouble,
Quentin explains to Shreve, was innocence. He rehearses the story
(as it came from his grandfather via his father) of Sutpen's fall out
of the Edenic communal setting of his childhood in the mountains
of West Virginia—where "the land belonged to anybody and every-
body"—into the postlapsarian world of Tidewater Virginia, "a
country all divided and fixed and neat with a people living on it all
divided and fixed and neat because of what color their skins happened to be and what they happened to own, and where a certain
few men not only had the power of life and death and barter and
sale over the others, but they had living human men to perform
the endless repetitive personal offices . . . that all men have had to
do for themselves since time began . . ." (pp. 221–22). The rude
shock of his initial encounter with the antebellum Southern way of
life, administered to him by the black servant who sent him from
the front door of the big house, awakened the young Sutpen to the
hard "facts" of life in the real world: slavery, caste, prejudice, and
the power of ownership. In that prolonged moment of shaken innocence, during which he ponders and contemplates this novel
phenomenon of actuality, Sutpen comes to recognize what was necessary and required if one were to succeed in that world—much
like the innocent James Gatz (not yet become Jay Gatsby) climbing
aboard Dan Cody's yacht to discover the rules of the world's game.
Hence came Sutpen's design.

If he is reminiscent of Jay Gatsby, he is also very similar to Joe
Christmas of *Light in August*. Like Joe, Sutpen was not born bad nor

was he, in the usual sense of the term, simply corrupted. Like Joe, he was educated by the "best" teachers, educated in the "proper" ways of the Southern system. Both characters are exactly the product of the society in which they must function. The evil they subsequently do, we cannot help but feel, results from their training, and hence their careers will seem to be pathetic and even to have a distinctly tragic cast.

The rest of Sutpen's early life, then, follows naturally from his epiphany, his discovery of the way of the world. He goes like any romantic adventurer to Haiti to make his fortune. He works on a rich plantation, puts down a rebellion there, and consequently takes the boss's daughter to wife. It is very much the career of Conrad's Lord Jim on Patusan, including even the Eastern bride: Eulalia is Sutpen's Jewel. But here reality intrudes into Sutpen's life as it did into Jim's; human voices wake him, so to speak, and Sutpen discovers the taint of blackness in Eulalia's blood—a distinct disqualifier. His later explanation to General Compson is calm and "rational": "I found that she was not and could never be, through no fault of her own, adjunctive or incremental to the design which I had in mind, so I provided for her and put her aside" (p. 240). A good pupil, he had learned the rules well. Eulalia and their son, Charles, just would not do. Having corrected that misstep, Sutpen removed to Mississippi, there to begin again the founding of his dynasty, the realization of his design, according to the Southern system as he had learned it.

In time, however, Sutpen the product would become almost indistinguishable from the producers. Sutpen himself lived into the role which the South had presented for his admiration and emulation. And as he participated in its life, he necessarily assumed (even if unwittingly and unintentionally) responsibility for its fate. Early and late in the novel Sutpen is included in the group of Southern leaders responsible for the fiasco of the Civil War. In Miss Rosa's earliest accounts, she explains that Sutpen had possessed in her eyes the heroic stature and shape of the legendary Confederate leaders—"even if only from association with them" (p. 19). And she adds the general condemnation that will be uttered again in the novel:

> " . . . Oh, he was brave. I have never gainsaid that. But that our
> cause, our very life and future hopes and past pride, should have been
> thrown into the balance with men like that to buttress it—men with

valor and strength but without pity or honor. Is it any wonder that
Heaven saw fit to let us lose?" [P. 20]

The disabused Wash Jones, most devout worshipper of Colonel
Sutpen, makes the same association at Sutpen's death. Clarified vision
is at last vouchsafed him on his full realization of how his granddaughter Milly had been abused and abandoned: "Father said that
maybe for the first time in his life he [Wash] began to comprehend
how it had been possible for Yankees or any other army to have
whipped them—the gallant, the proud, the brave; the acknowledged
and chosen best among them all to bear the courage and honor and
pride" (p. 290). Finally, toward the novel's close, the same note of
general condemnation is sounded as Quentin and Shreve, speaking
now with the one voice, place responsibility for defeat squarely on the
shoulders of those who were chosen to lead the Confederate troops,
"not through training in contemporary methods or aptitude for
learning them, but by the divine right to say 'Go there' conferred
upon them by an absolute caste system" (p. 345). And Sutpen has
been established as one of these. He has been created in their own
image, and in the novel (in Quentin's recreation of his life and career), Sutpen is their representative, almost their Frankenstein mon-
ster. If he lacks something of their chivalrous pretensions, their pro-
fession that *noblesse oblige,* he is then the naked *reductio ad absurdum* of
the essence and behavior of the Southern pseudoaristocrat; he is the
type stripped of its cosmetic blandishments. When the Southern establishment rejected him via the "monkey nigger" at the door of the
big house, it created its own avenging fury. The note of vengeance
sounds quite clearly enough in Sutpen's recitation of his first lesson:
"So to combat them you have got to have what they have that made
them do what the man did. You got to have land and niggers and a
fine house to combat them with" (p. 238). Sutpen becomes something
very like the South's demon.[3]

Of course the parallels between Sutpen's career specifically and
the history of the South generally are obvious; his career is a micro-
cosmic emblem of the Southern macrocosm. Understanding of
Sutpen yields understanding of the South, for Quentin and for us.
Sutpen's Hundred was established upon two evils that taint the actions of most of Faulkner's Southern pseudoaristocrats—piratical
land procurement (and several characters in Yoknapatawpha apparently got their land rather dubiously from old Ikkemotubbe) and

inhuman use of human beings, especially of the enslaved Negroes. Sutpen's casting aside Eulalia and Charles, fathering Clytie, and driving his band of wild Negroes are all culpable features of his preparation to establish his estate and found his dynasty. His use of people as pawns is not restricted to blacks, as he used Coldfield to procure a wife and Ellen, in turn, to provide the necessary male heir, but it is the novel's central concern.

The chickens come home to roost; the nemesis appears with the return of the son he has denied, Charles Bon. And of course he must be denied again—and finally. In the midst of the Civil War, the great American fratricidal holocaust, Sutpen obliges Henry to murder Charles. Now the bitter irony is that with that fratricide Sutpen loses both his sons, for the darker brother is dead and the "legitimate" heir has disappeared, is in fact as good as dead. (And the typical Faulknerian equation of fratricide with suicide is again patently evident.) Furthermore, Sutpen's inhumanity has turned most vengefully against himself: the impelled fratricide has broken his dynasty. There is, too, the additional irony that Sutpen's seed has been more fertile than he thought or could have desired, as Charles's progeny continues in a line stretching toward the furthest horizon—"grandsons and great-grandsons springing as far as eye could reach" (p. 271).

The postbellum attempt to recoup and reconstruct proves too much for the old man. His desperate attempt to refound his dynasty drives him to behavior as inhumane and vicious as ever. He proposes to Miss Rosa a trial at procreation, and then imposes that trial on Milly Jones. Her failure to produce a male heir (whom he presumably would have legitimized) provokes Sutpen's heartless response, "Well, Milly; too bad you're not a mare too. Then I could give you a decent stall in the stable" (p. 286), and causes Wash Jones to rise like the Grim Reaper and slay him. The sense of fit retribution is inescapable. Sutpen's heartlessness, however it was instilled, seems to merit the fate that has descended on him. And insofar as the novel has made him the South's representative, we feel that the South too has earned the wrath of the gods. We are liable to recall Quentin's thoughts at the outset, about Miss Rosa's motivation in telling him Sutpen's story: *"It's because she wants it told, . . . so that people whom she will never see . . . will read it and know at last why God let us lose the War: that only through the blood of our men and the tears of our women could He stay this demon . . ."* (p. 11).

The two principal allusions Faulkner has employed in this novel augment that sense of merited vengeance, of deserved divine punishment. The first, obvious and frequently commented upon, is the allusion to the biblical story of King David carried by the very title of the novel.[4] That allusion has properly enough encouraged identification of Thomas Sutpen with David, Charles Bon with Amnon, Judith with Tamar, and Henry with Absalom. The title, echoing the words of David's lament over the death of his son ("O my son Absalom, my son, my son, Absalom! would God I had died for thee, O Absalom, my son, my son!" 2 Sam. 17:33), tends to restrict the allusion to that part of David's story which immediately precedes and accounts for Absalom's death. But the significance of that allusion is enhanced and its application more sharply focussed and defined by the appearance within the novel of a most important reiterated allusion to classical myth.

The allusion is established by Quentin's father and then reiterated by Quentin himself. Mr. Compson comments on Sutpen's naming his progeny: "Yes. He named Clytie as he named them all, . . . with that same robust and sardonic temerity, naming with his own mouth his own ironic fecundity of dragon's teeth" (p. 62). Quentin recalls this much later in the novel as he tells Shreve (with fuller knowledge now) that Sutpen "named them all—the Charles Goods and the Clytemnestras and Henry and Judith and all of them—that entire fecundity of dragons' [*sic*] teeth as father called it" (p. 266). But the allusion has evidently become familiar between them, for as Shreve rehearses with Quentin Sutpen's postwar attempt at reconstruction he makes the appropriate application—this time only implicitly: "with [Wash] Jones for clerk and who knows maybe what delusions of making money out of the store to rebuild the plantation; who had escaped twice now, got himself into it and been freed by the Creditor who set his children to destroying one another before he had posterity . . ." (p. 181). Quentin picks up the allusion at once ("*He sounds just like father* he thought") and makes explicit its application:

Mad impotent old man . . . who looked about upon the scene which was still within his scope and compass and saw son gone, vanished, more insuperable to him now than if the son were dead since now (if the son still lived) his name would be different and those to call him by it strangers, and whatever dragon's outcropping of Sutpen blood the son might sow on the body of whatever strange woman would therefore carry on the tradition, accomplish the hereditary evil and harm. . . . [Pp. 181–82]

Now the allusion to the myth of Cadmus (sower of dragon's teeth)[5] is important because of its parallels to the story of David and Absalom. The two stories share several features, and their presence together focusses the relevance and controls the application of each to Sutpen's career. (1) Both stories involve the founding of kingdoms or dynasties—David his house and control of Jerusalem, Cadmus the city of Thebes. (2) Both tell of fratricide, of internal strife within the respective families, and also of enmity between fathers and sons. (3) In both, the fratricidal strife results from the principals' incurring divine wrath; it descends upon David and Cadmus as a punishment earned. David has sent Uriah to certain death in battle in order to take Bathsheba unto himself. In chapter 12 of the second Book of Samuel we read the prophecy that follows God's displeasure with David, "Now therefore the sword shall never depart from thy house" (verse 10), and "Behold, I will raise up evil against thee out of thine own house" (verse 11). Absalom kills Amnon, turns against David, and is himself finally killed. Cadmus slays the dragon that has killed his men when they violated its sacred wood and spring; bereft, he is told to sow the dragon's teeth to produce new offspring. Since the dragon was sacred to Mars, however, Cadmus' crop is a mixed blessing: the armed sons who sprout from the soil fall upon each other in lethal civil war and warn Cadmus not to interfere. (4) In both stories we have the case of "ironic fecundity," as both David and Cadmus have, in a sense, more sons than they can manage (which is also the case with Thomas Sutpen). (5) Both stories, finally, include a character who might be called the abused sister. Amnon's incestuous rape of Tamar, a crucial item in Absalom's career, has its counterpart in the threatened relationship of Charles Bon and Judith Sutpen. While there is no exact counterpart to this in the Cadmus myth, a kind of displaced equivalent may be seen in the fate of Cadmus's sister, Europa, seized and carried off by Jupiter disguised as a bull; and Cadmus's peregrinations have as their original motive the recovery of Europa. In spite of the inexact similarity, one sees that in both stories as in Faulkner's novel, the themes of unjust war and improper love play a prominent part.

These two important allusions—to Absalom and to the dragon's teeth—lend breadth of significance to the story of Thomas Sutpen and serve to give it the dimensions of myth. Furthermore, those features of the two which receive particular emphasis serve, in turn, to cast a searching light upon the crucial features of Sutpen's career as it is recreated for and by Quentin Compson: the earning of divine displeasure and the consequent internal, fratricidal strife. Now this is not to equate Sutpen fully with King David or with Cadmus;[6] his career certainly does not promise the calm and happy outcome of either of those figures. And whether his career even has the distinctly tragic cast that has often been claimed for it seems rather dubious. It seems to me that the tragic possibilities are to some extent undercut, both by the controlled relevance of the two allusions just discussed—i.e., controlled to emphasize the punitive suicidal fratricide—and also by Faulkner's strategy here of situational repetition, in a word, by what I have been calling the theme of the Second Chance.

The crisis in Thomas Sutpen's career occurs when Henry brings Charles Bon home from college with him at Christmastime (appropriately) in 1859. The meeting is critical as a repetition of the past— the father facing again that son who he earlier decided could not form any part of his grand design, and obliged once again to decide whether or not to recognize him. The Second Chance is offered, the opportunity to make the correct moral choice which would justly compensate for the earlier moral failure. Of course Sutpen must fail again, lacking the wherewithal—the moral imagination, the simple humanity, the "pity or honor"—to do otherwise. Sutpen's reported language exactly expresses the Second Chance theme and his repeated moral dilemma:

> I chose, and I made to the fullest what atonement lay in my power for whatever injury I might have done in choosing.... Yet I am now faced with a second necessity to choose, the curious factor of which is not ... that the necessity for a new choice should have arisen, but that either choice which I might make, either course which I might choose, leads to the same result.... [Pp. 273–74][7]

There is in Sutpen's attitude to this reappearance something almost equivalent to the *anagnorisis* of classical drama—a little like Macbeth's recognition of Macduff. He sees, thus, that he has no right option open to him, that whatever response he makes will lead to the destruction of his design, i.e., to "the same result." And as always, of course, Faulkner manages to make Sutpen's specific dilemma representative of the Southern dilemma in general, drawing an explicit parallel between the appearance of Charles at the door of the big house of Sutpen's Hundred and the much earlier appearance of the boy Thomas Sutpen at the door of the big house on another Southern plantation. Quentin gives his father's account of the confrontation:

> " . . . and Henry said, 'Father, this is Charles' and he—" ("the demon," Shreve said) "—saw the face and knew . . . that he stood there at his own door, just as he had imagined, planned, designed, and sure enough and after fifty years the forlorn nameless and homeless lost child came to knock at it and no monkey-dressed nigger anywhere under the sun to come to the door and order the child away. . . ." [P. 267]

The South has once again affirmed its principles of caste, of exclusiveness and discrimination and segregation, as Sutpen fulfills his representative role.

He rejects Charles the second time in two steps, first through refusal of him as potential fiancé on the grounds of threatened incest, and second—the "trump card"—through refusal on the grounds of threatened miscegenation. Although Quentin's father says that Sutpen did not call Charles's reappearance "retribution, no sins of the father come home to roost," Sutpen's very comparing Charles's position at the door now with his own many years ago would suggest that some fear that history would further repeat itself might well have haunted Sutpen's thoughts—that his vengeful response to rejection might be repeated by Charles. Hence he is obliged to make sure by taking that second step which will get rid of Charles once and for all through death. The pathetic irony is provided by Charles's convincing explanation to Henry, now armed with the knowledge Sutpen trusts will lead to Charles's death, that he would have made no exorbitant demand whatsoever:

> —And he sent me no word? . . . No word to me, no word at all? That was all he had to do . . . He would not have needed to ask it, require it, of me. I would have offered it. I would have said, I will never see her again before he could have asked it of me. . . . He didn't need to tell you I am a nigger to stop me. He could have stopped me without that, Henry. [P. 356]

But Sutpen could not run the risk. His trouble, Quentin insists (quoting his grandfather), was innocence. Sutpen's reported actions and comments argue persuasively, however, that his trouble was much rather overweening pride, first rudely awakened by the initial rebuff that started his vengeful design to take shape. His trouble was hubris. Sutpen's design reflected his learned desire to transcend the normal human condition, to aspire to godhead and so overcome the human facts of mutability and mortality. His attitude is like that of Horace Benbow, who wanted peace from the turmoil of life's constant change. Horace, like the speaker in Keats' "Ode on a Grecian Urn," envies the constancy of life depicted on the urn; and Sutpen is different only in that he will actively and vigorously attempt to create that sort of constancy himself and impose it upon his life. His establishing Sutpen's Hundred—the Be Sutpen's Hundred like the old time Be Light—is eloquent evidence of his hubristic intention to overcome mutability, to fix life; and his conception of the dynasty he will found suggests something like an intention to overcome even mortality.

In the midst of the holocaust of the Civil War, Sutpen could sit calmly, suspended in irrelevant hiatus, in the office of Quentin's grandfather to discuss his future, his whole career, "as if there were no haste nor urgency anywhere under the sun . . . and [he had] a thousand days or maybe even years of monotony and rich peace, and he, even after he would become dead, still there, still watching the fine grandsons and great-grandsons springing as far as the eye could reach . . ." (p. 271). Definition of Sutpen's attitude and aspiration benefits particularly from Faulkner's interesting choice of verb: Sutpen will not "die," he will "become dead" and be "still there." Further emphasis is added by the repeated reference to the two valuable tombstones Sutpen ordered from Italy and had delivered and hauled about with him during the war—and the gaunt and spent troops "speaking of the two stones as 'Colonel' and 'Mrs Colonel' . . . " (p. 189). Two such references precede by only a few lines Quentin's depiction of Sutpen imagining that endless row of heirs springing as far as the eye could reach. Sutpen's Hundred, the endless progeny, the very tombstones are interchangeable emblems of Sutpen's design to transcend and flout the inevitable factors of the human condition—of the Southern pseudoaristocrat's desire to fix and perpetuate the status quo of glorious antebellum existence. The Urn attitude.

The more healthy and humane Judith expresses the folly of that attitude by a modest counterstatement of the theme in terms which insist on specific comparison with Sutpen's aspiration. Mr. Compson tells of Judith's bringing to Quentin's grandmother a letter from Charles Bon (the first in four years) and asking her to dispose of it— to keep it or destroy it:

As you like. . . . all of a sudden it's all over and all you have left is a block of stone with scratches on it . . . and after a while they dont even remember the name and what the scratches were trying to tell, and it doesn't matter. And so maybe if you could go to someone, the stranger the better, and give them something—a scrap of paper— something, anything . . . at least it would be something just because it would have happened, be remembered even if only from passing from one hand to another, one mind to another, and it would be at least a scratch, something, something that might make a mark on something that *was* once for the reason that it can die someday, while the block of stone can't be *is* because it never can become *was* because it cant ever die or perish. . . . [Pp. 127–28; Faulkner's italics]

These words constitute an emphatic statement of the human necessity of recognizing mutability and mortality as twin facts of life. Failure to do so, Judith's request implies, means failure to be truly alive and human oneself and leads to inhuman regard and treatment of actually living things. It is Sutpen's failure (as the references to the block of stone encourage us to see) and thus responsible for his baleful view of those who come into contact with him, who are just so many tombstones to be fashioned to mark his place. His constant attitude is that of the speaker in Keats's ode, jealously admiring the fortunate youth on the Grecian urn: "She cannot fade . . . ,/ For ever wilt thou love, and she be fair!" And Judith's homely comments about the block of stone that cannot be *is* because it never can become *was* directly counter and correct his attitude, as one might conceive of Wallace Stevens's poetry directly countering the words spoken to the bold lover on Keats's urn:

> Death is the mother of beauty, hence from her,
> Alone, shall come fulfillment to our dreams
> And our desires. Although she strews the leaves
> Of sure obliteration on our paths. . . .
> ["Sunday Morning"]
>
> Beauty is momentary in the mind—
> The fitful tracing of a portal;
> But in the flesh it is immortal.
> The body dies; the body's beauty lives.
> ["Peter Quince at the Clavier"]

Indeed, this theme of "*was*-ness" echoes quietly but definitely elsewhere in the novel, as it does at intervals throughout the whole Yoknapatawpha Saga. Miss Rosa herself has caught a glimpse of the

truth which Judith's homely utterance expresses. (Rosa's choosing to
tell her tale to Quentin may be seen as an equivalent to Judith's
choosing to give Charles's letter to Quentin's grandmother.) She
recalls the years of patient deprivation which Southern women experienced during the Civil War and offers this explanation of their
dilemma and their strength:

> . . .*there was left only maimed honor's veterans, and love. Yes, there should,
> there must, be love and faith: these left with us by fathers, husbands, sweet-
> hearts, brothers, who carried the pride and the hope of peace in honor's van-
> guard as they did the flags; there must be these, else what do men fight for?
> what else worth dying for? Yes, dying not for honor's empty sake, nor pride nor
> even peace, but for that love and faith they left behind. Because he* [Charles]
> *was to die; I know that, knew that, as both pride and peace were: else how to
> prove love's immortality?* [P. 150]

And the thrust of that final rhetorical question establishes the same
point as Judith's comments about the perishable letter.

Even Henry seems to have shared this idea. Mr. Compson characterizes him early as "the provincial . . . who may have been conscious
that his fierce provincial's pride in his sister's virginity was a false
quantity which must incorporate in itself an inability to endure in
order to be precious, to exist, and so must depend upon its loss,
absence, to have existed at all . . . the brother realizing that the sister's virginity must be destroyed in order to have existed at all . . . "
(p. 96). Henry's ability to face the realization of that idea is of course
another matter—but the idea is there and develops a bit further the
countertheme to Sutpen's Urn attitude. His difficulty in facing the
real possibility of Judith's losing her virginity is compounded by the
fact that her fianc´e is Charles Bon and that part of Sutpen's means
of rejecting Charles a second time is to discover to Henry that he is
half brother to him and Judith—the discovery of threatened incest.
The second part of course is Sutpen's "trump card," the disclosure
that Charles is Negro. That knowledge involves Henry in the pattern
of the Second Chance: he, like his father thirty years earlier, must
choose to accept or reject this relative with "tainted" blood, and he
has the chance to do right where his father had chosen to do wrong.
Henry, alas, proves tragically to be his father's son, the full inheritor
of commitment to the rules governing Southern social organization
that his father had learned.

Henry has as much difficulty (according to Shreve's conception)

accepting the incestuous union of Charles and Judith as he had accepting Charles's morganatic marriage to the octoroon woman in
New Orleans: "Jesus, think of the load he had to carry, born of two
Methodists (or of one long invincible line of Methodists) and raised in
provincial North Mississippi, faced with incest, incest of all things . . ."
(p. 340). Henry's recollection that kings and dukes "have done it"—
especially the Lorraine duke named John something, excommuni-
cated by the Pope—seems to have made the union of Charles and
Judith finally acceptable to him. Shreve's emphasis on Henry's reluctance to face incest seems to put his version of Henry at odds with Mr.
Compson's version, which concluded with the following explanation
of Henry's attitude to his sister's virginity:

> In fact, perhaps this is the pure and perfect incest: the brother realiz-
> ing that the sister's virginity must be destroyed in order to have ex-
> isted at all, taking that virginity in the person of the brother-in-law,
> the man whom he would be if he could become, metamorphose into,
> the lover, the husband; by whom he would be despoiled, choose for
> despoiler, if he could become, metamorphose into the sister, the mis-
> tress, the bride. Perhaps that is what went on, not in Henry's mind but
> in his soul. [P. 96]

Mr. Compson's amplification indicates two salient features of
Henry's attitude (features which Faulkner typically associates with his
Southern heroes): first, the incest is conceived of as being consum-
mated *vicariously,* and second, this incest is *narcissistic*—as incest perhaps always is ultimately. The first of these features recalls Popeye
and his use of Red to service Temple Drake (and it even anticipates
somewhat Flem Snopes's relationship with Eula Varner in *The Hamlet,*
where he achieves a kind of *ex post facto* vicarious paternity via the
prior service of Hoake McCarron). The effect of that comparison is to
impute to Henry the impotence that scarred Popeye (and Flem). The
second feature recalls Horace Benbow's love of his significantly
named sister, Narcissa, and Quentin's love of Caddy, tending to make
explicit here what is everywhere implicit in the Yoknapatawpha Saga,
that the incestuous attitude of the pseudoaristocratic Southerners is
introverted, reductive, and finally self-destructive; is indeed the emblem of, or synecdoche for, the typical Southern aristocratic attitude
in general.

Furthermore, juxtaposing Mr. Compson's and Shreve's versions
of Henry's attitude to incest clarifies another facet of Henry's *Weltan-*

schauung: it offers the contrast between the idealist view (the "pure and perfect"), the merely cerebral contemplation of the potential intercourse, and the realistic view of that intercourse as a physical, palpable actuality. The former, Henry could manage; the latter caused him grief. And even the terms on which he can at last accept the actuality are themselves clouded with the romantically ideal: "kings have done it! Even dukes!" And in all of this Henry emerges more and more clearly as the typical Faulknerian representative of the Southern attitude; for Henry is as much a son of the South as he is a son of Thomas Sutpen.

Of course the most blatant function of the question of incest as it presents itself to Henry is to set up the wretched contrast between the terms upon which he makes his decision about Charles—the terms of his Second Chance. That theme, by the way, is particularly insisted on by Faulkner's narrative strategy. First, Henry's dilemma about Charles is placed in the same context as the account of Sutpen's shock at having to make his second choice—face his Second Chance—regarding Charles; and second, that context includes also the repeated reference to Sutpen's emblematic tombstones:

> " . . . Sutpen came home in '64 with the two tombstones and talked to Grandfather in the office . . . Sutpen must have known about the probation too, what Henry was doing now: holding all three of them— himself and Judith and Bon—in that suspension while he wrestled with his conscience to make it come to terms with what he wanted to do just like his father had that time more than thirty years ago. . . . "
> [P. 270]

That specific comparison is repeated a few paragraphs later, when Quentin's account has followed Sutpen into 1865: "And he (Grand-father) didn't know what had happened: whether Sutpen had found out in some way that Henry had at last coerced his conscience into agreeing with him as his (Henry's) father had done thirty years ago . . ." (p. 276). Thus, when we come upon the confrontation of Henry and Charles as they discuss Henry's dilemma, we are well prepared to see the choice and the basis for the choice as a reitera-tion; for there again Charles's reference to having given Sutpen the choice (already the Second Chance)—*"I have been giving him the choice for four years"* (p. 357)—echoes the sense of repetition of the two passages quoted above.

The basis on which Charles is to be rejected is either the threatened incest or the threatened miscegenation. We know Henry has managed to come to terms with the former, and we face the bitter recognition that he cannot come to terms with the latter. Charles puts it to him: *"So it's the miscegenation, not the incest, which you cant bear"* (p. 356). And he continues to press him, threatening now to go through with his pursuit of Judith, and pointing out to Henry the only way to stop him. He gives Henry the pistol and urges him on— *"Then do it now, he says."* At this moment of crisis Henry's response is the simple and tragically laconic *"You are my brother"* (p. 357). Charles is, however, relentless and drives Henry to the act he must commit— the fratricide which is always tantamount to suicide.

So Henry—and, by the usual extension, the South generally—has faced the Second Chance and rejected it in rejecting his brother. He is his father's son, and with his father shares a representative role. He has proven to be as exclusive, segregationist, and destructive as Thomas Sutpen—the South's demon. And the reports of Shreve and Mr. Compson prompt us to conclude, from his attitude to his sister, that he is in his way as unwilling to face the actual world of mutability, and thus as anxious to fix or to escape it. Henry is, finally, as enamored of the Urn existence as was his father; and he is heir to his father's hubristic attitude. Henry's motivation in rejecting Charles is a refusal to recognize him as a fellow human being—in spite of the spontaneous and tragic claim of brotherhood.

This shared hubristic attitude is, then, the tragic flaw in these quasi-tragic figures, Henry and Thomas Sutpen. They are not, however, truly tragic. Their shared flaw is not simply a blemish on an otherwise admirable character; it is the very heart of their being. And as they are the South's representatives, one may say that the "flaw" is the very base of the whole Southern structure. That somewhat architectural metaphor is proven apt and justified by Faulkner's own use of it at two junctures in the novel. In recounting the death of Ellen Coldfield, Mr. Compson observes that it occurred "in bed in a darkened room in the house on which fateful mischance had already laid its hand to the extent of scattering *the black foundation on which it had been erected . . ."* (p. 78; my italics). The metaphor is resumed much later when Quentin recalls his father's account of Mr. Coldfield, who "hated the country so much that he was even glad when he saw it drifting closer and closer to a doomed and fatal war . . . that day when the South would realize that it was now paying the price for having *erected its economic edifice not on the rock of stern morality but on the shifting sands of opportunism and moral brigandage"* (p. 260; my italics). The "flaw," then, is the fundamental and pervasive evil that has led to the frustrating of all of Thomas Sutpen's ambitions, of all of Henry's expectations, and hence to the collapse of the South in the Civil War. It was the disease which only that feverish holocaust could arrest, as Quentin terms it at the novel's outset:

> He was a barracks filled with stubborn back-looking ghosts still recovering, even forty-three years afterward, from the fever which had cured the disease, waking from the fever without even knowing that it had been the fever itself which they had fought against and not the sickness, looking with stubborn recalcitrance backward beyond the fever and into the disease with actual regret, weak from the fever yet free of the disease and not even aware that the freedom was that of impotence. [P. 12]

Impotence. The very word is like a knell, tolling for Henry, ironically for Thomas, and certainly for the whole South they represent. The moral brigandage—the racism, the more general disregard for human beings displayed by Sutpen, the irresponsible manipulation—all of that terrific evil has brought its own frustration and destruction. The two familiar themes thus come together: the "flaw" which is responsible for the rejection of the Second Chance is the very evil which reflexively destroys its principal agents.

While the story of Thomas Sutpen does not, I believe, carry for us or even for Quentin, the full impact of tragedy, its final impression is no more pessimistic, no less morally instructive than true tragedy. We have seen and understood, not simply that Sutpen and his South were bitterly frustrated and defeated, but also for what reasons— why God let them lose the War. We are perfectly prepared to answer Sutpen's naive though not innocent question: "You see, I had a design . . . the question is, Where did I make the mistake in it, what did I do or misdo in it, whom or what injure by it . . ." (p. 263). The mistake, the flaw (as Quentin may well want to see it), has been clearly identified, described, defined, and dramatized; and we recognize it as the evil which proves self-destructive. One looks vainly perhaps for hopeful signs of the Saving Remnant—unless it be in that ironically unrecognized progeny of Sutpen's, the product of his ironic fecundity springing (as it "bleaches out") as far as eye can reach: the descendants of Charles Bon.

This is what Quentin has seen and what he has enabled us to see and contemplate. His vision of it all, however, we must call "tragic" in the more colloquial sense of the term, since for him it can only be depressing. Particularly in that he can so readily identify with Henry Sutpen, and especially with that facet of Henry that attracts him cerebrally to his sister—a principal symptom of the Southern "disease." In his own attitude to Caddy, as we found it in *The Sound and the Fury,* he imitates the fond Henry and shares with him that tendency to impotence, to self-defeat, ultimately to suicide. The merely cerebral approach to life, which refuses commitment to actual life, which denies reality, is his perhaps even more strongly than it was Henry's. As Quentin and Shreve collaborate on putting the last touches to their portrait of Charles Bon, they consider whether part of the attraction to Judith may not indeed have been the possibility of incest itself. It is Shreve's turn—

> " . . . because who (without a sister: I dont know about the others) has been in love and not discovered the vain evanescence of the fleshly encounter; who has not had to realize that when the brief all is done you must retreat from both love and pleasure, gather up your own rubbish and refuse . . . and retreat since the gods condone and practise these and the dreamy immeasurable coupling which floats oblivious above the trameling [sic] and harried instant, the: *was-not: is: was:* is a perquisite only of balloony and weightless elephants and whales: but maybe if there were sin too maybe you would not be permitted to escape, uncouple, return.—Aint that right?" [Pp. 323–24]

Quentin's reply is "I don't know"; but he, unlike Shreve, indeed *has* a sister and therefore *does* know. And he cannot but recognize in this something of his own attitude—the desire to escape the weariness, the fever, and the fret here in this realm of relentless mutability. Quentin, like the speaker in Keats's ode, covets the Urn existence, even if it be an infernal existence. Here, then, is a distinct anticipation and explanation of Quentin's attempt to resolve his dilemma as recorded in *The Sound and the Fury*—his "confession" of incest:

> . . . it was to isolate her out of the loud world so that it would have to flee us of necessity and then the sound of it would be as though it had never been . . . if i could tell you we did it it would have been so and then the others wouldnt be so and then the world would roar away. . . . [P. 220]

The passage echoes his early thoughts of the "confession" which add a specific note that returns us again to *Absalom, Absalom!* "Because if

it were just to hell; if that were all of it. Finished. . . . Nobody else
there but her and me. If we could just have done something so
dreadful that they would have fled hell except us. *I have committed
incest I said Father"* (*Sound and Fury*, p. 97; Faulkner's italics). We
recall that it was not actual incest ("i was afraid to i was afraid she
might and then it wouldnt have done any good") but the idea of it
that Quentin wanted; and that too strengthens his identification with
Henry. The cerebral or vicarious incest only would do for both
young men. And the final element in the parallel encouraging identification is exactly this conception of incest as a means of escape to
hell. Quentin imagines Henry thinking about his incestuous Lorraine duke: *"he could say now, 'It isn't yours nor his nor the Pope's hell that
we are all going to: it's my mother's and her mother's and father's and their
mother's and father's hell, and it isn't you who are going there, but we, the
three—no: four of us. . . . And we will all be together in torment and so we
will not need to remember love and fornication . . ."* (pp. 347–48). Not so
exclusive a hell as what Quentin imagines for him and Caddy, but
sufficiently similar an escape.

Quentin's early twentieth-century world we saw in *The Sound and
the Fury* lacks even the pretension of glamorous chivalry that deco-
rated the antebellum South: it is a world in which his brother Jason
feels at home in the company of the Snopeses and will become head
of the family. It is not Quentin's world. His is the world of Thomas
and Henry Sutpen as he has recreated it in *Absalom, Absalom!* in most
terrifically believable detail. He is indeed a barracks filled with stub-
born back-looking ghosts. As Quentin says during his chill colloquy
with Shreve, their two voices frequently joined in single utterance,

*Yes, we are both Father. Or maybe Father and I are both Shreve, maybe it took
Father and me both to make Shreve or Shreve and me both to make Father or
maybe Thomas Sutpen to make all of us.* [Pp. 261–62]

Absalom, Absalom! is indeed Quentin's story. It is about him and his,
and about who made him so: Thomas Sutpen and beyond him the
whole South. What other final words, then, could Quentin utter
than *I dont. I dont! I dont hate it! I dont hate it!*

I think that when at last you dare to face
The purity of death, you find the wan,
Remembered innocence of childhood scenes. . . .

Radcliffe Squires, "Mark Twain"

VII

The Unvanquished

In this novel of 1938, perhaps his most explicitly optimistic, Faulkner has delineated a portrait of the true hero as he traces the development of Bayard Sartoris from the age of twelve to the age of twenty-four. As we watch Bayard grow from boyhood into manhood, we see him learn and embody those virtues which Faulkner would have us cherish—the virtues of love, courage, responsibility, and honor. The education of Bayard's character is of course carried out in "Southern" terms; but as is usual with Faulkner, the implications of those terms are extended finally well beyond the boundaries of the southern United States. Bayard learns love for the land; he learns brotherly love and, most important, love for his darker brother; and increasingly he learns responsibility. The whole lesson in miniature is contained in the opening scene of the novel, just as the "living map" the two boys are making in their play contains Vicksburg in miniature. The necessary virtues are there, expressed dramatically in the boys' game:

Ringo and I had a living map. Although Vicksburg was just a handful of chips from the woodpile and the River a trench scraped into the packed earth with the point of a hoe, it (river, city, and terrain) lived, possessing even in miniature that ponderable though passive recalcitrance of topography which outweighs artillery, against which the most brilliant of victories and the most tragic of defeats are but the loud noises of a moment. To me and Ringo it lived, if only because of the fact that the sunimpacted ground drank water faster than we could fetch it from the well, . . . the two of us needing first to join forces and spend ourselves against a common enemy, time, before we could engender between us and hold intact the pattern of recapitulant mimic furious victory like a cloth, shield between ourselves and reality, between us and fact and doom.[1]

Here, in terms of play, we see the recognition of and respect for the solid power of the land, the willing recognition of the need to work together—black and white—to create and sustain something vital, and the readiness to work responsibly. As the novel continues, the play quickly hardens into reality and these "represented" virtues are likewise realized as grim actuality tests the growing Bayard. He is faced finally with the question of whether he has the proper love and courage to accept with honor the responsibility of being The Sartoris—the head of the family.

Bayard's relationship with three members of his family, Granny, Drusilla, and his father—specifically his involvement in and attitude toward the careers of those three and the principles according to which they functioned—defines his development. Certainly Bayard's connections with Ringo, Uncle Buck McCaslin, and Aunt Jenny are of importance, but the other three relationships control the central line of the action.

Miss Rosa Millard, Bayard's Granny, figures importantly in his young life. She has given him as a child the foundation of his religious and ethical training. She has taught him the importance of honesty: Bayard indeed recalls that he has never been whipped for anything except lying. She has taught him to be clean of speech: she washes his mouth out with soap whenever she hears him swearing. She has taught him respect: she even insists on his referring to the dubious Ab Snopes as *Mister* Snopes, until that crucial moment when Snopes has proved himself quite unworthy of respect. And clearly Granny has taught Bayard to pray—for forgiveness and for guidance. He also learns—not by precept but by example—to assume responsibility for the less fortunate, who must depend upon the strong and capable for their welfare. In the bleakest days of the Civil War he sees Granny call upon her shrewdness and courage in the mule-trading business to provide for the needy of the Reverend Fortinbride's congregation—or for anyone gathered into the Sartoris neighborhood. And finally, Granny's murder at the hands of the wretched Grumby gives Bayard the chance to prove his love, his courage, his willingness to assume responsibility, as he rises to hunt down the killer and avenge his grandmother's death with what his society has taught him to recognize as honor.

That is not all, however. From the story of Granny's career—narrated by an older, mature Bayard, who arranges highlights, gives uninsistent emphasis, and selects details from among the plethora of early impressions—emerges another lesson, sternly moral and difficult to accept. Although Granny's career is recalled with deep affection and presented with compelling honesty, so strong is the fondness of his memory of Granny, that it threatens to cloud over the significance of her behavior. John Lewis Longley, Jr., for example, offers the appealing suggestion that "Granny's death is the direct result of wrong actions taken for the best of reasons. . . . Her death comes when she is unable to break off the pattern of her new habits."[2] If we examine the terms of this suggestion in connection with the episodes in the novel itself, however, we may want to modify it rather severely. In particular we must look sharply at "the best of reasons" which Granny had for her actions, and consider whether the persistence of new habits or of old contributes more to her death. A strict moralist might claim that Granny's "wrong actions" begin with her deception before the Yankee officer whose horse Bayard and Ringo have shot. Any reader, however, will certainly recognize that her accepting the one hundred ten mules (she had asked for "The mules, Old Hundred and Tinney") and ten chests of silver marks the first step on that slippery primrose path which leads her finally into the den of Grumby and the jaws of death. To be sure, she determines to use this windfall to provide for the unfortunate. And one can be persuaded all too easily to forgive her for capitalizing on the army's gullibility and confusion to procure additional means of caring for the victims of the war. Yet there is another aspect to Granny's actions of Pity and Mercy. She is, after all, a Southern lady; she is mother-in-law of John Sartoris and aunt of Drusilla Hawk; in short, Miss Rosa Millard, bless her heart, represents the Southern establishment which foundered in the Civil War—that fever (as Professor Wilkins calls it) which cured the disease. She is habituated to this role; this is the old habit which persists beyond any new she may have subsequently assumed. Granny's perfectly understandable comments to one of the "freed" Negroes rushing toward their homemade Jordan serves as an eloquent emblem of her basic code. She stops by the almost exhausted woman: " 'Who do you belong to?' Granny said. . . . 'If I give you something to eat, will you turn around and go back home?' " (pp. 95–96). Perfectly understandable and sensible. Her initial question, however, recalls the outburst by Loosh, just a few pages earlier, on the question of ownership: "Let God ax John Sartoris who the man name that give me to him. Let the man that buried me in the black dark ax that of the man what dug me free" (p. 85). And the two passages are thus erected into significant juxtaposition. Beneath her actions of generosity, there is, after all, the profound motive of maintaining the status quo. The old pride, the exclusiveness, the basic segregation, all are functioning. For Granny is doing her best—and we must not be distracted by the rhetoric—"to keep things going," to continue in the old dispensation.

Those "wrong actions" were undertaken for *what Granny believed* were "the best reasons," as her interesting prayer makes clear. Yet we seriously misread the novel if we fail to see that it exposes the *worst* which lies at the core of those best reasons: the evil which Faulkner repeatedly discovers to have been gnawing at the very foundation of the magnificent Southern edifice—a failure of true brotherly love in the exploitation of human life which slavery unavoidably was, the exclusive, restrictive, introverted, and reductive pride of race. Beneath the superficial humor of the scene in which the crusty old lady talks to *her* God, the ringing tones of pride are quite discernible. "I did not sin for gain or for greed," she sensibly begins; "I did not sin for revenge." Then the voice of the real Granny emerges: "I defy You or anyone to say I did." The proud Southern lady continues,

> I sinned first for justice. And after the first time, I sinned for more than justice; I sinned for the sake of food and clothes for Your own creatures who could not help themselves—for children who had given their fathers, for wives who had given their husbands, for old people who had given their sons to a holy cause, even though You have seen fit to make it a lost cause. [P. 167]

There is, furthermore, another element in Faulkner's nondiscursive presentation of the career of Miss Rosa, which we may barely have learned to recognize by this point of the Yoknapatawpha Saga. Granny earns the association of Ab Snopes. Thus far we have met (in the major novels) Byron Snopes and quite briefly Montgomery Ward Snopes and have got a thumbnail forecast of Flem's career in *Sartoris,* and we have caught just a glimpse of I. O. Snopes and Mink Snopes in *The Sound and the Fury;* but perhaps that is enough to alert us to the significance of the intrusion of Ab Snopes into Granny's life. Where evil exists so do Snopeses: they are the symptoms of moral and social disease, as much the sign as the agents of evil. Byron is given the chance to flourish because of Narcissa Benbow's provocative prurience; Monty Ward comes to Horace, whose fear of actual life itself constitutes an evil. It is with Jason Compson that I. O. and Mink are associated—the first in connection with Jason's stock market endeavors, the second with Jason's horrible literal bargain to let Caddy see her baby "for a minute." Granny's initial success in the mule business has conjured up Ab Snopes. We notice the ominous comment, "Ab and Granny got along all right" (p. 136), and worry.

These features of Faulkner's presentation of Granny's life in *The Unvanquished* encourage us to see into the heart of her "wrong actions" and to perceive there the heinous, diseased core. Certainly she is attractive, what we easily (all too easily, as I say) call a well-intentioned old lady, and she is for the most part sympathetic. But the mark of familiar evil is there. And as usual in Faulkner's fiction, the evil works to its own destruction. Finally, then, we can accept as absolutely accurate Ringo's diagnosis of Granny's trouble. He and Bayard have hunted down Grumby, nailed him like a coon hide to the cabin door, and brought home his severed right hand to lay on Granny's grave, so that honor is satisfied. Nevertheless—

> "It wasn't him or Ab Snopes either that kilt her," Ringo said. "It was them mules. That first batch of mules we got for nothing."
> [P. 211]

Granny's reasons, alas, were not finally "the best," for even in her new habit of dishonest mule trading and even in her intention to provide for the needy, it was the old habit—keeping things as they were, maintaining as far as possible the status quo—that persisted.

It is most useful to consider next the role of Drusilla Hawk in the experience of Bayard Sartoris. Certainly Drusilla and John are closely associated in their influence on Bayard, and his crucial decision at the close of the novel involves immediately his attitude to both of them. Yet to consider Drusilla and Granny together for a moment will enable us to recognize more clearly certain important features of the code, the tradition, the old habit which persists and which swaddles Bayard. From the outset Drusilla is an attractive character. She is young and vital, and she has been terribly touched by the war. Her young fiancé, Gavin Breckbridge, was killed at Shiloh. She feels terribly the evident loss of her whole way of life.

We cannot forget her bitterly ironic explanation to Bayard of what
has happened:

> Living used to be dull, you see. Stupid. You lived in the same house
> your father was born in, and your father's sons and daughters had the
> sons and daughters of the same Negro slaves to nurse and coddle; and
> then you grew up and you fell in love with your acceptable young
> man, and in time you would marry him, in your mother's wedding
> gown, perhaps, with the same silver for presents she had received; and
> then you settled down forevermore. . . . But now you can see for your-
> self how it is; . . . you don't have to worry now about the house and the
> silver, because they got burned up and carried away; and you don't
> have to worry about the Negroes, because they tramp the roads all
> night waiting for a chance to drown in homemade Jordan; and you
> don't have to worry about getting children to bathe and feed and
> change, because the young men can ride away and get killed in the
> fine battles; . . . and then [you can] say, 'Thank God for nothing.'
> [Pp. 114–15]

We understand, and our sympathy goes out to her. Even more as we
see how her mother and the other ladies—Mrs. Habersham, Mrs.
Compson, et al.—willfully misunderstand her joining John's troop
like a subaltern Joan of Arc.

These ladies contribute much to moulding Drusilla into a representative figure. As she is, in their eyes, already a wonderful representative of an ideal, her riding with John's troop, astride, dressed
like a man, is all the more lamentable. Bayard relates what his Aunt
Louisa has put into her letter of high-flown rhetoric:

> . . . how when Gavin Breckbridge was killed at Shiloh before he
> and Drusilla had had time to marry, there had been reserved for
> Drusilla *the highest destiny of a Southern woman—to be the bride-widow of a
> lost cause* . . . [p. 219; my italics][3]

The figure of the bride-widow represents Southern aspirations as
Faulkner typically depicts them. She bears some relationship to the
Lady of the Courtly Love tradition: chastely desirable and safely
unattainable—"safely," not simply for herself but also, and indeed
principally, for those who desire her; because while potential lovers
apparently want to possess her, actually possessing her would oblige
them to accept proper responsibility for her—and that burden, as
Faulkner's fiction tragically demonstrates repeatedly, they do not
want; also, once "possessed," she ceases to be the unchanging, virgi-

nal representative figure. Quentin Compson is the earliest unambiguous paradigm of that unwilling lover; his type includes Horace
Benbow, Isaac McCaslin, and Gavin Stevens—indeed, his name is
legion. It is furthermore significant that the bride-widow figure is so
often the object of *incestuous* desire. Obviously this expresses the
tendency of love to turn in upon itself, to keep itself "in the family,"
which is not only separatist and exclusive but, carried to its extreme,
becomes reductive and finally self-destructive. Another aspect of the
situation is that the "lover" is protected by the taboo against incest,
so he is safely (in Faulkner's irony) held—fixed in impotent conti-
nence. As "bride," then, Drusilla is unavailable as sexual partner for
anyone other than her groom; as "widow," she is unavailable even to
the groom. She is Faulkner's equivalent of the "still unravished
bride" of Keats's ode. Changeless, she stands, thus, for the status quo
which the Faulknerian Southerners cherish and intend to sustain.
Another example is Narcissa Benbow as viewed by Horace; yet
another is Caddy Compson as Quentin (at least) wished to keep her;
and she recurs repeatedly under various guises.

So Drusilla fails the ladies, as they see it, in two ways: first, by riding
about dressed like a man and second, by "carrying on" with Cousin
John (they quickly assume that she is pregnant). Consequently, they
exert pressure on Drusilla to make her give up riding with the troop
and don woman's clothes, and then to make her and John marry. And
we must not fail to notice that Faulkner manages to state his familiar
theme of incest—and for the usual purpose, i.e., as a means of expressing the self-destructive self-love of the exclusive, introverted,
restrictive Southern society in its jealous pride of race and blood.
Although denied, the question of incest is raised—once quite explicitly and once by implication. Aunt Louisa's lament about Drusilla and
her destiny continues, "she had not only become a lost woman and a
shame . . . but . . . at least thank God that Father and Drusilla were
not actually any blood kin, it being Father's wife who was Drusilla's
cousin by blood and not Father himself" (p. 219). So John and Drusilla marry—when they finally find time to remember to do so.

And Drusilla grows into her role and in fact grows to relish it and
take it for her own. She becomes the priestess of the cult, the symbol
of the Southern code by which Sartorises and their ilk fashion their
life and behavior. Significantly, Drusilla turns her most seductive
attentions to Bayard, the heir apparent to the Sartoris seat. Before
we see the actual seduction, Faulkner very effectively poses Drusilla

in her symbolic role which will dominate the concluding movement of the novel. Summoned from the University at Oxford, Mississippi, by Ringo with news of his father's death, Bayard returns home to be greeted by Drusilla, just as he had known she would be

> in the yellow ball gown and the sprig of verbena in her hair, holding the two loaded pistols (I could see that too, . . . see her in the *formal* brilliant room arranged *formally* for obsequy . . . the face calm, almost bemused, the head simple and severe, the balancing sprig of verbena above each ear, the two arms bent at the elbows, the two hands shoulder high, the two identical *duelling* pistols lying upon, not clutched in, one to each: *the Greek amphora priestess of a succinct and formal violence*) [P. 252]

I have italicized some of the terms which emphasize the ritual quality of the scene as it exposes Drusilla's role, her almost symbolic function. The formality of the scene strikes us; the pistols, unmistakably duelling pistols, reiterate the insistent code; and Drusilla is the priestess of this formal rite of violence and death.

Upon his arrival, and now accompanied by the chorus of George Wyatt and other members of his father's old troop, Bayard is acutely aware of the ritual drama now being staged and of himself as an additional actor making his potentially heroic entrance:

> they all followed, still with that unctuous and voracious formality. Then I saw Drusilla standing at the top of the front steps, in the light from the open door and the windows like a theater scene, in the yellow ball gown and even from here I believed that I could smell the verbena in her hair, standing there motionless yet emanating something louder than the two shots must have been—something voracious too and passionate. . . . I seemed . . . to watch myself enter that scene which she had postulated like another actor while in the background for chorus Wyatt and the others stood with the unctuous formality which the Southern man shows in the presence of death. . . . [P. 269]

The question is whether Bayard will don the traditional dramatic mask and reenact with unctuous and voracious formality the fixed ritual of vengeance and death, or whether he will be able to revitalize it and redeem it, to redefine the idea of courage and honor which it seems intended to express. The appeal of the formal rite, focussed in its fascinating priestess, is strong and inevitable. And as Drusilla offers him the ritual utensils we are again made acutely aware of the nature of the appeal. She in fact presents herself as the

hero's appropriate consort, offering the pistols as a distinct symbol
of potent manhood:

> "Take them, Bayard," she said, in the same tone in which she had said
> "Kiss me" last summer.... "Take them.... you will remember me
> who put into your hands what they say is an attribute only of God's,
> who took what belongs to heaven and gave it to you. Do you feel
> them? the long true barrels true as justice . . . the two of them slender
> and invincible and fatal as the physical shape of love." [P. 273]

Despite the spell cast by the rhetoric of the passage, we recognize the
irony of the symbolism: here the phallic symbol of the physical shape
of love is destructive, its ejaculation carries the power of death, not
of life.

The impact of the scene is heightened by a flashback which has
been interposed between Bayard's accurate forecast of the scene
which will greet him (quoted above) and the realization of that forecast; it is his memory of Drusilla's initial appeal to him—her initial
seduction, to which he refers in the passage immediately above. The
flashback is of crucial importance because its narrow compass throws
together into fruitful proximity several significant motifs. Bayard
remembers that he and Drusilla were discussing his father's dream
of triumph in the midst of Reconstruction, and with specific reference to John's management of the first election; that leads to their
argument over the necessity of killing to achieve a worthwhile end.
In the midst of that Drusilla affirms her belief that there are worse
things than killing and being killed and her idea of the *summum
bonum:* "the finest thing that can happen to a man is to love something, a woman preferably, well, hard hard hard, then to die young
because he believed what he could not help but believe and was what
he could not (could not? would not) help but be" (p. 261). Then she
commands him, "Kiss me, Bayard." Here again the understated
theme of incest is uttered in much the same way as it was in connection with Drusilla and John. There is no actual incest, of course, but
the theme is presented. Bayard refuses Drusilla's imperative: "No.
You are Father's wife." To which the insistent Drusilla replies, "And
eight years older than you are. And your fourth cousin too. And I
have black hair. Kiss me, Bayard." She will not be denied. This
immediate juxtaposition of the topics of killing and kissing, of death
and love most distinctly anticipates Drusilla's seductive offering of
the pistols as "the physical shape of love." Quite as significant, fur-

thermore, is the briefly interwoven reference to Bayard's killing of Grumby to avenge Granny's death.

This collection of scenes, featuring the voracious and passionate nature of Drusilla's appeal to and influence upon Bayard, serves to impress us sympathetically with the burden—effectively represented by the pervasive and persistent odor of verbena—which Bayard carries as he makes his difficult way to the decision confronting him at the close of the novel. How will the demands of courage, love, responsibility, and honor be served? As the priestess bids, or otherwise? How will he fill the role of The Sartoris?

Colonel John Sartoris as a recognizable type of hero has influenced Bayard as have Granny and Drusilla. We do not get a particularly clear view of John in the early parts of *The Unvanquished*, where he appears mainly as the ideal hero, larger than life-size, capable of Herculean accomplishments. For our view of him there depends upon the wide-eyed and awe-smitten focus of Bayard as a boy. Evidently John is courageous, as responsible a head of the family as his military duties permit, shrewd and resourceful, and a man of honor. Yet, from the earliest pages, we are given glimpses of his dangerous pride and his determination to lead in whatever ventures he is involved with, and there may be something more which helped persuade his original regiment to vote him out of command. We begin to get a surer sense of Colonel John in the closing hours of the war and especially during the period of Reconstruction. Bayard does well to speak of his father and Thomas Sutpen together, for, whatever their initial differences, Colonel Sartoris and Sutpen undergo a similar development. Their evident virtues—of courage, industry, resourcefulness, and so on—are warped by the frustrating experience of the war and turned monstrous. When Colonel John loses command of his regiment and organizes his band of raiders, we see his certain courage become a kind of frantic recklessness almost without point. And as he moves into postwar life, that military courage degenerates into needless, capricious antagonism and finally to the cruel callousness of murder. His pride is inflated into overweening vanity; his responsibility turns to tyranny; his honor is finally proven hollow; of love he is evidently quite bereft.

But perhaps that is too bald a representation of John Sartoris, making him sound too much like the villain of melodrama, a characterization Faulkner is careful to avoid. Our sympathy is involved by Faulkner's explanation of Colonel John's dilemma; he does seem victimized to some degree. As a soldier, he has been obliged to kill, and as George Wyatt says, "I know what's wrong: he's had to kill too many folks, and that's bad for a man" (p. 260). And as a citizen of the defeated South, a man like John Sartoris feels acutely the effect of the opportunist horde of carpetbaggers and scalawags, the "new foe whose means we could not always fathom but whose aim we could always dread" (p. 228).

In part, John Sartoris seems victimized by fate's confronting him with problems without correct solution, dilemmas in which there is no right option. The election in Jefferson offers the crucial example of his dilemma. Colonel John sees that Jefferson is threatened with what is virtually a rigged election, in which the newly enfranchised blacks have presumably been herded together until it is time for them to be guided to the polls to vote as they have been told. John's choices are either to let the rigged election proceed, or to take the law into his own hands and control the election himself. Neither of these is a good option, and there seems to be no other. Insofar as Sartoris is really the victim of the situation, he earns our sympathy. One might say of him what has been said of Granny Millard, that he has had to resort to wrong actions for the best reasons.

Yet the truth is that John Sartoris is victimized by his own evil. The situation which grips him and offers him no acceptable option is ultimately the result of the traditional Southern arrangement that blacks be kept (as a general rule) disenfranchised and uneducated. John objects to the disturbing of that arrangement by carpetbaggers like the Burdens, not to the fact that the election is rigged. Specifically, he objects (1) that blacks are being allowed to vote, and (2) that Cash Benbow, a black, is a candidate for office.

> Father had told the two Burdens before all the men in town that the election would never be held with Cash Benbow or any other nigger in it and . . . the Burdens dared him to stop it. [P. 232]

And Colonel John defends what he believes in and does so with what he would call honor. When he goes to seize the ballot box, he gracefully allows the Burdens to shoot first; then he gracefully kills them both. After explaining to the townspeople that the election will be held at his home and that Drusilla will be the voting commissioner, the colonel goes like a man of honor to report to the sheriff on what he has done. His statement to Jefferson is moving: " 'Don't you see we are working for peace through law and order?' he said" (p. 239).

But the irony is crushing: Sartoris law and order, he means, and evidently acceptable to the majority of the white citizens of Jefferson—acceptable because familiar, the old status quo.

It is even less easy to defend John Sartoris's harassment and gratuitous taunting of Ben Redmond, originally his partner in the railroad company and his opponent in the election for the legislature. One is tempted to say that John got what he deserved, that his constant provocation of Redmond produced the only possible result—death at Redmond's exasperated hands. We pause tentatively at George Wyatt's generous and plausible explanation of John's actions: that he has had to kill too many people in the past (as a soldier, one supposes he means). Yet Bayard's explanation is more convincing; he sees the motive in "Father's violent and ruthless dictatorialness and will to dominate" (p. 258). That will, we recall, has long been visible in Colonel John, although the violence and ruthlessness may be later embellishments due to the influence of the war, as George Wyatt implies.

We can see, certainly, the extent to which the experience of the war has aggravated certain characteristics of John Sartoris and thus regret its effect; but we must not overlook the fact that the tendencies and aims which motivated his behavior in the war are precisely those which in large part were responsible for the war: not just pride, but pride of race and blood; not just the will to dominate, but the determination to enslave and to keep enslaved as far as possible a definite section of the human family. And as his courageous fighting in the Civil War was a defense of the way of life (the status quo) in which that pride and that will predominated, so are his postwar efforts directed toward its reestablishment. One sees, furthermore, that he will continue to resort to the means of violence in his attempt to restore the old way as he did in his attempt to defend it. Finally, the honor in question is defined by the way of life that fostered it and which expects to be sustained by it; it is embodied in the formal rite of which Drusilla appears as the high priestess.

While it is true, then, that in various respects the career of John Sartoris has the shape of a tragic drama, Colonel John himself is something less than satisfactory as a tragic hero. He is heroic only in the restricted context of the Southern way of life, and Faulkner's concern is to call seriously in question the virtues and values of that way of life. John Sartoris's role is really that of a kind of antagonist which young Bayard must confront and overcome in the comic drama of which Bayard is the true hero. Or rather, that antagonist and what he represents are to be redeemed by Bayard's superior moral action. None has seen more clearly than Bayard, surely, what virtues—however tainted—did in fact reside in his father; and Bayard is thus willing to do his utmost not to dishonor his father and not to fail the demands of the highest code of honor as he answers the summons from home on his father's death.

Thus, as Bayard returns to Jefferson and then walks forth to meet his father's slayer, he carries the tremendous burden of the influence upon him of the three characters we have been principally concerned with, chiefly Drusilla and Colonel John Sartoris. The persistent and pervasive odor of verbena and all it means—Drusilla and her awful attractiveness, the aroma of honor, and the weight of accumulated tradition of the Southern romantic heroes represented by his slain father—accompany him like the Furies.[4] It will be a difficult task to act against the general expectations, against the specific demands of Drusilla and the tacit exhortation of the dead John Sartoris. We are made acutely aware of the agony which accompanies this crucial trial, and our sympathy is painfully involved as we share Bayard's thought: *"At least this will be my chance to find out if I am what I think I am or if I just hope; if I am going to do what I have taught myself is right or if I am just going to wish I were"* (p. 248). So it is with tremendous relief and a sense of superlative triumph that we watch Bayard face Redmond completely unarmed. He has won a superior victory not only over his father's slayer but over the ritual code of violence.

It is of primary importance to understand what resources Bayard was able to call upon to achieve that victory, and also what the significance of that victory is for the society in which it was achieved. Most immediately, of course, we are aware of two items of Biblical teaching that are buzzing in Bayard's head to conflict with the seductive influence of the odor of verbena: "Who lives by the sword shall die by it," and "Thou shalt not kill." The teaching has obviously been imparted to him initially by Granny, but fostered and reenforced by Professor and Mrs. Wilkins, with whom he has rooms while at the University. The Biblical interdict against taking human life, then, functions in Bayard's decision to face Redmond unarmed. Bayard's espousal of this teaching is tested for us immediately prior to his decision about facing Redmond. In the flashback which precedes the depiction of his return to Jefferson, Bayard recalls discussing with

Drusilla his father's dream and the value of human life. She explains his dream of raising the whole country by its bootstraps; Bayard makes a fumbling reply:

> "But how can they get any good from what he wants to do for them if they are—after he has—"
> "Killed some of them? I suppose you include those two carpet baggers he had to kill to hold that first election, don't you?"
> "They were men. Human beings."
> "They were Northerners, foreigners who had no business here . . . A dream is not a very safe thing to be near, Bayard. . . . But if it's a good dream, it's worth it. There are not many dreams in the world, but there are a lot of human lives. And one human life or two dozen—"
> "Are not worth anything?"
> "No. Not anything." [Pp. 256–57]

The scene does more than test Bayard's espousal of the teaching against killing. It extends the range of significance of Bayard's imminent decision to embrace most prominently the real question at issue in Colonel John's refusal to accept the rigged election—racial and social discrimination. The issue, in fact, is the whole basis of the society on which has been constructed the pseudoaristocratic system and its sustaining formal code. Bayard's experience has also prepared him to face the full implications of the challenge he confronts. His association with and intimate understanding of Ringo have evidently had a salutary effect on him. We know that he recognizes differences between himself and his young friend, but gratefully they are simple human differences and not those attributable to race. Bayard often enough reminds us, indeed, that the difference in skin color had ceased to be a concern to them. Of course the important lesson about confraternal cooperation is broached in the very first scene of the novel (as I have pointed out above), where Bayard observes that he and Ringo must work together if they are to keep their "South"—their living map—from falling. To this important influence must be added what Bayard knows about the system Buck and Buddy McCaslin have used to prepare their black workers for freedom and independence. We do not see anything of the McCaslin system at first hand, but as Bayard rehearses what he has been told of it, we notice the juxtaposition of two familiar themes fundamental to Faulkner's ethical view and present in the companionship of Bayard and Ringo: respect for the land and respect for human integrity. Amodeus and Theophilus McCaslin

believed that land did not belong to people but that people belonged
to land and that the earth would permit them to live on and out of it
and use it only so long as they behaved and that if they did not behave
right, it would shake them off just like a dog getting rid of fleas. They
had some kind of a system of bookkeeping ... by which all their
niggers were to be freed, not given freedom, but earning it, buying it
not in money from Uncle Buck and Buddy, but in work from the
plantation [P. 54]

Bayard has had the preparation necessary to make the right decision in his moment of crisis. He has seen into the heart of society
and has grasped what Faulkner evidently would have us see and
cherish as the necessary virtues. Bayard knows *and does not forget* the
importance of true brotherly love and of proper respect for the
land. He has known and loved the typical actors in the Southern
drama—the grand old lady in Granny Millard, the Southern belle in
Drusilla Hawk, the traditional heroic Southern gentleman in Colonel
John Sartoris with his library stocked with the inevitable Scott,
Cooper, and (delicious irony) Dumas. He has known them and loved
them for their good qualities before he has grown into maturity and
its attendant obligation to judge them. He has learned something
about courage and love and responsibility and honor as those typical
Southern actors have taught him, by both precept and example, to
understand those virtues—in Southern terms. Bayard's task at last is
not so much to overcome those virtues in their Southern definition
as it is to transcend them by giving them broader definition in more
general human terms. In that way he can redeem them and perhaps
the individuals and the society which would live by them.

It is significant, surely, that Bayard's intention is accepted and
even encouraged by Aunt Jenny: "You are not going to try to kill
him. All right. . . . Don't let it be Drusilla, a poor hysterical young
woman. And don't let it be him [Col. John Sartoris], Bayard, because
he's dead now. And don't let it be George Wyatt and those others
who will be waiting for you tomorrow morning. I know you are not
afraid" (p. 276). Then, after the fact, George Wyatt shows gratifying
comprehension of what Bayard has accomplished: " 'Well by God,'
he said again. 'Maybe you're right, maybe there has been enough
killing in your family without—Come on' " (p. 289). These representatives of Bayard's society have approved his decision, showing
clearly the hopeful signs of redemption. Drusilla Hawk remains,
who had in effect charged him with betrayal after recognizing intu-

itively that he would not perform the rite of violence as she had
bidden him. Yet even her final gesture hints at reluctant approval of
Bayard's way. We know she has gone to Montgomery, to her brother
Dennison; but when Bayard at last goes up to his room he finds on
his pillow a sprig of verbena—"filling the room, the dusk, the evening with that odor which she said you could smell alone above the
smell of horses" (p. 293). Surrendering in tribute her familiar badge
of honor, Drusilla would seem to be tacitly acknowledging the way
Bayard has chosen as preferable to the form she had urged him to
accept.[5]

Bayard's action has been courageous, of a courage which is positive and creative, not that which destroys. Like Fielding's Captain
Booth (in *Amelia*), Bayard has already proven himself—before the
final test—capable of the fierce courage that the old dispensation
had understood and demanded. He had killed Grumby in hot vengeance and brought back his trophy. He has no need to prove
himself again in that way, but can rise to the superior and more
affirmative manner of serving the demands of honor—and no less
courageously. Nor, obviously, does he refuse responsibility, or simply turn his back on evil and wash his hands of it. He will step
firmly into his role as The Sartoris, but will merely redefine and
redeem that role to make it more humane and also more loving.

The love that Bayard exhibits is that more general and more
difficult love of humanity—the old brotherly love urged on us by
both religious and philosophical dicta. He has had to refuse Drusilla's desperately attractive offer to participate in her *liebestod*. His
choice is positive and vital, and he emerges as the true hero, superior to those with whose legacy he has been left. To say it again, he
has not triumphed over Granny, Drusilla, and Colonel John, but
transcended them. Their commitment to the old ways, pride of race,
the maintenance essentially of the *status quo*, brought their own defeat upon them, rendering them incapable of fruitful functioning in
the modern world. Insofar as the old Southern way was evil at its
root and base, their commitment to its maintenance and continuation is likewise evil. The retribution is expressed in Faulkner's persistent theme of the Self-Destructiveness of Evil. Drusilla again remains, perhaps not destroyed, but saved and redeemed by what
seems to be her tacit acceptance of Bayard's decision, her recognition that he has accepted the Second Chance offered to The Sartoris
and successfully met its demand. (Both the recurrence in the Sarto-

ris family of the Christian names "Bayard" and "John" and the repetition of the demand to face Redmond—and to face him *unarmed,* as
Colonel John originally announced he would and Bayard actually
did—serve to give emphasis to the Second Chance theme in this
novel.)

The Unvanquished offers one of the few examples of Faulkner's
depiction of the Second Chance successfully accepted—the opportunity to try again at performing precisely that task which had earlier
met with failure. Bayard Sartoris has courageously faced the challenge with superior understanding and love, has accepted his difficult responsibility and fulfilled the sternest and highest demands of
honor. Certainly much remains for Bayard to do, and Faulkner does
not explore the specific program of actions he must undertake. But
he has carefully shown us what Bayard has become, what qualities he
possesses, what virtues he embodies. And Bayard has been proven in
his crucial test. In a very real sense it does not matter so much what
program we would have him follow: no program of improvement
will succeed unless there are heroic figures like Bayard to carry them
out. On the other hand, we can place some confidence in characters
who *are* what Bayard has proven himself to be, and trust that what
he will *do* will simply reflect what he *is.*

Bayard Sartoris is the Faulknerian standard against which we may
measure numerous other characters in the Yoknapatawpha Saga
who gain the knowledge that Bayard has gained, but who fail for
one reason or another to become what that knowledge should make
of them—what it has made of Bayard. He is the most accomplished
and successful representative, thus far, of the Faulknerian Saving
Remnant.

Movement Two

No wonder then so many die of grief,
So many are so lonely as they die;
No one has yet believed or liked a lie,
Another time has other lives to live.

W. H. Auden, "Another Time"

> . . . beauty, like a Sunday school,
> Humiliated men and turned them old.
>
> Radcliffe Squires, "Mark Twain"

VIII

The Hamlet

Among the most fascinating of Faulkner's creations is the group or swarm or tribe of proliferating characters called, arrestingly, Mink, Ike, Eck, and Flem, Orestes and Virgil, Saint Elmo, Lancelot, and Byron, Montgomery Ward, Watkins Products, Wallstreet Panic, etc., and all sharing the surname *Snopes*. From beneath whatever wet rock they emerged, they quickly make their nearly ubiquitous presence felt as they scuttle across myriad pages of the Yoknapatawpha Saga, most of them leaving a trail of grey-green slime—or something worse. They are important collectively as representing Faulkner's conception of the worst sort of human evil, the threat of redneckism in its most blatantly dreadful form; and that importance is focussed in the marvellous character of Flem Snopes. But more than that, Faulkner came to realize the remarkable potential of the Snopeses as a convenient means to develop and bring to ultimate fulfillment certain themes with which he was concerned throughout his career, and especially those with which I am concerned in this study. And as he employs the Snopes clan to develop those themes, he is able to give full and final form and expression to his fundamentally optimistic attitude to the human condition, his faith in mankind.

Very nearly the earliest creation of Faulkner's fictional county, the Snopeses were at least contemporary with his creation of the opposite pole of Yoknapatawpha society, the Sartorises of *Flags in the Dust*, with whom the Snopeses there share the stage. In his introductory note to *The Mansion*, the last novel of the Snopes Trilogy, Faulkner states simply, "This book is the final chapter of, the summation of a work conceived and begun in 1925," referring to the beginning of the Snopes chronicle as it exists in the "Father Abra-

145

ham" manuscript (now in the Arents Collection of the New York
Public Library); that manuscript sketches briefly the general lines of
the whole Snopes story as it was to be developed in the trilogy, *The
Hamlet, The Town,* and *The Mansion.* Essentially a skeletal resume of
the career of Flem Snopes, it gives full development only to an early
episode in that career—the great pony auction, which is familiar to
Faulkner's readers as the short story "Spotted Horses" (originally
published in *Scribner's,* 89 [June 1931], 585–97), and now incorpo-
rated in *The Hamlet.* Snopeses, indeed, are absent from only two of
the seven Yoknapatawpha novels of the thirties.

Yet the publication of *The Hamlet* in 1940 marks the beginning of
the fully detailed treatment of the Snopes material. It develops the
initial stages of the rise of Flem—the paradigm of Snopesism, the
super-Snopes. He is characterized according to two significant principles, both of which depend on the fact that he and the Snopeses
generally are parasites; their host is the evil (potential or actual) of
humanity. The first principle of development follows obviously from
the initial assumption: Snopeses appear wherever they can take advantage of human frailty, human weakness, human sinfulness. They
represent Evil in an ambivalent way: they are apparently evil themselves—they commit evil acts, are evil agents; but in addition to that
their presence indicates that human evil (or at least the distinct tendency or liability to do evil) was already present before them.
Faulkner spoke of them as being "like mold on cheese."[1] The second
principle of development is their perverseness; they represent the
unnatural—the corruption, spoiling, frustration, or misdirection of
natural (and hence *good*) tendencies.

Faulkner has typically characterized evil as action against nature.
From his earliest presentation of antebellum corruption at the foundations of the magnificent Southern edifice which crumbled in the
1860s, Faulkner has realistically equated the sin of slavery and the
folly of agricultural abuse, figuratively equating exploitation of human beings and exploitation of the land. Both abuses are wrong
because both are unnatural—that is, both involve mistreatment of
God's creation. A similar equation predominates in the rehearsal of
the Snopes Saga, and especially in the first novel of the trilogy, *The
Hamlet.*

The two principles of development mentioned above find their
expression in *The Hamlet* worked out in terms of cows, horses, goats,
and of course "the land" on the one hand, and of human (romantic)

love on the other. To begin with what is perhaps the most salient and arresting and therefore memorable aspect of this thematic development, Ike's love affair with Houston's cow, it must be admitted that, considered as a discrete episode, it is merely a burlesque depiction of enormous monstrosity. Of course, it is not presented as an isolated episode, but benefits from the total context of the novel, including other liaisons between male and female, and other associations with cows, just as it benefits from the texture provided by its poetic prose. Therefore, as a functioning part of the whole structure and pattern of the novel, Ike's affair with the cow becomes something quite other than it would appear if considered in isolation, or as a piece of biography. It also benefits from whatever faint echoes it awakens of mythic representations of other such associations—Europa, Io, Pasiphae, et al.

Ike Snopes is an idiot, yet his devotion to his beloved is as selfish as true love always is: he *wants* the object of his love, and, at the same time, he is as ready for selfless sacrifice, for gallant protection, for unstinting care for the wants and needs of the beloved as a true lover always is. Ike goes through fire to save his beloved from the burning barn; he gets food for her, graces her brow with a garland of posies, gives her the relief from a heavy udder that milking affords. When Jack Houston discovers them together his epithet for the cow is, in the context in which it is uttered, singularly inappropriate: "you damn whore." There is further irony in Houston's plan to punish Ike and cure him forevermore of courting cows by the tried and true method of making him feed and milk this one; for we have already seen Ike freely attending to those very tasks:

> He sets the basket before her. She begins to eat. The shifting shimmer of incessant leaves gives to her a quality of illusion as insubstantial as the prone negative of his late hurrying, but this too is not so: one blond touch stipulates and affirms both weight and mass out of the flowing shadow-maze; a hand's breadth of contact shapes her solid and whole out of the infinity of hope. He squats beside her and begins to draw the teats.[2]

Not only has Ike anticipated Houston in this, he has undertaken those chores freely and prompted by love, not under the duress of threat or as a punitive task.

The comparison between Ike's association with his beloved and Houston's marriage to Lucy Pate is encouraged by the role which

Houston's stallion plays in the frustrating of his and Lucy's liaison.[3] And as far as commerce with cows is concerned, we have these situations: the farmer from whom Ike steals food for the cow wants to impound her and collect the one-dollar pound fee from Houston, just as Houston will demand a one-dollar pound fee from Mink Snopes for having pastured and kept his heifer. Both might have the law on their side in asking the pound fee, but both strike us as meanly and morally unjustified in demanding it, especially Houston in punishing (almost gratuitously) the severely impoverished Mink. There is, in the two cases of the pound fee, a reflection of Faulkner's theme about using nature and her products as means of barter, using them for exploitation. (And it will not do to pose the rhetorical question: "What do people raise cattle for if not for barter?" The whole tenor of the passages in question and the particular focus through which they are presented prevent us from responding to them otherwise than as I have suggested: Houston and the farmer are interested in both cases in gouging an easy buck out of somebody by means of those respective cows.)

It is relevant to consider here another set of amorous associations including Ike Snopes and tacitly imposing comparisons upon the reader. The three principal Snopes liaisons include Ike, Mink, and Flem. And because of the novel's manner of presenting Eula Varner, the comparison between the liaisons of Ike and Flem is primarily most salient. Eula's "entire appearance suggested some symbology out of the old Dionysic times—honey in sunlight and bursting grapes, the writhen bleeding of the crushed fecundated vine beneath the hard rapacious trampling goat-hoof" (p. 95). Young Labove, the aptly named school teacher, sees in the eleven-year-old Eula "that ungirdled quality of the very goddesses in his Homer and Thucydides: of being at once corrupt and immaculate, at once virgins and the mothers of warriors and of grown men"; and he feels that her entrance into his schoolroom brings "a moist blast of spring's liquorish corruption, a pagan triumphal prostration before the supreme primal uterus" (pp. 113–114). She is divinely and essentially female, fecund, genial; and her size, her mammalian precocity, and her pastoral passivity suggest a bovine (or vaccine) quality in Eula. One of the Homeric goddesses of whom she reminds the school teacher may well be "ox-eyed Athena." In any case, the comparison is to be made; and from virtually any point of view, Flem suffers in the comparison with Ike. Put as simply as possible, Flem takes Eula not at all for herself, but for the use he can make of her as a lever against Will Varner to gain the Old Frenchman's Place and to raise himself in the world. She is for Flem a means of barter. The only "use" to which he does not put Eula is that for which she is so superlatively qualified—for love, for motherhood. That he does not "use" Eula in the natural way is quite apparent; that he constitutionally *cannot* do so is suggested by every trait of his characterization in *The Hamlet.*

Finally, Lump Snopes's making money out of Ike's affair with the cow (if that is the advantage Lump hopes to gain) by turning it into a peep show for the boys of the town appears far more perverse than Ike's innocent amour. Once again, an enterprising Snopes exploits and, in the most pejorative sense, uses natural living things. Evil is expressed in terms of the abuse of nature.

Horses function similarly in *The Hamlet.* They too, of course, are *natural,* nature's representatives, and as characters relate to them, so do we relate, sympathetically or antipathetically, to the characters. Houston's stallion is something of a special case. It seems clearly to stand for his natural masculine tendencies, tendencies which, like Caddy Compson's generous capacity for love, are good in themselves but require control. Houston's unwillingness to be domesticated, his returning to Lucy Pate reluctantly as though to his doom, is expressed (appropriately enough) in terms proper to horse-breaking:

> He was bitted now, even if it did not show so much yet. There was still the mark of space and solitude in his face, but fading a little, rationalised and corrupted even into something consciously alert even if it was not fearful; the beast, prime solitary and sufficient out of the wild fields, drawn to the trap and knowing it to be a trap, not comprehending why it was doomed but knowing it was, and not afraid now—and not quite wild. [P. 214]

One need hardly observe that this is not the attitude with which to embark on matrimony. The point here, however, is that the figure of Houston's stallion objectifies or realizes the equine metaphor: "if that blood and bone and muscles represented that polygamous and bitless masculinity which he had relinquished, he never said that" (p. 214). He doesn't need to, of course, for Faulkner has expressed that idea with strikingly dramatic immediacy. The stallion, bought (appropriately) "as if for a wedding gift," is his natural masculinity— natural, but *wild* simply because it rebels against the control that domesticity would require and impose.[4] It (the stallion and all that it represents) kills what Houston would most love if he could. The marriage, dominated by the unfortunate attitudes of both Houston and Lucy, is "unnatural" and thus perverse; and what does violence to nature provokes violence in return.

Much the same function is served in *The Hamlet* by the Spotted Horses, the Texas ponies Flem has brought to town to sell. Natural beings like Houston's stallion, they show their retributive wildness when misused, and wreak havoc among those gullible and simple folk who think they have something to gain, a bargain is to be theirs in this traffic in natural goods. (The ponies are Flem's, of course, and his is the chief misuse of nature in the Spotted Horses affair; that he emerges unscathed makes of him an apparent exception to the rule I am proposing, but that point will be treated fully below, as we consider the ultimate winding up of his career in *The Town* and *The Mansion*.)

The Spotted Horses episode (still the most satisfactorily separable portion of the novel) expresses in extremely interesting terms the theme of the perversion of the natural. Three features of the narrative particularly seize our attention. First, the prevalence of water imagery, especially as associated with the ponies; second, the contrast between the ponies' harm to those who would "make use" of them and their carefully sparing the innocent who want nothing of them; third, the antipathetic involvement of Mrs. Littlejohn in the whole affair. I take it that the water imagery associated with the ponies reenforces our impression of their naturalness, and as these natural creatures penned up become increasingly fierce, so the "water" dammed up threatens inundation when it breaks free. The horses are likened to "dizzy fish in a bowl . . . hysterical fish" and "phantom fish"; their movement is "fluid"; they "flow" and "swirl" and rush "in purposeless and tireless surges"; they move, "clotting"; they "eddied." And so on, again and again, persistently. When finally they burst out and flow all over the countryside creating general mayhem, wreaking havoc, inflicting serious hurt on Henry Armstid and only slightly less on the Tulls, we recognize that Flem's manipulation of this "stream" has made it fierce and destructive. In his abuse of this natural force, Flem threatens to overcome much of the countryside and all that is caught in the maleficent tide he has loosed. The water imagery persists to the bitter conclusion as poor Mrs. Armstid approaches Flem in a futile attempt to regain her five dollars:

she seemed to progress without motion like a figure on a retreating and diminishing float; a gray and blasted treetrunk moving, somehow intact and upright, upon an unhurried flood. [P. 317]

And the motif is further carried out in the minor but typically expressive detail of Flem's reaction to Mrs. Armstid. "Snopes raised his head and turned it slightly again and spat neatly past the woman, across the gallery and into the road." And again, "He turned his head slightly and spat again, neatly past the gray garment [Mrs. Armstid], into the road. . . ." One is tempted to insist here on the (Flegmatic) source of the "unhurried flood" upon which Mrs. Armstid is wafted away.

Among the actors and spectators of the great pony auction, one little central figure of appealing innocence is spared by the lethal wave of spotted horses—Eck Snopes's boy Wallstreet Panic. The beasts' careful treatment of him is portentous. We see little Wall in his diminutive overalls peering into the barn at the horses through a knothole in the door; then they burst out—

> he vanished utterly beneath the towering parti-colored *wave* full of feet and glaring eyes and wild teeth . . . revealing at last the gaping orifice and the little boy still standing in it, unscathed, his eye still leaned to the vanished knot-hole.
> "Wall!" Eck roared. The little boy turned and ran for the wagon. The horses . . . rushed up quartering and galloped all over the boy again without touching him as he ran. [P. 283; my italics]

Below the surface of the whole frankly comic scene, created in the tradition of the Keystone Cops' pell-mell pursuits, the serious significance of Wall's escape is perfectly perceivable. Twice more the experience is repeated, with the ponies again demonstrating that discernment and care of the innocent—not only of Wall but once of Mrs. Armstid as well.

> Then the whole inextricable mass crashed among the wagons and *eddied* and divided about the one in which the woman [Mrs. Armstid] sat, and rushed on down the lane. . . .
> The men in the lot, except Henry [Armstid], got to their feet and ran toward the gate. The little boy [Wall] once more had not been touched, not even thrown off his feet. . . . [P. 302; my italics]

And finally—

> the horse whirled and rushed back up the hall, where Eck and the boy
> now stood .... The boy did not move, and for the third time the
> horse soared above the unwinking eyes and the unbowed and un-
> touched head ... soared outward, hobgoblin and floating, in the
> moon. [P. 303]

The ponies' discerning treatment of the innocent and unspoiled
little Wall recalls the similar experience of the innocent Ike with
Houston's horse on the occasion of rescuing the cow from the burning barn. Repeatedly the half-crazed animal comes bearing down on
Ike alone or Ike with the cow, but always avoids him, usually soaring
over him as the spotted horse soared over little Wall. The significance of these occurrences seems perfectly obvious.

The third feature of this episode involving the spotted horses is
the role of Mrs. Littlejohn. Her association with Ratliff confirms (if
confirmation, indeed, is needed) her opposition to Snopesism and
her harsh judgment of the fools who are willing gulls to the enterprising Flem. But emphasis and dramatic emotional appeal are
achieved by extending the dominant water symbology to embrace
Mrs. Littlejohn. If the function of that imagery is to express Flem's
control and perverse use of these specific examples of natural force
which then overflow and sweep away the foolish populace, Mrs.
Littlejohn's activity eloquently expresses her freedom from that victimization—in the very terms in which that victimization is presented. Mrs. Littlejohn is busy, throughout the pony auction, washing clothes. That occupation is insisted on by the narrative. We are
never allowed to forget the fact that while Flem's influence is surg-
ing over the townsfolk in constantly threatening waves, she is busy
employing water effectively and in one of its proper and natural
uses (and we note appreciatively how Faulkner has fused the realistic
and the figurative to achieve the dramatic expression appropriate to
his point).

> Mrs. Littlejohn was in the yard again.... She carried an armful of
> clothing and a metal-ridged washboard ... she moved across the yard,
> still looking into the lot [where the ponies eddy and swirl], and
> dumped the garments into the tub, still looking into the lot.... Mrs.
> Littlejohn turned away and began to bail water from the pot into the
> tub, though after each bucketful she turned her head and looked into
> the lot again. [Pp. 288–89]

References to her activity—her banging the pail against the rim of the tub, her rhythmical pumping up and down on the washboard, her line of clothing hung up to dry, and so on, regularly punctuate the action. And then as the flood of ponies spills out of the lot to drown the countryside, one stray trickles onto Mrs. Littlejohn's veranda and into her house. Her manner of overcoming this intrusion is notable. The horse

> whirled again and rushed on down the hall and onto the back porch just as Mrs. Littlejohn, carrying an armful of clothes from the line and the washboard, mounted the steps.
>
> "Get out of here, you son of a bitch," she said. She struck with the washboard; it divided neatly on the long mad face and the horse whirled and rushed back up the hall, where Eck and the boy now stood. [P. 303]

Another touch is given to Mrs. Littlejohn's portrait as it figures in this panorama when she and the unfortunate Mrs. Armstid are discussing the possibility of appealing to Flem to return the five dollars. They are washing dishes.

Only the goats remain. Their role, although certainly miniscule, forms a part of the animal pattern we have examined. Again, the use of the goats is not in any sense simply a legitimate business undertaking. Ratliff, who ought to have known better, is merely trying both to set up a trap to catch Flem Snopes in his greed and to combat his use of Mink's and Ike's notes. In addition to that, the goat episode plays a significant role in contributing to the characterization of the attractive Ratliff, chief opponent of Snopesism. The trouble for Ratliff lies in his attempt to beat Flem Snopes at his own game—a tactic ultimately bound to failure, moral as well as practical. One does not undertake to defend the Marquis of Queensbury's rules by entering the ring armed with brass knuckles. So Ratliff's subsequent efforts to combat Flem by tackling him at his game cancel his minor success with the goats. Most memorable is his attempt to outsmart Flem in the matter of the buried treasure on the Old Frenchman's Place, when he even employs old Dick, wise in the lore of nature's ways, with his divining rod.

This leads us to the next important element in the general theme of nature as developed in *The Hamlet*—the importance of the land. Respect for the land is a major motif in Faulkner's ethical system, receiving perhaps its fullest development in *Go Down, Moses*, where exploitive barter in land and the implicit disregard of man's mere tenantship—not ownership—couples with barter in human beings to form the most heinous sin which Faulkner allows the young Isaac McCaslin to discover for us. *The Hamlet* expresses the same ethical attitude.

The principal piece of land in the novel is of course the Old Frenchman's Place. The novel begins, indeed, with a description of that old plantation and its surroundings.

> Frenchman's Bend . . . had been the original grant and site of a tremendous pre-Civil War plantation, the ruins of which . . . were still known as the Old Frenchman's place. . . .
> . . . His dream, his broad acres were parcelled out now into small shiftless mortgaged farms for the directors of Jefferson banks to squabble over before selling finally to Will Varner. . . . [P. 3]

Frenchman's Bend is something like a "company town" and old Will Varner is the company. The land is largely *his;* most of the tenant farmers and sharecroppers farm *his* land; they gin their cotton at *his* mill; they get their furnish at *his* store—"in six-bit dollars," as his son Jody "pleasantly" admits to Flem Snopes. Will Varner *uses* the land and its produce and the commerce derived from it for all it is worth, occasionally using his female tenants for pleasure as well. But he has everything so well set up—the need for his responsible attention is so minimal—that he hardly needs to attend to his affairs. He simply owns body and soul the folks who depend on Varner land and attendant conveniences for their very existence. The relationship between him and them is not unfriendly, is at times almost cordial and quite definitely human, alas, after all. He is a manipulator and exploiter nonetheless.

Trouble begins when Flem Snopes arrives and puts his foot on the bottom rung of the Horatio Alger ladder by undertaking to assist Will Varner. Flem's gradual takeover of the management of Varner affairs simply makes blatantly explicit the half-hidden, apparently quiescent evil latent in Varner's grip on the land and on the lives dependent on it. The focus sharpens when Will Varner discovers he needs a son-in-law to go with his pregnant daughter Eula, and Flem proves to be as accommodating as ever. Flem helps out Eula and the family by marrying her; in return, of course, he gains the indebtedness of the Varners, the position of the fellow who marries the boss's daughter, and the Old Frenchman's Place. Clearly,

Flem has made a deal, and the trade has been in terms of land and
Eula. It becomes apparent in due time that Flem is both unwilling
and unable to care for either of them as they properly require. In
neither case can he assume responsibility for a fertile relationship.
And he will *use* both subsequently as means to further his own progress up the ladder. If Will Varner is a manipulator, Flem Snopes is
manipulation itself.

Since he had never actually done anything with the Old Frenchman's Place, Will Varner considered its role in the bargain with Flem
to be rather slight. Flem will make the most of it, however; and in his
arrangement to turn the Old Frenchman's Place to "good use," i.e.,
as an item of barter in an advantageous trade, Flem's behavior reflects the ultimate in human greed benefitting from the ultimate in
human gullibility. It also paves the way to Flem's final upward step
in the novel and his apparent triumph over his principal antagonist,
V. K. Ratliff. A possible value in the Old Frenchman's Place—apart
from the strictly agricultural in which Flem would not be interested—lies in the treasure reputedly buried there since Civil War days.
It is that empty value which Flem trades on and in which he induces
Ratliff, Bookwright, and Armstid to become interested. They are
taken in, and Ratliff tries to beat Flem at his own game. Flem has, of
course, salted the land, after having made sure that he has been seen
"secretly" digging for the treasure himself, with three bags of coins
for Ratliff and friends—or, indeed, anybody—to find. Flem's last
victorious gesture in the novel is typical and impressive. Pausing to
watch the gulled Ratliff and the mad Henry Armstid futilely digging
in the earth, Flem impassively spits.

The finishing touch to this particular theme is Ratliff's having
enlisted the aid of old Uncle Dick to help him find the buried riches.
There seems to be a particular perversity in involving Uncle Dick,
full of years and lore. He brings a peachfork (doctored up with a
pendant "tobacco-sack containing a gold-filled human tooth") to
serve as divining rod. Uncle Dick with his paraphernalia offers a
clear parallel to the old system of determining where to dig a well, of
finding one of the basic riches of the earth. And Uncle Dick's using
his peachfork in an attempt to find buried treasure anticipates Lucas
Beauchamp's using the gold-divining machine similarly in *Go Down,
Moses*. Uncle Dick unconsciously underlines the irony of his position
and, by extension, of Ratliff's and the others' as well, when he utters
his advice:

"Ye kin dig and ye kin dig, young man," the reedy voice said. "For what's rendered to the yearth, the yearth will keep until hit's ready to reveal hit." [P. 343]

The old man's words anticipate those of Molly Beauchamp when she protests to Roth Edmonds (in *Go Down, Moses*) Lucas's folly with the gold-divining machine: "Because God say, 'What's rendered to My earth, it belong to Me unto I resurrect it. And let him or her touch it, and beware.' . . ."[5] The peachfork does its work (as a well-handled willow fork finds water), but the "treasure" proves as deceptive (appropriately) as the gold Lucas will seek in *Go Down, Moses* proves illusory. Ratliff has let himself sink to the level of violating nature—has, in more ways than he intended, put himself on a par with Flem Snopes.

The theme of love closely associates and mutually illuminates these nature themes in *The Hamlet*. As we have already glimpsed, the association is quite obvious in most instances. At the center of the novel are Flem Snopes and Eula Varner, and just as Flem is willing to speculate in, i.e., to *abuse*, in the novel's terms, land (the Old Frenchman's Place) and nature's animals (goats and especially the spotted horses), so is he willing to take on those very terms the pregnant and unwed daughter of his boss. Indeed, Eula and the Old Frenchman's Place figure equally in the deal with Will Varner. And just as Flem has no intention (and finally, we realize, no ability) to act as proper husbandman of the Old Frenchman's Place so he has neither intention nor ability to act as Eula's proper husband.

Faulkner's characterization of Eula as the female principle, a figure of quite blatant fecundity, reinforces this association. She simply waits, passively for the most part, for the figure strong enough, potent enough, courageous enough, and (in a sense the most important qualification) responsible enough to be her active, fecundating partner. Furthermore, descriptions of Eula emphasize in almost literal (or at least opaquely figurative) terms her earthiness, her similarity to the land. Complementarily, the female quality of the land— its feminine undulations, its female potential for fecundity—heightens the similarity. The eloquent pathos (comic though its appearance sometimes is in the novel) of Eula's career derives from the failure of a properly qualified consort—potent, courageous, and responsible— to present himself and claim her as his partner. The inescapable implication is that imitative magic would take effect, as in the primitive fertility rites it was expected to do, if the proper consort did appear and couple with the waiting Eula: the rivers would fill, the crops would burgeon, and the flocks and herds would multiply. Instead, the encouragingly named Labove appears and desires, is strong and evidently potent, but fails of the necessary courage to grasp and cleave to what might have been his. Then it is Hoake McCarron's turn. He seems much nearer to the anticipated ideal, but he lacks the sense of responsibility that must accompany the strength, potency, and courage (of a kind) which he clearly possesses. Labove ironically senses his own failure, which shows through his somewhat sardonic anticipation of the pathetic future awaiting Eula in the wretched partner who will claim her, as if by default,

> ... the husband which she would someday have. He would be a dwarf, a gnome, without glands or desire, who would be no more a physical factor in her life than the owner's name on the fly-leaf of a book ... the crippled Vulcan to that Venus, who would not possess her but merely own her by the single strength which power gave, the dead power of money, wealth, gewgaws, baubles, as he might own, not a picture, statue: a field, say. [Pp. 118–19]

That is Flem, who, although completely devoid of the necessary qualities, makes Eula his property through his cleverness and opportunism.

Many of the other "love affairs" in the novel reflect on the central union of Flem and Eula, and furthermore gain by the comparison. Most important are those which involve other Snopeses—I. O., Ike, and Mink. Insofar as they are truly Snopeses (Eckrum, not a "true" Snopes, is obviously an exception) they share in the Snopesian corruption. Or rather they share in the general Snopesian function of indicating the corruption which is already there, which has, so to speak, attracted them and given them their *raison d'être*. The evil that Snopeses do is always to a considerable extent the responsibility of the rest of society. Snopeses somehow realize (by a kind of *reductio ad absurdum*) the evil already potentially or latently present in society. As they take advantage of the moral decay already begun, they are the sign perhaps even more than the agent of evil and corruption— the scab on the moral sore, or (in Faulkner's own terms) the mold on the cheese. I. O. is, of course, a fool and a congenital ne'er-do-well, and he is hypermarried—a bigamist. Ike's case is much more important. As I have argued above, his affair with the cow is simply perverse if considered out of context, but in the context of the novel,

Ike's devotion, lapt as it is in soft Lydian prose, is perhaps the purest in the novel. One cannot avoid comparing his love with Flem's, especially when the bovine qualities of their respective paramours help encourage the comparison. Furthermore, the most indelible flavor of perversity arises, not from Ike's love of the cow, but from Lancelot Snopes's turning that union into a peep show for the Toms on the store's gallery.

Mink's is a somewhat different case, though not less relevant, and particularly expressive. It is not easy to prepare a brief for Mink as a superlative lover, but in some degree he must be so considered. The plantation owner's daughter, whose breadth of experience in such matters would seem to qualify her as a connoisseur, has chosen him as her partner. Reviewing certain salient features of Mink's relationship with his wife will increase our understanding of that somewhat strange union. As he returns from killing Houston, he sees the figure of his wife waiting for him, framed in the doorway of their wretched cabin. That image, developed subsequently to give it a particular emphasis, merges first into the initial vision Mink had of his wife—"in the savage lamplight . . . in the open door of the messhall in that south Mississippi convict camp where he first saw her nine years ago" (p. 220). Then, after Houston's murder is discovered and Mink is being sought, he comes to Will Varner's to find his wife—

> She came out of the front door, running, framed again for an instant by the lighted doorway as when he had first seen her that night at the lumber camp. . . . The feeling was no less strong now than it had ever been. . . . [P. 235]

Each recurrence of the image brings additional recall of Mink's past, with special emphasis upon his attraction to the woman. Her appearance in the lighted doorway is like her being framed in a picture or ensconced like the figure of a goddess in an important niche in the temple built for her shrine, her place of adoration. Mink recalls his first view of her, he "heard the loud voices and saw her framed in the open door, immobile, upright and unlistening, while those harsh loud manshouts and cries seemed to rise toward her like a roaring incense. He went no further" (p. 236). Mink's single and unswerving devotion and commitment to Yettie began at that moment; and his first taste of her "made a monogamist of him forever, as opium and homicide do of those whom they once accept" (p. 238). The simile, of course, is harsh and threatening; yet if it was not love that there engulfed Mink, we have no name for what it was—and we have no right to call it anything else.

But it is a love which, like all truly Snopesian love, has been perverted. I do not mean that Mink's love is perverse, in the usual sense of the term; we are meant to feel that his love and love-making are strong and intense and rather exceptional—that his amorous qualities have the strength of virtue, but have somehow gone wrong, have not achieved their fullest potential. The key statement is Yettie's observation. Her judgment in such matters we can accept as based on wide experience:

> they were married. . . . They returned to his native country, where he rented a small farm on shares. They had a second-hand stove, a shuck mattress on the floor, the razor with which he still kept her hair cut short, and little else. At the time they needed little else. She said: "I've had a hundred men, but I never had a wasp before. That stuff comes out of you is rank poison. It's too hot. It burns itself and my seed both up. It'll never make a kid." [P. 238]

Nor is their union simply one of lust. At least until the miserable consequences of Houston's death wrench them apart, they love with honor and respect and a willingness to sacrifice. Poor Yettie rushes about proclaiming Mink's alibi when the crime itself remains undiscovered and her husband unaccused. Even more—like Ruby Goodwin working for her man (in *Sanctuary*)—Yettie has gone to Will Varner's and earned ten dollars to help Mink escape. Mink's sense of honor and fairness, however, prevents him from accepting that sacrifice, and he spurns the ill-gotten gains as he had refused even to consider robbing the dead Houston. "I could not love thee, dear, so much / Loved I not honor more." Poor admirable Mink!

Finally, we are made to feel that Mink's peculiarity as a lover—not so much his almost obsessive concern with honor, perhaps, but especially his hot waspish sexuality—results from his social and economic conditioning. Mink is small and skinny, and the picture of the abject, grinding poverty in which he lives speaks with horrible eloquence of the years, the generations, of deprivation and of malnutrition that have produced this strange little man. The impressive if somewhat diminutive sting of Mink's sexual service would seem appropriate to his size. But he is fiercely monogamous, fiercely moral, fiercely proud. The singleness of Mink's devotion (for all its fierceness)

serves as a striking contrast to the cold and opportunistic attitude of
Flem to his partner, Eula. If Mink is in some ways less than satisfactory, his failure results from generations of misfortune, of under-
nourishment, of drastic social injustice, of the lack of means and
opportunity to do better. While much the same may be said of Flem,
the argument in his case is severely diminished in effectiveness because of his characterization: he is mean and deadly, and evidently
willfully so. Mink represents love twisted, truncated, and perverted—but recognizably *love,* nevertheless; Flem represents simply
the absence of love—its negation, in fact.

The contrast of Mink with Jack Houston further strengthens his
role. While marriage has trapped both Mink and Houston, Houston
reacts with reluctance, regret, and submission; Mink does not. His
trap is the pressure of social inequality and crass injustice. Furthermore, while Houston is giving up his wild, polygamous freedom,
Mink willingly and eagerly cleaves to his spouse in that fierce spirit
of monogamy we have already noted. Mink is pathetic but admirable, even though we regret his apparently gratuitous murder of
Houston in *The Hamlet.* Even that regret is greatly modified by subsequent development in *The Town* and *The Mansion,* where we are
given a much fuller and more sympathetic exposé of the Mink-
Houston affair. While Mink disappears from our view in *The Hamlet,*
he returns to play a role of great importance in the denouement of
the Snopes drama, and it is thus important that we recognize the
potential value in the comparatively brief development of Mink's
love affair in this initial volume of the trilogy. He serves, in any case,
to add to the development of the theme of love in *The Hamlet.*

The themes which I have isolated for discussion—love, exploitive
barter and abuse, and nature—of course cross, merge, and illuminate each other brilliantly. They function admirably as the terms
which Faulkner's ironic mode employs to involve and guide our
sympathies and antipathies, to dilate our consciousness and instruct
our moral understanding. And they all contribute to Faulkner's development of the larger theme, the definition and illustration of
Evil; and this is preparation for the working out of the dominant
theme of the Self-Destructiveness of Evil, which working out is a
complex and extended concern of the whole trilogy.

Taken alone, *The Hamlet* presents the horrifying comedy of Flem
Snopes's successful career. Its counterplot is the tragedy of V. K.
Ratliff, and of all the rest of Frenchman's Bend. Yet here, as so

frequently elsewhere in Faulkner's fiction, the narrative mode is fundamentally ironic; and the novel's statement is basically moral and, as is usually the case with tragedy, basically affirmative, positive, hopeful. Flem's apparent success is carefully defined in terms which make its horror quite understandable and sensibly impressive. Similarly, the apparent failure of Flem's adversaries—Eula (passively) and Ratliff (actively)—is quite clearly defined and explained. The novel's moral statement is thus eloquent and readily available. Our satisfaction derives from our seeing the action of evil made understandable, from our recognizing precisely in what the evil consists, and from our being shown exactly how specific attempts to combat that evil are liable to fail. By the same token we are enabled to understand exactly how the evil might successfully be confronted and its agents overcome. The ironic presentation of Flem's success makes that understanding available to us.

Nevertheless, *The Hamlet* does end with Flem triumphing over his antagonist, Ratliff. But here we must insist again on the necessity of regarding the novel as but one part (albeit successfully separable and satisfyingly self-contained) of a larger whole, the Snopes trilogy, and ultimately of the total opus of the Yoknapatawpha Saga. For just as full understanding and appreciation of the separable pieces which comprise *Go Down, Moses* depend on our reading them as parts of the unified whole which *Moses* demonstrably is, so we must complete the projected trilogy in order fully to grasp the import of its component parts.

Video meliora proboque,
deteriora sequor.

Ovid, *Metamorphoses*, VII

IX

Go Down, Moses

Go Down, Moses (1942) occupies a special place among Faulkner's important works. One part of it, "The Bear," is not only his best known piece of fiction but also the one that has elicited the most critical commentary. The frame of specific temporal reference is further extended here than in all of his other major fiction. Following the familiar practice of the first dozen years or so of the Yoknapatawpha Saga—that of doubling back over ground already crossed in order to discover and examine the antecedent cause of the growing evil already exposed—Faulkner has in *Go Down, Moses* gone furthest into his characters' history, to the virtual discovery of the New World; yet this novel bursts into our own time, into the middle years (appropriately) of the Second World War. While much has been settled, fictionally, by *Go Down, Moses* and by the critical commentary it has received, a close rereading of the novel will reveal certain unanswered questions and unresolved difficulties. Those answers and resolutions can best be found in our rereading by attending to the nature of the novel's focus on Isaac McCaslin—surely the Moses of the novel's title—and by looking closely at his role and its implications for this land of ours where a "Pharaoh" takes precedence over a King.

Mr. Cleanth Brooks has made the interesting suggestion that *Go Down, Moses* might have been more usefully entitled *The McCaslins*, "for the book has to do with the varying fortunes of that family."[1] I would modify that suggestion only to emphasize that the book has to do with Ike's understanding of and finally his contribution to the fortunes of that family. The crucial question facing Isaac McCaslin is "What does it mean to be one of the family?" In terms of the novel's metaphor, the family is, of course, the McCaslins; in terms of the broadest significance of that metaphor, however, the family is the human family. To answer such a crucial question, one must know and understand the family heritage—must recognize the virtues and the source of goodness whence they derive, as well as the sins and the source of evil which promotes them; one must also understand what has been and what now can be done to foster the former and combat the latter. In dealing with this question and the problem of answering it satisfactorily, Faulkner has offered a combination of dramatic expression and discursive narration in the various pieces which make up *Go Down, Moses*.

The novel is clearly enough Isaac's from the opening lines onward. Yet the beginning statement about "Uncle Ike" is left suspended, to be finished later. And that is, I think, the initial clue to the novel's three-part structure. The first three stories ("Was," "The Fire and the Hearth," and "Pantaloon in Black") portray Isaac's heritage; this permits us an objective view of the features, the good and the evil, which characterize his heritage, and allows us to make our balanced judgment of it. The second part ("The Old People," "The Bear," and "Delta Autumn") presents us with Isaac's discovery of that heritage, his education in its good and evil. We not only have his experiences but are privy to his thoughts about those crucial experiences. Since we already know, from reading the first part, what Isaac must learn, we can better sympathize with him as he discovers—sees and defines for himself—the good of the wilderness and the evil of exploitation; and, more important, we can judge the decisions he subsequently makes on the basis of his understanding of his heritage. The first part shows the scene upon which Ike will enter; the second shows us Ike's reaction to that scene. The third part ("Go Down, Moses") serves as the conclusion, which not only rounds off the action of the novel but also points ahead to the consequences which will follow from Ike's experience and his reaction to it.

The virtues discovered in *Go Down, Moses* are, most simply expressed, respect and love for God's creation and the courage to accept the responsibility which that respect and love demand. The source of goodness whence those virtues spring is God's creation itself, or, more properly, right knowledge of God's creation. The sins and wickedness discovered in the novel are, of course, the opposite of that—lack of respect and love, or failure of courage when some respect and love have been awakened.

We are led gently into the heart of the matter by the initial "Was." The hearty joviality and lusty romp may easily camouflage the more serious concerns of the story. It certainly has some highly humorous moments, and if we do not look very hard or more than once at its shenanigans, we will not recognize until we get further into the novel the horror of the actual situation. Uncle Buck and Uncle Buddy McCaslin can hardly be called evil men; it is easy to sympathize with them and even to feel that they deserve their significant names—Theophilus and Amodeus—as men who do love God. The rollicking chase after Tomey's Turl is funny until we realize the fact that Buck and young Cass are hunting a human being, one who is running because he wants to be with the girl he loves. Thus, the activity of Buck McCaslin is objectionable on two counts: it is opposed to the virtue of respect for God's creature Terrel (and by extension Tennie), and also to the genial virtue of love. The deceptive camouflage benefits from the parallel theme of Miss Sophonsiba's hunting of Buck. We are at first amusedly aware of the jangling, roan-toothed, toddy-sweetening bait and of the trap into which Buck finally falls as into a feather bed, but our attention is deflected or at least somewhat amazed in the concluding poker game, where the story's emphasis has apparently shifted to the question of Buck's freedom. We all cherish freedom and are thus hoping that Buddy will win the poker hand. But the stakes are human beings, and there is more than Buck's freedom in the ante—or rather, the crushing irony is that while Buddy can win Buck's freedom, nothing in the game can win freedom for Tomey's Turl and Tennie. The awful fact of the condition of slavery is muffled under a chuckle, but it is there. Similarly, in the Beauchamp hyperbole at Warwick, the miserable code which depends upon the institution of slavery for its support and sustenance—the exclusive, introverted, and gentle code of the pseudoaristocratic way of "the Old South," the "Southern gentleman," and the "Southern Belle"—holds sway.

"Was" has opened the story of the McCaslin heritage *in medias res.* Our attention is directed to an episode in the life of the middle generation of McCaslins—the twin sons of old Carothers McCaslin, first of that name in Yoknapatawpha County, and the father and uncle of Isaac McCaslin, last of that name (legitimately) in Yoknapatawpha County. "The Fire and the Hearth" is concerned with two other branches—the white Edmondses, descended from the distaff side, and the black Beauchamps, descended from old Carothers

McCaslin's left hand. Three closely related features of the novel's principal concern emerge strongly in this story: proper respect for the land, love, and the responsible courage to sustain that respect and love. So far as the present moment of the story is concerned, Lucas's folly over the gold-divining machine is the main event. He has been tricked into believing that he can gain rapid and unearned riches from the earth in the form of buried coins. The very way in which the earth's temptation is phrased clearly enough indicates the folly of Lucas's attempt. As the broken vessel crumbles it seems to Lucas that the earth has placed the seductive coin in his palm, but then as the paragraph ends we hear the unambiguous chuckle which accompanies the donation of that tempting morsel. Molly's explanation of why she wants a divorce underlines the significance of Lucas's pursuit of these riches: she is afraid Lucas will call down God's curse. "Because God say, 'What's rendered to My earth, it belong to Me unto I resurrect it. And let him or her touch it and beware.' "[2] She repeats this to Roth Edmonds as "the curse of God that's gointer destroy him or her that touches what's done been rendered back to Him" (p. 122). In effect it is the long-tried love of Lucas and Molly, so effectively symbolized by the fire which he built on their hearth on their wedding night and has kept alive ever since, that overcomes Lucas's folly. He refuses the divorce and gives up the machine—even refuses Roth's conspiratorial willingness simply to put it away for further use at a later date, when Molly won't know.

Two additional comments are needed here. First, that the application of Molly's simple but profound observation about God's earth and the attendant curse extends beyond Lucas's folly with the gold-divining machine to embrace all exploiters of the land. After Molly has given Roth her explanation of Lucas's evil behavior and Roth is left alone, he wanders out on his own land and Molly's words recur to him: "There was a moon now, blanched upon the open cotton almost ready for picking. The curse of God. He knew what she meant, what she had been fumbling toward" (p. 122). The juxtaposition of this brief scene and that of Molly's complaint about Lucas's folly, and (within this brief scene) of the "open cotton" and "the curse of God," manages to give eloquent emphasis to Molly's point and to extend its implications to embrace all those who seize illegitimately the riches of the earth. For what Molly has said in reference to Lucas's behavior with the gold-divining machine, Roth sees has reference to himself and his cotton exploitation. Furthermore,

Molly's notion of God's curse and Roth's recognition of what she had been fumbling toward will be reflected strongly in the twenty-one-year-old Isaac McCaslin's condemnation of his cursed heritage (and there, to anticipate a little, what has been scarcely explicit in this scene involving Roth and Molly will emerge in flat statement). Isaac will claim he has set himself

> against the tamed land . . . which old Carothers McCaslin . . . tamed and ordered or believed he had tamed and ordered it for the reason that the human beings he held in bondage and in the power of life and death had removed the forest from it and in their sweat scratched the surface of it . . . in order to grow something out of it which had not been there before and which could be translated back into the money he who believed he had bought it had had to pay to get it and hold it and a reasonable profit too. . . . [P. 254]

And the whole of the novel, of course, is redolent of Faulkner's vision of a society as guilty of agricultural as of social abuse.

The second comment is that Lucas's folly with the gold-divining machine is not typical of his behavior. The flashbacks to his life as a young man impress on us the fact that he has been a sober, responsible, and reliable farmer, who has prospered from his labors. It is not that Lucas benefits from whatever proddings of conscience made his grandfather leave him a legacy of a few hundred dollars, but rather from the recognition of his reliability and responsibility shown by Cass Edmonds, who had built a house for him and Molly and "allotted Lucas a specific acreage to be farmed as he saw fit as long as he lived or remained on the place" (p. 110). He is known as one to be trusted—even to farm "as he saw fit."

Here we see that important feature of responsible respect for the land—respect which Lucas (being human and hence imperfect) has momentarily lost in succumbing to the temptation of easy riches. We also see, in that lengthy flashback, the two other salient features of the novel closely combined: love and responsible courage. And their appearance in Lucas is all the more impressive considering the circumstances against which he has to contend. At the birth of Zack Edmonds's son, Roth, Lucas is dispatched to fetch the doctor and almost loses his life doing so, while Molly is summoned to care for the new born baby as wet-nurse, for she herself has just given birth to Henry. Since Zack's wife dies in childbirth, Molly remains at Edmonds's. Lucas suffers through several months the absence of his

wife, yet keeps alive that symbolic fire on his hearth. When he finally
determines to demand his wife back, we see the supreme example of
the strength of Lucas's love and of his dauntless courage in risking
death to regain his beloved. And it is easy to believe that (as Lucas
thinks to himself) the single misfired shell in his pistol did contain
the two lives, his own as well as Zack's; for his own pride and courage would have obliged him to accept the rope and the kerosene too
for the death of Zack, if the pistol had not misfired. Nor was this
foolhardy, thoughtless courage. Lucas knew very well the apparent
hopelessness of his position. "How to God . . . can a black man ask a
white man to please not lay down with his black wife? And even if he
could ask it, how to God can the white man promise he won't?"
(p. 59). For there is Lucas, fully cognizant that he is confronted with
the awful fact of miscegenation, which we recognize again as
Faulkner's tellingly dramatic synecdoche for slavery.

Henceforth Lucas will behave toward Zack as toward a fellow
man, not a superior. When he has to address him by name (which he
avoids doing whenever possible) he calls him Mr. Edmonds, not Mr.
Zack, which is the subservient, "nigger" term of address. Young
Roth has recognized early this tacit statement of (at least) equality,
and has managed rightly to grasp its basis: *"It was a woman*, he
thought. . . . *And by God Lucas beat him. . . . Even a nigger McCaslin is a
better man, better than all of us"* (pp. 115–16). This recognition comes
to the boy Roth as though in consequence of his having one day
asserted his difference from Lucas's son Henry—his playmate since
birth—and hence his superiority: "one day the old curse of his
fathers, the old haughty ancestral pride based not on any value but
on an accident of geography, stemmed not from courage and honor
but from wrong and shame, descended to him" (p. 111). The narrow
exclusiveness of the master class and its regularly claimed *droit du
seigneur* (in and out of season) are closely joined in the context to
underline the dominant evil of the situation in which Lucas has
found himself and in which he nevertheless had the courage to act,
to accept the responsibility for claiming what his love and his sense
of human justice obliged him to claim. Lucas acted like a man, and
he demands no more than to be accepted as one. When Roth comes
to Lucas's at Molly's prompting to settle the question of a divorce,
Lucas says to him flatly, "I'm a man . . . I'm the man here. I'm the
one to say in my house, like you and your paw and his paw were the
ones to say in his" (p. 120). This in turn echoes his earlier statement

to Zack, when he went to demand the return of Molly—" 'I'm a nigger,' Lucas said. 'But I'm a man too' " (p. 47).

The very foolishness of Lucas's succumbing to the temptation of the gold-divining machine serves to heighten by contrast our sense of his nobility as it emerges in the flashback to his earlier life; and we see the unmistakable reflections of it in his behavior toward Roth Edmonds and indeed finally toward Molly. Lucas is and has been the man he claims to be. He has the necessary virtues of respect for God's creatures and of love, and he has likewise the courage to accept the responsibility for what he rightly respects and loves. This discovery of human virtue in the son of Tomey's Turl, whose pursuit we were invited to laugh at and whom we were permitted to dismiss as a rather shrewd but inhuman clown (in "Was"), comes as a bracing contrast.

In the subsequent story, "Pantaloon in Black," one aspect of Lucas's life gains special emphasis by the illumination reflected from the profoundly pathetic love of Rider and Mannie. The association of that young couple of newlyweds, so soon separated by death, with Lucas and Molly is made quite specific: "they married and he [Rider] rented the cabin from Carothers Edmonds and built a fire on the hearth on their wedding night as the tale told how Uncle Lucas Beauchamp . . . had done on his forty-five years ago and which had burned ever since . . ." (p. 138). The distraught Rider is driven in his despair to a horrible death (the very death which Lucas had been ready to accept for the sake of gaining vengeance on Zack Edmonds); and the wretchedness of Rider's—and, by extension, of all blacks'—situation is bitterly expressed in the naive comment of the sheriff's deputy: "Them damn niggers . . . they aint human . . . when it comes to the normal human feelings and sentiments of human beings, they might just as well be a damn herd of wild buffaloes . . ." (p. 154). The irony is almost unbearable. But the sheriff's deputy is reiterating that attitude of exclusiveness, of lack of charity and simple human brotherhood, which Faulkner indicates was not confined to the "aristocrats" alone. Here again is an example of what young Roth had recognized as the old curse of his fathers.

This first section of three stories presents quite clearly enough those sins of disrespect for and hence exploitation of the land and of human beings which are regularly the basic concern of Faulkner's fiction. And in the character of Lucas Beauchamp we find embodied the virtues of respect for the land and people, of generous and effective human love, and of stoutly courageous responsibility. A tragic qualification is that because of the peculiar institution which restricts Lucas's field of influence—that way of life which, Faulkner's work persuades us, was responsible for the demise of the old South and prevents the successful rise of a new South, and a new North too—his virtues cannot effect all the good they otherwise might.

The next group of three stories presents the same heinous sins as Ike McCaslin discovers them—discovers them to have existed even among the aborigines of this brave New World of ours—and the stories also show us Ike discovering the virtues necessary to combat those sins. And in the scope of these stories we also see the tragic failure of one so enlightened to act on his knowledge.

"The Old People" is best seen as the immediate preparation for the important discoveries Isaac will make in "The Bear." It is Isaac's story (as indeed the whole novel is)—the story of "his maturing, of that for which Sam had been training him all his life some day to dedicate himself" (p. 173). And it is about the shooting of a buck when Ike is twelve—or, rather, the shooting of two bucks. After Ike successfully shot his first buck, Sam Fathers marked him with its hot blood, as a ritual of initiation into the mystery of the hunters. But as the story's final comment on that ritual marking insists, it has a broader significance: "Sam Fathers had marked him indeed, not as a mere hunter, but with something Sam had had in his turn of his vanished and forgotten people" (p. 182); and "Delta Autumn" will tell us, as old Isaac recalls this experience, that "there was something running in Sam Fathers's veins which ran in the veins of the buck too" (p. 350). That "something" seems to have been a sense of the basic goodness in God's creation, in the unspoiled Edenic wilderness, in what we might call man's *real* estate. To be initiated into the knowledge of that everlasting spirit—that he may dwell in it and it in him—is to "participate" in its immortality:

> the white boy [Isaac], marked forever . . . the first worthy blood which he had been found at last worthy to draw, joining him and the man [Sam] forever, so that the man would continue to live past the boy's seventy years and then eighty years, long after the man himself had entered the earth as chiefs and kings entered it. . . . [P. 165]

The buck itself which Ike had shot, having the characteristics of the fixed and immutable which suggest eternal existence, further contributes to this quality of the experience. Ike does not see the buck approach: "the buck was there. He did not come into sight; he was just there . . ." (p. 163). In this, it anticipates the behavior of old Ben, the famous bear. And Ike's memory of the experience insists on the quality in question: "the buck still and forever leaped . . . still out of his instant of immortality the buck sprang, forever immortal" (p. 178). Faulkner may have persuaded us, but we should be glad of some confirmation of this quality of the experience; and that will be granted in the closing episode.

But first we might recall Sam's qualifications for the role of mentor to young Isaac. The brief biographical sketch of Sam makes two points. First, he descends from two lines of "natural" races, both of which were royal: "all his blood on both sides, except the little white part, knew things that had been tamed out of our blood [Cass tells Ike] so long ago that we have not only forgotten them, we have to live together in herds to protect ourselves from our own sources" (p. 167). And Sam's nobility is attested to by the likeable plebeian Boon—"a mastiff" (we need later to recall), "absolutely faithful"— who also has Chickasaw blood like Sam. And second, the little white part of his blood stridently proclaims that Sam has been enslaved— and not only by the white man, but by his own people, as the brief history of Ikkemotubbe relates; yet he is free in a very important sense, for his soul is his own. One sees in Sam's eyes at times a certain expression, not the mark of servitude, but of bondage; he is (Cass says) "Like an old lion or a bear in a cage" (p. 167). He is in this much like Lucas Beauchamp, a Lucas less civilized, perhaps. Both are independent, proud, and confident, and, in spite of their victimization by society, fundamentally "free." Thus Sam retains and can pass on to young Isaac knowledge of that "something" inherited from his own African and Chickasaw ancestors and nurtured by his constant communion with the wilderness, the knowledge that brings maturity and the freedom all men can enjoy in spite of whatever bondage society places on them.

That Sam's marking of Isaac in that ritual of initiation has the significance I have claimed is confirmed in the final paragraphs of the story. Boon has sighted a great, fourteen-point buck just as they are all leaving camp, and they all disperse to find stands and await the buck's appearance. Ike *senses* that the buck has returned, noted their presence, and faded back into the cane—then he hears Walter Ewell's rifle, which never missed. Sam bids the impatient and disappointed Ike to wait. The magnificent buck appears to them, passes close to them, and even as Ewell's horn still sounds its triumphant note, Sam greets the buck: "Oleh, Chief . . . Grandfather." And when they reach Walter Ewell, they see he has shot a little spike buck. Walter comments, "But just look at the track he was making. It's pretty near big as a cow's. If there were any more tracks here besides the ones he is laying in, I would swear there was another buck here that I never even saw" (pp. 184–85). That superlative buck symbolizes, of course, the undying spirit of the wilderness—the "something" that runs in Sam's veins and in the veins of all the natural creatures of the wilderness, where it is *realized,* incarnate. Finally, Ike urgently relates this experience to Cass, insisting on the truth of his vision—of which he perhaps only imperfectly grasped the significance at the time—and fearing that his cousin will not believe him. But Cass supplies the confirmation we have been await-ing (with Ike) as he replies calmly, "I know you did. So did I. Sam took me in there once after I killed my first deer" (p. 187).

The second stage of Isaac's initiation is given much fuller develop-ment in "The Bear." To begin with, the story gives us to understand that Ike is being prepared to enter the mystery of the hunters, whose life in the wilderness is guided by certain rituals of behavior and whose role as hunters demands certain qualities in the men themselves. When Ike has evidently proved to Sam Fathers's satisfac-tion that he possesses (at least potentially) those necessary qualities— honor and pride and pity and courage and love—he is given the final test of self-reliance. He must strip himself of the last aids of civilization, watch and compass and gun, and face the wilderness on his own. When he does so, he is granted his first vision of Ben, the bear. Like the magnificent buck in "The Old People," Ben does not come into view, he just suddenly materializes:

> . . . he saw the bear. It did not emerge, appear: it was just there, immobile, fixed in the green and windless noon's hot dappling . . . looking at him. . . . Then it was gone. It didn't walk into the woods. It faded, sank back into the wilderness without motion. . . . [P. 209]

Ike has thus become one of the family of hunters, has entered the mystery of the hunters' fraternity.

The next stage of Ike's progress is his joining the party in actual pursuit of old Ben—the yearly pageant-rite. The final act of this ritual drama, as Faulkner encourages us to consider it, begins with Sam's finding and preparing the special dog, Lion, for the pursuit of

old Ben, and the hunters' consequent drawing of the first blood.
And the climax is Sam's arranging the rather stiffly ritualistic, pag-
eant-like death of old Ben and staging it for Ike's evident edification.
It is quite apparent that Ben's death means Sam's and Lion's death
as well, and that coincidence perhaps needs a word of comment.
The death is a combination of a *coup de grâce* and a sacrificial killing.
Ben the bear and the wilderness it represents are threatened—Ben
by his advanced age, and both him and the wilderness by the severe
inroads made by the voracious progress of civilization. Sam himself
has had enough, and thus he prepares as honorable a death as he
can for the remarkable bear and for himself—associated as he is with
that threatened wilderness, and being himself (as "The Old People"
tells us) "like an old lion or a bear in a cage."

Ben's death is sacrificial in that he dies that Ike might live—truly
live—and furthermore, that all that Ben represented and embodied
be absorbed by Ike and therefore continue to live in him as he had
lived in it. Ben, of course, is the incarnation of the Good of the
wilderness, the spirit which need not die because some incarnation
of it dies. Sam apparently believes that he has found in Ike a figure
particularly worthy of the special participation in the special pageant
of Ben's death: his hope is, surely, that Ike will continue to carry in
him the immortal spirit of the wilderness.

The other half of Isaac McCaslin's preparation is his discovery of
the evil with which his heritage is touched, complementing most
necessarily his discovery of the Good; both discoveries occur in his
sixteenth year. As he pores over the family ledgers kept by his father
and his Uncle Buddy, he discovers that to be one of the family is to
participate in the shame of the family's evil. He finds that his heritage is fearfully tainted. And the trouble is the usual one—failure of
respect for God's creation. Old Carothers McCaslin has participated
in the "sin" of Ikkemotubbe by involving himself in the act of barter
which procured him his first piece of land, the McCaslin property.
At the moment of trade, the land which Ikkemotubbe swapped to
Carothers for a horse "ceased ever to have been his forever . . . and
the man who bought it bought nothing" (p. 257). Isaac's explanation
of this fundamental error reminds us of Molly's explanation of her
objection to Lucas's use of the gold-divining machine.

> Because He told in the Book how . . . He made the earth first and
> peopled it with dumb creatures, and then He created man to be His

overseer on the earth and to hold suzerainty over the earth and the
animals on it in His name, not to hold for himself and his descendants
inviolable title forever . . . but to hold the earth mutual and intact in
the communal anonymity of brotherhood, and all the fee He asked
was pity and humility and sufferance and endurance and the sweat of
his face for bread. . . . [P. 257]

The initial wrong is extravagantly compounded, however, by the
peculiar institution of human exploitation which made possible the
way of life the McCaslins and their ilk chose to establish in the South.
And in order to give piquancy to the horror of that institution,
Faulkner presents it to Isaac—as he does so often elsewhere—by
means of his sexual synecdoche. The Ledgers focus on old Carothers's miscegenation, his buying Eunice for his own pleasure—"who
never went anywhere any more . . . and who did not need another
slave, had gone all the way to New Orleans and bought one" (p. 270).
We watch Ike discovering the evidence of the most personal abuse of
the general evil of slavery, recalling our experience earlier of Lucas's
victimization (or at least threatened victimization) by the same practice at the hands of Zack Edmonds. It is another way of the aristocratic
white master's imposing his will on those other human beings whom
he considered a race apart—and inferior.

This attitude of exclusiveness, of rigid discrimination, expressed
in the Southern landowners' strict limitation of his society to his own
kind, is also sharply focussed in Faulkner's synecdochic use of the
theme of sex. Ike discovers that not only has his grandfather Carothers got a daughter by Eunice, but that he has got a son in turn on
that daughter—"*His own daughter His own daughter. No No Not even
him*" (p. 270), is Ike's horrified response. Here miscegenation is compounded by incest to form a most compelling emblem of the South's
complex attitudes of exploitation, introversion, and finally self-
destruction. That is the heritage of Isaac McCaslin. To be one of the
family is to accept that burden as it is set out in the family history,
the Ledgers. And more than just the McCaslin family is implicated,
as Isaac has recognized, for those Ledgers

contained a chronological and much more comprehensive . . . record
than he would ever get from any other source, not alone of his own
flesh and blood but of all his people, not only the whites but the black
one too, who were as much a part of his ancestry as his white progeni-
tors, and of the land which they had all held. . . . [P. 268]

Now Isaac has seen it all. He has had his vision of the Good once
he proved to Sam Fathers he was worthy to be granted that vision
and the subsequent communion as part of the fraternity of hunters;
and he has seen the worst face of Evil—exploitation of God's creation, the land and the wilderness and His human creatures. And as
he achieves his majority, we watch to see how he will respond to the
heavy responsibility which descends to him in the McCaslin inheritance. His response is to repudiate that inheritance: "1888 the man,
repudiated denied and free" (p. 281)!

How are we to judge that response? A fair judgment is made
difficult because our sympathies have been so fully enlisted with Ike.
He has certainly seemed to be as worthy of Sam's special care as Sam
appears to have believed; and he has clearly and eloquently commented upon and condemned the evils that men have done. Isaac
does know what he is inheriting, what plagues the human condition.
So much of the appealing philosophizing about mankind in "The
Bear" comes from Ike that it is very difficult to see him as anything
but a good and wise man. And as a venerable old man, the old Uncle
Ike who was introduced to us at the very beginning of the novel and
is at last in "Delta Autumn," he seems to have grown only wiser.

Readers have praised Isaac for repudiating that seriously tainted
inheritance. How good of him, they say, to wash his hands of evil, to
have nothing to do with it. But those readers overlook that the
cursed heritage nevertheless remains for someone to accept, and
that the evil he turns away from still remains evil. Furthermore, they
have missed the fact that Isaac has repudiated only the responsibilities of that inheritance, retaining at least some of the benefits. Admittedly, the glorious rhetoric of certain passages concerning the
repudiation is distracting. Here, for example, is Ike's account of his
decision to become a carpenter after his repudiation:

> . . . not in mere static and hopeful emulation of the Nazarene . . .
> but (without the arrogance of false humility and without the false
> humbleness of pride, who intended to earn his bread, didn't especially
> want to earn it but had to earn it and for more than just bread)
> because if the Nazarene had found carpentering good for the life and
> ends He had assumed and elected to serve, it would be all right too for
> Isaac McCaslin. . . . [P. 309]

Admirable (one thinks); touching! But the paragraph continues, "He
had forgotten the thirty dollars which McCaslin [Edmonds] would

put into the bank in his name each month. . ." (p. 310). (He seems also to have forgotten the sum: it was fifty dollars.)[3] The other benefit he retains is the right to act as the figure of charity with the money old Carothers left to his illegitimate descendants—the children of Tomey's Turl and Tennie (whose romance we saw threatened in "Was"). Isaac has "retained of the patrimony, and by his own request [notice], only the trusteeship of the legacy," for that is quite the sort of rewarding "responsibility" he cherishes. He can play the role of good old Uncle Ike being kind to the darkies. Of serious responsibility he wants none at all, for the risk is too great, as Ike's analogy between himself and the biblical son of Abraham clearly states. He calls himself "an Isaac born into a later life than Abraham's and repudiating immolation: fatherless and therefore safe declining the altar because maybe this time the exasperated Hand might not supply the kid" (p. 283). Our Isaac will run no risks, which fact makes his unctuous "nonemulative" imitation of the Nazarene—the supreme figure of sacrifice in the Christian world—rather monstrously ironic.

Other characters in the story seem to be in little doubt about what Isaac is doing. Major de Spain refuses to believe what he sees, "Because I don't believe you just quit. It looks like you just quit but I have watched you in the woods too much and I don't believe you just quit even if it does look damn like it" (p. 309). We remember Lucas Beauchamp's observation about Isaac's turning apostate to his name and lineage by relinquishing his heritage "to live . . . on the charity of his great-nephew [Zack Edmonds]" (p. 40); and Isaac's later recognition of Lucas's opinion of him—

> *Fifty dollars a month. He knows that's all. That I reneged, cried calf-rope, sold my birthright, betrayed my blood, for what he too calls not peace but obliteration, and a little food.* [Pp. 108–9]

And throughout the long fourth section of "The Bear" Cass Edmonds stoutly opposes Ike's repudiation, claiming he is merely escaping, fleeing his responsibilities. Cass points out to Ike that, from any point of view, he is the proper inheritor, agreeing that his inheritance from old Carothers is indeed cursed and was consequently never Carothers's to bequeath to anybody, but countering with the argument that he must then consider himself Sam Fathers's heir. Ike still refuses: "Sam Fathers set me free," he blandly responds. Cass accepts that, tactically, and asks how long the others, the Negroes, must wait for their freedom.

Ike's reply to that leads us to what has been another little problem for some of Faulkner's critics. Ike answers, "It will be long. I have never said otherwise. But it will be all right because *they will endure*—" (p. 299; my italics). This is another of Ike's statements which, to a superficial view, appears wise and generous. He is indeed referring to a real virtue he has observed in the Negroes he has known, and furthermore is echoing a statement of Faulkner himself about his black characters. In his appendix to *The Sound and the Fury* he had written of the blacks, "They endured." (One thinks of the vexed critical commentary which that laconic summation has provoked, including the most misguided—an attempt to explain why Faulkner used that plural pronoun to refer to Dilsey!) Since the time of his speech in acceptance of the Nobel Prize for Literature, where he couples "endure" with "prevail," there seems little justification for missing the point that Faulkner meant something quite positive and affirmative by "endure"—not simply "being able to take it."[4] Just as clearly, however, Isaac McCaslin intended the term to mean something passive, the almost abject absorption of punishment; this becomes apparent when we consider the various occasions on which he uses the term. He admits to Cass that the Negroes are victims of economic bondage: " 'Yes. Binding them for a while yet. . . . But not always, because they will endure. They will outlast us because they are—'[and here occurs a very important interruption, which I will comment on in a moment] . . . Yes . . . Because they will endure. They are better than we are. Stronger than we are' " (p. 294). That may still not sound too bad, only rather ambiguous, perhaps; but we must also recall his use of the term in haranguing the improvident husband of Fonsiba, Lucas's sister, where "endure" has inescapably a desperate passivity:

> This whole land, the whole South, is cursed, and all of us who derive from it. . . . Granted that my people brought the curse onto the land: maybe for that reason their descendants alone can—*not resist it, not combat it*—maybe just *endure* and outlast it until the curse *is lifted*. Then your peoples' turn will come because we have forfeited ours. But not now. Not yet. Don't you see?" [P. 278; my italics]

Ike promises that he and his ilk will do nothing against the curse but simply wait (*endure*) until it "is lifted" by that always unidentified actor absent from verbs so used in the passive voice. Nor will the

Negro be allowed to do anything about it, according to Ike, at least "Not now. Not yet." The final touch to this particular scene derives from Ike's exasperation at Fonsiba and her pretentious husband. Unwilling to take any responsibility, they simply claim "I'm free!" Thus, a dozen or so pages later, when Ike is claiming he has been freed, and using again the term "endure," this eloquent scene comes back in our minds and most poignantly colors poor Isaac's righteous nonsense—"Sam Fathers set me free."

For as Lucas knew, and as Isaac knew he knew, the irresponsible repudiation of his McCaslin heritage is a betrayal, a cowardly escape. Ike had been seeking unearned peace. As he faces those stern arguments from Cass, Ike thinks, "I could say I don't know why I must do it but that I do know I have got to because I have got myself to have to live with for the rest of my life and all I want is peace to do it in" (p. 288). Again we must be careful not to be deceived by the rhetoric here. When we hear someone talking about having to live with himself, we are ready to hear him say (or have already understood the tacit implication) that even if no one else were to know the evil of the action in question he at least would know and how could he do it and live with himself knowing . . . and so on. Ike further seems to be echoing faintly the common supplication "Give peace in our time, O Lord"; which may be all very well, but in Isaac's mouth it has the nasty odor it had late in the 1930s when Britain's diplomatic sell-out to Hitler was said to have brought "peace in our time." The peace is escape. And a disturbing discovery is that Ike's continued pursuit of the life of a hunter, into which he had been so admirably initiated as a promising youth, has after all been just that—an escape; and all his talk about the inroads made on the hunters' terrain by civilization and "progress" has been the talk not of a staunch opponent but a frightened victim.

If the novel impresses on us this interpretation of Isaac's repudiation, it also indicates quite unmistakably why he lacks the courage to face his responsibilities—or, rather, explains in other terms just what that failure of courage consists of. And the "other terms" exert an effective emotional appeal upon the reader. Ike's failure of courage is expressed as a failure of power, a distinct impotence. For the other terms indicate that good old Uncle Ike lacks the important virtue of love. Faulkner focuses on this aspect of Isaac's character most sharply in "The Bear," and by his familiar means of the synecdochic use of sex. He manages it clearly, if subtly, by the dramatic

method—scrupulously avoiding the discursive. The long dialogue
between Isaac and Cass which dominates part 4 of "The Bear" is
interrupted by chronological shifts—flashbacks and previews—re-
sulting in juxtapositionings which comment with tacit eloquence
upon the attitudes which the two men express.

A brief résumé of Ike's life follows his exhortation to Fonsiba's
husband to be patient and, if possible, provident (for himself and his
wife): "and that was all: 1874 the boy; 1888 the man, repudiated
denied and free; 1895 and husband but no father, unwidowered but
without a wife . . ." (p. 281). Rich but puzzlingly laconic, the phrases
seem to gain nothing in clarification from their immediate context;
preceded by the scene with Fonsiba and her husband, who are
"free," and followed first by a statement of Ike's which places responsibility for lifting the curse, etc., upon God's shoulders (who
"must accept responsibility for what He Himself had done in order
to live with Himself" [p. 282]), and second by his explanation of his
unwillingness to be a latter-day Isaac. But as the fourth section of
"The Bear" draws to its close, a scene between Ike and his wife sends
a bright ray of illumination over that brief résumé and hopefully
lights up its informative context as well, showing us Ike's powerlessness (if not impotence in the strictest literal sense) in his love-making
as a husband, which expresses by extension his general impotence in
all vital affairs. His wife has gone to the farthest lengths in her
attempt to persuade Ike to resume his inheritance; she makes the
strongest and most direct appeal of love that she knows how—

> her face strained and terrible, her voice a passionate and expiring
> whisper of immeasurable promise: 'I love you. You know I love you.
> When are we going to move?' . . . 'Stand up and turn your back and
> shut your eyes:' . . . and he heard the bed and turned and he had
> never seen her naked before, he had asked her to once, and why: that
> he wanted to see her naked because he loved her . . . but after that he
> never mentioned it again . . . and not looking at him now, she didn't
> need to, the chaste woman, the wife, already looked upon [by] all the
> men who ever rutted and now her whole body had changed, altered,
> he had never seen it but once and now it was not even the one he had
> seen but composite of all woman-flesh since man that ever of its own
> will reclined on its back and opened, and out of it somewhere, without
> any movement of lips even, the dying and invincible whisper: 'Prom-
> ise:'. . . . [Pp. 312–14][5]

"Delta Autumn" refers again and quite specifically to Ike's relationship with his wife and establishes clearly the connection between

his failure of love and his failure of courage which prompted his repudiation of the McCaslin inheritance. Old Uncle Ike reviews his long life, from the beginning of his initiation at the hands of Sam Fathers, through the decision which brought him to where he is— "past seventy and nearer eighty than he ever corroborated any more, a widower now and uncle to half a county and father to no one," as the opening lines of the novel had told us. And so he presents us with the rehearsal of his attitude at the crucial moment:

> but at least he could repudiate the wrong and shame, at least in princi-
> ple, and at least the land itself in fact, for his son at least: and did,
> thought he had: then . . . the first and last time he ever saw her naked
> body, himself and his wife juxtaposed in their turn against that same
> land, that same wrong and shame from whose regret and grief he
> would at least save and free his son and, saving and freeing his son, lost
> him. . . . he had had a wife and lived with her and lost her, . . . lost her,
> because she loved him. But women hope for so much. [Pp. 351–52]

At least Isaac cannot be accused of hoping for so much. His case amply distinguishes between optimism and procrastination, between hope and despair. In cherishing his convenient view of the Negroes' ability to "endure" and his reiterated counsel of "Patience," Isaac has exhibited the cowardly and loveless procrastination of despair.

The last word on this important characterization of Ike McCaslin is provided by the young woman who appears at the hunting camp carrying Roth Edmonds's baby. Ike gives her the money Roth has left for her and urges her to leave. She has two points to make, however, before she departs. First she puts the blame for Roth's weakness and irresponsibility squarely upon Ike's shoulders: "You spoiled him. You and Uncle Lucas and Aunt Mollie. But mostly you" (p. 360). She explains that he spoiled Roth by giving to his grandfather (Cass) the land that didn't belong to him "by will or even law"—the land, she need not add, that is still rightfully Isaac's. And then, in response to Ike's frantic advice that she forget Roth and marry someone of her own "race," she utters that beautiful rhetorical question which virtu-ally annihilates the quivering old man in his long underwear:

> "Old man," she said, "have you lived so long and forgotten so much
> that you don't remember anything you ever knew or felt or even
> heard about love?" [P. 363]

Then she is gone, and old Uncle Ike, father to no one, returns to the comfort of his cocoon; he lies down again in bed and draws the blanket up to his chin, hugging to himself—whether he fully recognizes it yet or not—his impotent self-righteousness.[6]

It is quite true, of course, that Isaac has clearly seen and properly identified the evil which has made the McCaslin land a cursed heritage; and we would do wrong to take from Ike credit for that clear-sightedness. It is with his decision about what to do with that cursed heritage, however, that we must be most alertly concerned. And we must recognize the extent to which Faulkner has gone in expressing Ike's failure of courage and love as the reason for that decision. Even the best of Faulkner's readers are liable to miss this point, and with the best will in the world. In commenting upon Isaac's wife, Mr. Cleanth Brooks suggests that she cannot or will not understand and share her husband's repudiation of the inheritance: "Few human beings—and especially few women, so Isaac thinks—are capable of making the renunciation of material things that is the door to freedom."[7] But it is not the renunciation of material things that is the point at issue here so much as the refusal to accept the onerous responsibility of the general human heritage of a fallen world. Like many of his literary compatriots, Faulkner knew that commitment to *things,* to the merely material aspect, is a denial of life; he also knew that one does not affirm life by turning one's back upon the material world—"fallen" though that world admittedly is. One of the difficult lessons taught by Huckleberry Finn's trip down the Mississippi River is that real freedom is possible only *within* society, *within* that cursed material world. Hawthorne, Twain, and James all give eloquent testimony in their fiction to their recognition that one can not renounce the material world, that one is obliged to live there, though not necessarily on its terms. This is part of their commonly shared Miltonic heritage. Hester Prynne can escape briefly into the wilderness and let her hair down with Arthur Dimmesdale, but that is only a temporary possibility and no decision of "permanent" escape can thus be realized; Isabel Archer can return to the sheltering confines of Gardencourt, but again only temporarily, for she too must return to "this base ignoble world" and Gilbert Osmond, and there make her responsible decision; and Huck Finn's decision to "light out for the territory ahead of the rest," to escape the responsibility of coming to terms with civilization, is permanent only as death is permanent—it is no solution for living. Huck's "territory" has its equivalent in Robert Frost's woods which are "lovely, dark and deep": one returns to actual life from either only when one recognizes that he has promises to keep and can find the strength and courage necessary to keep them. For Isaac McCaslin and for Huckleberry Finn, as for Ernest Hemingway's Nick Adams of *In Our Time,* the actual world is too demanding; so each escapes the burden of that real, material world—in the wilderness, in the territory, or in the woods along the Big Two-Hearted River.

To a considerable extent, Faulkner's use of the Theme of the Second Chance sharpens our grief and the tragic import of Ike's failure. Typically, the theme shows us not simply the repetition of misdoing, of the denial of Good, but within that repetition the opportunity to compensate for the earlier failure. And, as is most appropriate, the Second Chance is presented in terms of Love—the opportunity for Love. The Theme is "stated" in two ways, matching the mode of development within the first two large sections of the novel (1, "Was"—"Pantaloon" and 2, "Old People"—"Delta Autumn"). We and Ike observe the Second Chance offered and refused, and Ike enacts that refusal himself. The original evil is, of course, old Carothers McCaslin's sin of abuse of God's creation, expressed figuratively as well as literally by his acts of miscegenation and incest. "Delta Autumn" offers us the spectacle of one of Carothers' descendants—and, fittingly, a namesake, "Roth" Edmonds— having reenacted the old man's sins (if in somewhat attenuated form). His young mistress—Negro, granddaughter of Tennie's Jim—appears with Roth's baby on her arm. The compounded sin committed, Roth has the opportunity to do the right thing, to redeem his perversion of love; but again like his grandfather, Roth denies the girl's humanity by reducing their relationship to the terms of the cash nexus.

What makes this all the more poignant is that Ike himself had earlier repeated Carothers's gesture of denial, even though his act masquerades as a charitable act of mercy. He has discovered the legacy which Carothers left to his illegitimate descendants, through Tomasina's son Terrel and thence through Terrel's and Tennie's children, and has condemned "father's will" (as it is referred to in the Ledgers) as a mean evasion of responsibility:

> flinging almost contemptuously, as he might a cast-off hat or pair of shoes, the thousand dollars which could have had no more reality to him under those conditions than it would have to the negro, the slave who would not even see it until he came of age, twenty-one years too late to begin to learn what money was. *So I reckon that was cheaper than*

saying My son to a nigger, he thought. *Even if My son wasn't but just two words.* [Pp. 269–70]

Yet there is Isaac, doing little more than his grandfather had done, taking pity on the Negro, being merciful to Fonsiba and (on demand) to Lucas by bestowing upon them their share of the legacy, but doing nothing whatsoever to improve their status, leaving untouched the basic wrong of their condition.

> Pity would be no more,
> If we did not make somebody Poor:
> And Mercy no more would be,
> If all were as happy as we. . . .
> [from William Blake, "The Human Abstract"]

If we are faced with the question (often posed rhetorically) of what more Isaac could have done, we can always point to the attempts of his father and uncle, whose treatment of their slaves was considerably enlightened, especially in preparing them for responsible freedom by enabling them to earn their own land as they learned to accept the burden of ownership. But Ike will not even make a beginning. He is given his real Second Chance, however, in "Delta Autumn" with the appearance of Roth's mistress, the "doe" of the story. As though this self-styled disciple of the Nazarene were reenacting the experience of Peter on the Appian Way, fleeing his responsibility under the onerous persecution in Rome, Ike is confronted by the figure who represents those whose important essential being he had earlier denied; and he is given the opportunity to ask his equivalent of "Domine, quo vadis?" But he is terrified only and cannot wait to force upon her the money Roth has left—again resorting to the "cheaper" expedient. To underline the essential parallel between this opportunity and the earlier one, Faulkner has Ike resort to precisely the same admonition he had given Fonsiba's husband: "Not now! Not yet!" He has finally recognized the girl as a "nigger": *"Maybe in a thousand or two thousand years in America,* he thought. *But not now! Not now!"* (p. 361). He tells her flatly that he can do nothing for her and counsels her to return North and marry a man "in your own race": "That's the only salvation for you—for a while yet, maybe a long while yet. We will have to wait" (p. 363). It is most appropriate that Faulkner's Theme of the Second Chance couch itself in terms of love—even as the myth of Peter and his

vision in the Appian Way is a tale of love and of the courage it both
fosters and relies upon. Roth's "doe" responds eloquently with her
rhetorical question to Ike about love. The unwilling Isaac has failed
again of courage and love.

Much of the tragic impact of Isaac's failure derives from the fact
that he knows—and quite clearly at his best moments—just what he
is doing, just exactly how he is being apostate from what Sam
Fathers had taught him. We have seen his flat refusal to be "an Isaac
born into a later life than Abraham's" and the reason for that refusal. Even more striking, because of its immediate context, is Ike's
recognition that he is rehearsing his grandfather's evil. In the very
midst of his explanation to Cass that the Negroes will endure because they are better than we are, etc. (see above, p. 176), comes the
interruption of Ike's thought about

> his repudiation, that which to him too, even in the act of escaping . . .
> was heresy: so that even in escaping he was taking with him more of
> that evil and unregenerate old man who could summon, because she
> was his property, a human being because she was old enough and
> female . . . than even he had feared. [p. 294]

He does know, and at such moments can almost judge himself honestly for what he is. The fact of that self-knowledge both mitigates
and aggravates our sense of Ike's tragic failure. That he knows what
is right to do and yet cannot do it gives rise to pity for his case; that
he willfully fails to do the right, yet hypocritically rolls on his tongue
forever the rhetoric of righteousness, gives rise to the terror. The
tragic effect is there.

Isaac has learned much from Sam Fathers's initiation, though he
cannot act on his knowledge; yet he has missed the impact (or perhaps willfully mistaken it) of an important part of the initiation. Ike
refuses to face the fact of mutability and mortality, to accept the
essential quality of potential "was-ness" in the creation. In that refusal Isaac McCaslin is typical, representative of a familiar and ubiquitous Faulknerian character—the "good, weak hero."

We must reconsider a particular aspect of the ritual pageantry
associated with hunting in "The Bear," especially as it includes the
pursuit and finally the death of old Ben; and with that, the characterization and role of Ben as they compare with the development
and presentation of the magnificent buck whom Sam addresses as
"Chief . . . Grandfather" in "The Old People." We can best grasp

the significance of that aspect if we begin with an early statement about Sam's instruction concerning the worthy hunter's attitude toward the animals he kills, the creatures of God's wilderness. Sam had "consecrated and absolved" Isaac "from weakness and regret"—"not from love and pity for all which lived and ran and then ceased to live in a second in the very midst of splendor and speed, but from weakness and regret" (p. 182). But the consecration and absolution fail Ike at crucial moments, particularly when old Ben is concerned. Ike's attitude to the hunters has always been that "they were going not to hunt bear and deer but to keep yearly rendezvous with the bear which they did not even intend to kill." Hence Ike thinks of it as "the yearly pageant-rite of the old bear's furious immortality" (p. 194). Now the narrative does encourage us, at times, to think of old Ben as "immortal"; he thus plays a dual role, is in part the extraordinary but quite mortal bear, and also the indwelling spirit of the wilderness. Ben thus combines in himself the role of the several bucks shot in "The Old People" and of that magnificent fourteen-point buck whom Sam salutes just before that story ends (or perhaps of the buck that "still and forever leaped" in Ike's mind). It is clearly important, however, that we make the distinction between the two roles—one actual and literal, the other representative or symbolic. Ike is unable, because unwilling, to make that distinction. He will not even test it, run the risk of proving it. When he has his first experience of Ben and knows the old bear is looking at him, Ike "did not move, holding the useless gun which he knew now he would never fire at it, now or ever . . ." (p. 203); then when he and the overly brave little fyce actually ambush old Ben, Ike flings his gun down and runs over to pick up the frantic little dog. Sam chides him mildly for having failed to shoot—"you couldn't have missed him" (p. 212). Ike turns the same question on Sam, of course, but the effect is different; perhaps it finally determines Sam to make his lesson as explicit and graphic as he possibly can for Ike. He begins definite preparation for the elaborate ritual death of Ben.

A couple of succinct expressions in the poetry of Wallace Stevens clarify what Sam Fathers is up to: the occasional refrain of Stevens's "Sunday Morning," "death is the mother of beauty," and the slight expansion of that idea in one of the quatrains of "Peter Quince at the Clavier":

> Beauty is momentary in the mind—
> The fitful tracing of a portal;
> But in the flesh it is immortal.
> The body dies; the body's beauty lives.

Sam seems to want to make sure that, as a worthy hunter, Isaac will not regret the death of any particular "body"—a buck, old Ben, the wilderness itself—but rest secure in the knowledge that "the body's beauty lives." The formalized death of Ben would appear to be staged specifically for Ike's benefit, that he might realize in himself that beauty which had been incarnate in old Ben. After Lion has been readied to play his contributory role, the hunters draw first blood. Isaac's reaction is noteworthy—

> It seemed to him that something, he didn't know what, was beginning; had already begun. It was like the last act on a set stage. It was the beginning of the end of something. . . . [P. 226]

The reference to the stage helps suggest that the ritual drama of Ben's death is intended to have a mimetic quality, to be the imitation of an action that expresses a truth, even though in itself it may not be that truth or may only participate in it. The mimetic quality is further underscored by Faulkner's manner of depicting the actual death. As Boon, Lion, and Ben are locked in mortal combat, Boon's knife strikes home—

> For an instant they almost resembled a piece of statuary: the clinging dog, the bear, the man astride its back, working and probing the buried blade. Then they went down . . . then the bear surged erect, raising with it the man and the dog too, and turned and still carrying the man and the dog it took two or three steps toward the woods on its hind feet as a man would have walked and crashed down. It didn't collapse, crumple. It fell all of a piece, as a tree falls, so that all three of them, man dog and bear, seemed to bounce once. [P. 241]

The comparatively static quality of this pageant of death insists on its mimetic (or at least pantomimetic) significance, as though the actors in this formal rite represented the qualities they embody. Thus, while Lion, Sam, and Ben prove their mortality, the spirit that has been incarnate in them may yet live—and further, the very fact of the carnal death can make one cherish all the more dearly the spirit therein embodied. Since while the body dies the body's beauty lives, death (as Stevens's "Sunday Morning" puts it) is the mother of beauty.

Isaac has discerned in Ben's behavior something that would indicate he has grasped Sam's lesson—the necessity of accepting the inevitable fact of mutability and mortality:

> . . . an old bear, fierce and ruthless not just to stay alive but ruthless with the fierce pride of liberty and freedom, jealous and proud enough of liberty and freedom to see it threatened not with fear nor even alarm but almost with joy, *seeming deliberately to put it into jeopardy in order to savor it.* . . . [P. 295; my italics]

In Ike's view, it appears as if old Ben were insisting on his own mortality in order to appreciate his life the more—reaffirming his ability to become *was* in order fully to realize that he *is*. Yet with all this preparation, Ike's response is merely cerebral: he has grasped, intellectually, a good deal of Sam's very important lesson, but his heart is not involved. Consequently, he rejects the lesson, and largely because it carries with it the obligations of responsibility. McCaslin Edmonds confronts directly this failing in Ike, apparently recognizing quite clearly what is wrong. His tactic is to remind Ike of his failure to shoot Ben, and then with perfect appropriateness to quote from Keats's "Ode on a Grecian Urn":

> *"She cannot fade, though thou hast not thy bliss," McCaslin said: "Forever wilt thou love, and she be fair."*
> *"He's talking about a girl," he* [Isaac] *said.*
> *"He had to talk about something," McCaslin said. Then he said, "He was talking about truth. Truth is one. It doesn't change. . . . "* [P. 297]

Here Isaac has seized upon the metaphor and confused it with the reality it represents. He fails to make the distinction between "the girl" and "the truth" she embodies and represents, just as, by obvious analogy, he failed to distinguish between old Ben (and the whole wilderness as well) and the important immortal indwelling spirit animating Ben and the woods. He confuses "the body," which dies, and the "body's beauty," which lives.

This misapprehension, willful or not, of Sam's lesson helps explain a great deal of Isaac's regrettable behavior. For Isaac, death is not the mother of beauty, but of despair: once the lovely body dies—old Ben, the wilderness, the status quo—nothing beside remains. Hence, Isaac has committed himself to the girl on the Grecian Urn; he realizes that there is just exactly enough wilderness to last his lifetime ("the two of them . . . coevals . . . the two spans running out together"); and he hopes that the general status quo can be maintained just that long as well. He knows well enough that the change is coming—that the actual wilderness will be destroyed, and also that the injustice of continued slavery (under whatever post-Emancipation name) will be removed; consequently, his constant prayer is "not now! Not yet!"—for peace in his time, O Lord! Ike's wilderness is lovely, dark, and deep; he will make no real promises and hence have none to keep. Ike's vaunted repudiation is a repudiation of life; his bent, quite as much as Quentin Compson's, is distinctly suicidal. The peace Ike yearns for is in truth "not peace but obliteration."

Thus, once again, Faulkner has employed the Theme of the Self-Destructiveness of Evil. Isaac's evil, as we have seen, is a refusal to accept the family heritage because it is tainted and cursed. He washes his hands, refuses all responsibility for it. But the novel expands the sense of "family," stretches it to embrace virtually all of humanity; so to deny one's family heritage is to deny one's place in the communal human heritage. This, too, Isaac has done. His decision has indeed brought him "obliteration." The very opening note of the novel stresses the fact that Ike is without progeny—is "uncle to half a county and father to no one." And that note is sounded throughout the novel until Roth's "doe" gives her resounding stroke of condemnation to the shirking Isaac. And we cannot miss the point that following that final denial of family relationship—of human brotherhood—Isaac appears no more in the novel. To supplement and reinforce that impression, Roth's career likewise promises to be without issue—or at least without legitimate issue, or at most any issue for which he will accept responsibility. The heritage of old Carothers McCaslin has worn itself out. The denial of love and respect for God's creatures and the failure of the courage to accept responsibility for those creatures have been the flaws in Isaac McCaslin and in Roth Edmonds as they were in Isaac's grandfather. That line has worked out its own destruction. The McCaslin line is ended.[8]

We are left, then, with the brief third part of *Go Down, Moses*—the concluding story. Its title has the effect of a plaintive reiteration of the urgent admonition of the novel's title: go down, Moses. . . . The ostensible Moses, Isaac McCaslin, has thoroughly failed to heed that request, as we have seen. His role in "Go Down, Moses" is assumed by Gavin Stevens; and we might consider that here is the offer of a Second Chance, that perhaps a "Moses" with the necessary qualifications will now appear and that God's people—of whatever complexion—will be set free. We learn little about Gavin in this final story, only the essential fact that he will fail, as Isaac failed, by doing his bit—as the figure of Blakean pity and mercy—to maintain the status quo. The parallel between Isaac and Gavin is heightened by Gavin's involvement in the McCaslin heritage: (1) he is involved with Mollie (as she is now spelled) Beauchamp and the grandson of Carothers McCaslin's grandson, and (2) he focusses sharply the responsibility of Roth Edmonds for the young Samuel Worsham Beauchamp. Read alone, apart from the context of the novel, "Go Down, Moses" might look like a sweetly nostalgic tale of pleasant relations between the races down South—like something from a slightly updated Thomas Nelson Page. Mollie's grandson got himself in trouble. Gavin's help is enlisted, first to save the boy if possible, and then, discovering it is too late for that as he has already been executed for the murder of a Chicago policeman, to bring the body home, see it properly buried, and have due publicity entered in the paper. Gavin agreeably fills his avuncular role splendidly, carrying out his acts of pity and mercy in an exemplary way. (And Gavin's role here is a distinct repetition of his role in *Light in August,* where he similarly took care of Joe Christmas's remains for the Hineses and a distinct anticipation of the role he will play in the rest of the Saga.)[9] The story ends with everyone living happily ever after—except, of course, Samuel Worsham Beauchamp, and anyone else who has only this familiar Pity and Mercy (at best!) to depend on.

But when we read the story in its proper context, we appreciate how Faulkner has insisted on the parallel between Gavin and Isaac by involving Gavin in the problems of the McCaslin heritage. He is invited to enter personally into the career of the grandson of Carothers's grandson; furthermore, he focusses our attention on the role Roth Edmonds had already played in that young man's brief career. Faulkner has also given subtle but distinct emphasis to the novel's judgment of Isaac's failure of responsibility and, consequently, judgment of Gavin's action as successor to Isaac McCaslin. Mollie laments the fate of her grandson in biblical terms: "Roth Edmonds sold my Benjamin. Sold him in Egypt. Pharaoh got him—" (p. 371). Gavin remembers "that it was Edmonds who had actually sent the boy to Jefferson [where he was caught robbing Rouncewell's store] in the first place. He had caught the boy breaking into the commissary store and had ordered him off the place and had forbidden him ever to return" (p. 373). Having read the rest of the novel, and coming fresh from "Delta Autumn," we recognize Roth's washing his hands of the responsibility for young Samuel as a reiteration of his refusal of responsibility for his illegitimate child by the young woman who confronts old Uncle Ike. And we can quickly enough reckon that those two are of the same generation, both being great-grandchildren of Terrel and Tennie. Mollie's language, reminding us both of the Old Testament story of slavery and salvation and also of the Negro Spiritual from which the title of the novel and of this terminal story is taken, points again at the failure of Isaac McCaslin as the novel's ostensible Moses, and likewise at the failure of this second-string Moses, Gavin Stevens. Gavin will simply care for the niggers as niggers; like Isaac, he will leave the root evil of their condition untouched. Like Isaac, he will act—certainly out of pity and mercy—to maintain the status quo. Gavin's brief career in "Go Down, Moses" may lack the "certain magnitude" Aristotle demanded of tragedy, yet as an extension of or sequel to Isaac's career, its effect is tragic enough.

As usual in Faulkner's presentation of the "tragedy" of his good, weak hero, we find the cause of failure here carefully defined and the possibility of other options clearly expressed. In other words, in *Go Down, Moses* as in traditional tragic drama, we understand why this particular hero has failed and how he—and indeed we—might avoid that tragic failure. The effect is pitiable and terrible, to be sure, but by no means desperate; it is, in its way, hopeful, positive, instructive. To augment that effect Faulkner has relied upon another character—potentially one of the Saving Remnant—who possesses precisely those qualities the lack of which fostered Isaac McCaslin's failure. Lucas Beauchamp is presented, particularly in "The Fire and the Hearth," as capable of the love so sadly lacking in Ike. His courage in standing up to those who have wronged him specifically and generally is far beyond any demanded of Ike; and his responsibility in caring for his own is just exactly that which Isaac—for all his righteous rhetoric—flatly refuses. Furthermore, the basis for his accepting what Ike at every turn refuses, is just that attitude toward the fact of mutability and mortality which Ike cannot bring himself—for all of Sam's careful instruction—to accept. By

means of some few impressive touches, the novel encourages comparison between Lucas and Sam, and, perhaps even more significant, between Lucas and Ben. Like Sam, he is victimized by the white
blood in his veins; yet, by every action, he expresses the fact that his
problem is not servitude but bondage: his soul is distinctly his own.
Like old Ben, Lucas has the fierce and ruthless pride of liberty and
freedom and the fierce and ruthless desire for life that can see those
cherished features threatened fearlessly and almost with joy, seeming deliberately to put them into jeopardy the better to savor them.
Lucas apparently knows—as Sam wished Isaac to learn—that while
the body dies, the body's beauty lives. Consequently, Lucas is not
afraid of life and its demands, but bravely and lovingly affirms
them. And Isaac was more correct than he knew in asserting that
characters like Lucas will "endure." The novel also strongly expresses the idea that Lucas, or rather the "beauty" that Lucas embodies, will live, that it is free of mere carnal mortality. He is "Im-
pervious to time," thinks Roth as he contemplates

> the face which at sixty-seven looked actually younger than his own at
> forty-three . . . the face which was not at all a replica even in caricature
> of his grandfather McCaslin's but which had heired and now repro-
> duced with absolute and shocking fidelity the old ancestor's entire
> generation . . . a composite of a whole generation of fierce and unde-
> feated young Confederate soldiers. . . . *He is both heir and prototype si-*
> *multaneously of all the geography and climate and biology which sired old*
> *Carothers and all the rest of us and our kind, myriad, countless, faceless, even*
> *nameless now except himself who fathered himself, intact and complete.* . . .
> [P. 118]

That is, if anything, the face of the unvanquished, the spirit which
will not only endure but prevail—when the proper conditions are
fulfilled.

Although both Lucas and Isaac are absent from this final piece of
the novel, the difference in effect of the two absences is impressive.
We have seen what is virtually the end of Isaac as he wraps himself
up in his comforting blanket at the end of "Delta Autumn." To all
intents and purposes, Isaac is finished. Lucas has not been at all
accounted for in this way. He is, then, conspicuous by his absence,
since, once again, the acute need for those virtues he possesses is
stridently expressed by the action of Isaac's replacement. And again
it is Lucas's family which needs the benefit of his virtues. In a sense,

Lucas would be the successful Moses to which the novel's title addresses its urgent appeal. The very conditions of the society in which he is granted an unequal share make it impossible for him to fulfill that broadly liberating function. His potential is not recognized, or, in Isaac's mournful refrain, not now! not yet! Like the damp gust over the mountains in the closing movement of Eliot's *The Waste Land,* Lucas's vital and liberating potential is forever about to be realized.

Intruder in the Dust brings us a step closer to that realization.

> You realize while you were growing old
> The child had fooled you with a ruse
> Of drowning.
>
> Radcliffe Squires, "Mark Twain"

X

Intruder in the Dust

From its earliest pages, *Intruder in the Dust* (1948) urges its readers to recognize it as a sequel to the novel it followed by six years, *Go Down, Moses*. Our attention is focussed upon Lucas Beauchamp, one of the important characters of the earlier novel—perhaps even the Moses called to in the novel's title, if only he could be clearly seen and recognized. But beyond that, *Intruder* carefully situates Lucas in the McCaslin-Edmonds heritage by reviewing briefly in the novel's opening pages his descent from old Carothers McCaslin and his place on the land given him by Cass Edmonds. Furthermore, the lifelong white companion of his wife, Molly, emerges from her minor role in the closing section of *Go Down, Moses* to assume a major role in the sequel. We note only that Miss Worsham's name has been augmented to become the more substantial Miss Habersham. Then, Gavin Stevens, who assumed old Isaac McCaslin's role in the final section of *Go Down, Moses* and is there associated with Molly and Miss Worsham, also emerges with a major role in *Intruder in the Dust*.[1]

To read *Intruder* against the background of *Go Down, Moses* is to achieve a much richer experience than to read it alone as a discrete novel, as I will indicate during this discussion. The novel might well have been subtitled "The Education of Charles Mallison," had Faulkner wanted to underline the obvious. It is especially helpful, if we want fully to appreciate that education, to compare it generally with the education of young Isaac McCaslin. We learn at the very outset of *Intruder* that Chick is sixteen, and note the coincidence of his age and the age of Ike when he made his discovery of Good and Evil in "The Bear." Lucas Beauchamp is initially involved in Chick's education as Sam Fathers was in Ike's; the nature of that involvement and the results produced differ markedly, of course. Yet, what each boy had to learn was one and the same thing; we might call it, too simply, the importance of responsibly accepting membership in the human family.

The opening paragraph of this novel gives an innocent appearing statement of what is, nevertheless, the principal antagonist that Chick's education will have to overcome. It says simply—

> It was just noon that Sunday morning when the sheriff reached the jail with Lucas Beauchamp though the whole town (the whole county too for that matter) had known since the night before that Lucas had killed a white man.[2]

But it is a statement of the town's, or of the whole county's, prejudice. They *know* that Lucas has killed a white man. Of course we do learn soon enough that Lucas was found with a recently fired pistol in his hand standing over the dead Vinson Gowrie—pretty strong circumstantial evidence, to be sure. And a good bit of the action in the novel is devoted to preventing Lucas's lynching and assuring him a fair trial—quite as fair a trial as any black man in Mississippi might reasonably have expected. Yet that opening paragraph initiates a motif which is fully developed as the novel progresses: the statement of racial prejudice (and hence discrimination). The important preliminary step in Chick Mallison's education has to be the freeing of his mind from lessons of racial prejudice he has already learned.

Chick's education begins with the instructive, emblematic little episode (virtually mythopoeic) of his plunge into the water of the creek after which he is fished up again right at Lucas's feet and under his direction. Young Chick Mallison rejects this action of common human charity by offering money to Lucas to pay him for what he did. Of course Lucas refuses to be paid. For a good while Chick's major effort is his attempt to discharge this obligation to Lucas, but Lucas manages always to prevent Chick's doing so by countering gift with gift. Chick is disturbed both at his discovery that his debt is not something he can discharge once and for all, and by the fact that it is Lucas's unusual and unexpected behavior that prevents the discharge of it. Chick shares in his society's prejudice: "within the next year he was to learn [what] every white man in that whole section of the country had been thinking about him [Lucas] for years: *We got to make him be a nigger first. He's got to admit he's a nigger. Then maybe we will accept him as he seems to intend to be accepted*" (p. 18).

Chick thinks that the score has been settled when one day Lucas passes him on the Square without acknowledging him, without even seeing him. But later, the first crack in Chick's prejudice appears as he reflects on that apparent cut on the Square after learning that Lucas's wife had died just prior to the encounter. There is Chick, "thinking with a kind of amazement: *He was grieving. You don't have to not be a nigger in order to grieve*" (p. 25). Once made, the discovery is never forgotten, even though Chick tries hard to repress that knowledge and to confirm his commitment to his comfortable prejudice. A repetition of the encounter with Lucas and his repeated failure to acknowledge Chick seems proof at last that his obligation to Lucas has been fully discharged. Chick feels "free." Then, after Lucas has been apprehended in connection with Gowrie's death, Chick finds himself lingering on the Square, obviously concerned about Lucas's fate; but he argues with himself, fostering his old prejudice, trying to convince himself that Lucas is no concern of his.[3] The language of Chick's thoughts is revealing: "Because he was free. Lucas was no longer his responsibility, *he was no longer Lucas's keeper;* Lucas himself had discharged him" (p. 42; my italics). One can't avoid the echo of Cain's response, "Am I my brother's keeper?" Yet he still won't let go of the idea that Lucas simply reaffirms the stereotype of "nigger" and ought not to deny it. When he sees Lucas sleeping in jail, Chick concludes with relief that he is just a nigger after all: *"Only a nigger could kill a man . . . and then sleep like a baby . . . "* (p. 58).

In spite of that prejudice, however, Chick responds to Lucas's appeal; his better self gets the better of him and he goes to work with Aleck Sander and Miss Habersham to solve the murder mystery and clear Lucas's name. His action eloquently expresses his refusal to share in the community's prejudice, his refusal to oblige Lucas to "be a nigger," and his ability to see through the stereotype image to Lucas's real existence as a fellow human being—as his brother, in fact, whose keeper he must be. Chick finds his reward in seeing Lucas cleared completely of the charge against him. Chick is further alienated from his society by his sad disappointment at the subsequent reaction of the townspeople, the fellow members of the community to which he has always felt very strong ties; and the measure of his young maturity, the gauge of the success of his "education," is the extent to which he can judge the embarrassing behavior of the Town. "They ran," he exclaims again and again in a mixture of amazement, disappointment, and censure:

... the composite Face of his native kind his native land, his
people his blood his own with whom it had been his joy and pride and
hope to be found worthy to present one united unbreakable front ...
who ran, fled not even to deny Lucas but just to keep from having to
send up to him by the drugstore porter a can of tobacco not at all to
say they were sorry but so they wouldn't have to say out loud that they
were wrong. ... [Pp. 194–96]

Who, in the face of that condemnation, can speak on behalf of the
society to which Chick had aspired and which now shows itself so
unworthy? Gavin Stevens, of course, can and will and does—at
length—speak for them. And a good deal of what he says can touch
a strong sympathetic chord in many if not most readers; he is, in
fact, a sounder and more persuasive spokesman than Isaac McCaslin, whom he so strikingly resembles in his role and attitude. As
Gavin undertakes to defend the community against young Chick's
attack, we recognize that we are present at a situation like that in
which an older Ike McCaslin is offering his defense to his idealistic
younger self—to the boy in whom Sam Fathers had such high hopes.
For in his long dialogue with Cass in part 4 of "The Bear," Ike is
addressing his younger, better self quite as much as he is his cousin
Cass. Gavin claims that the responsibility for Sambo (as he calls the
Negro—and one wonders with how many layers of irony, intentional and unintentional, functioning here) is the South's; he asserts
that the South is defending its privilege of setting Sambo free, and
opposes himself to the "outlanders" of the North (and the East and
West, too) who believe that freedom and so on can be successfully
legislated. He bolsters that argument by the appeal to homogeneity.
The South is homogeneous, he claims, and is thus different from
most of the rest of the United States; and "only from homogeneity
comes anything ... of durable and lasting value" (p. 154). Furthermore, Gavin proceeds, Sambo is a homogeneous man too—has even
a better homogeneity than the whites'; and that is illustrated by his
having found roots in the land, and having cultivated patience and
the long view. Thus, Sambo and the white man should pool their
resources:

We—he and us—should confederate: swap him the rest of the economic and political and cultural privileges which are his right, for the
reversion of his capacity to wait and endure and survive. Then we
would prevail; together we would dominate the United States; we
would present a front not only impregnable but not even to be threat-

ened by a mass of people who no longer have anything in common
save a frantic greed for money and a basic fear of a failure of national
character which they hide from one another behind a loud lipservice
to a flag. [P. 156]

If Gavin's term "homogeneity" is a bit puzzling, we can see clearly
enough what he means by it. Cleanth Brooks quite rightly calls it "a
community of values that is rooted in some kind of lived experience."[4]
This is an appealing, or, at least, an understandable argument. We
are familiar with the values that derive from a sense of community—
particularly in the United States—and we have heard from artists
during most of the twentieth century about the grievous lack of communal experience. We live in cities and are alone, and (like W. H.
Auden's Unknown Citizen) we don't know who we are and neither
does anyone else. (Ask a new acquaintance where he comes from: he
can hardly give a simple answer, but begins with "Well . . . ," and may
tell you where he was born, "but. . . .") There remains, however,
something fundamentally unsatisfactory about Gavin's arguments.
They contain *some* truth; they are *plausible;* their rhetoric sways. So we
share sympathetically in Chick's tart reponse, "But you're still excusing it" (p. 204). For what lends credence to Chick's attack, what seriously undercuts Gavin's suave rhetoric, is the participation of Miss
Eunice Habersham in the cause of justice on Lucas Beauchamp's
behalf. If anyone has a proper claim to the homogeneity Gavin so
unctuously appeals to, it is she, Miss Habersham, "whose name was
now the oldest which remained in the county, . . . living in the col-
umned colonial house on the edge of town" (pp. 75–76); and who
seems to have acted out the idea of confederating, which Gavin proposes, in her own life with her close and persistent association with
Molly, Lucas's wife. She and Molly were "born in the same week and
both suckled at Molly's mother's breast and grown up together almost
inextricably like sisters, like twins, . . . until Molly and Lucas married,
and Miss Habersham had stood up in the Negro church as godmother
to Molly's first child" (p. 87).

Then, too, a close look at some of Gavin's supporting arguments
indicates that he is as committed, after all, to the status quo as was
Isaac McCaslin. Gavin has employed a term from Isaac's vocabulary,
and with virtually the same connotations, to talk about Sambo—
"endure." In one of his particularly cynical outbursts (the first clause
of which is itself embarrassingly revealing) he observes that "Not all
white people can endure slavery and apparently no man can stand

freedom . . . ; with one mutual instantaneous accord he forces his liberty into the hands of the first demagogue who rises into view. . . . But the people named Sambo survived the one and who knows? they may even endure the other" (pp. 149–50). And in his attack on the outlanders who want to force on the South laws based on the idea that man's injustice to man can be abolished overnight by police, Gavin sarcastically shrugs and says that Sambo will even stand up to that: "he will endure it, absorb it and survive because he is Sambo and has that capacity . . . the capacity to endure and survive but . . . what he survives to may not be worth having because by that time divided we may have lost America" (p. 204). One might be tempted to ask Gavin, in an idiom he would recognize: what doth it profit a man if he gain the whole country and lose his own soul?

It is at that point that Chick charges Gavin with "excusing" the community's behavior. With all these defensive demands that the South be left to solve its own problems, there is no mention of when the solution will be forthcoming—or even of when it will be broached. The implication is that it does not matter when, for Sambo has learned to "endure." Like Isaac McCaslin, Gavin cannot really stand the idea that things change, cannot really accept the notion of challenging the status quo. The familiar and heart-sickening cry of "Not now! Not yet!"—which Isaac habitually uttered—rises to Gavin's pursed lips almost unchanged.

> *Someday* Lucas Beauchamp can shoot a white man in the back with the same impunity to lynch-rope or gasoline as a white man; *in time* he will vote anywhen and anywhere a white man can and send his children to the same school anywhere. . . . *But it wont be next Tuesday.* [P. 155; my italics]

And there it is. (We note also in this brief excerpt another indication of Gavin's prejudice regarding Lucas's guilt—even though he has agreed to serve as Lucas's legal "defense.")

Although Gavin makes some telling points, his defensive argument is finally just embarrassing. In the context of his rather condescending attitude to Lucas and the Negroes generally, Gavin's suggestion of confederating sounds suspiciously like some "separate but equal" togetherness; consequently, his championing of the idea of "homogeneity" is liable to seem little different, after all, from the "aristocratic" Southerner's cherishing his exclusive, strictly defined, introverted, and ultimately reductive "pure blooded" society. Gavin does, after all, discriminate between his "homogeneity" and Lucas's. Chick Mallison's evident notion of community and the responsibilities it requires is considerably more enlightened than Gavin's. Chick's education has freed him from such distinctions as Gavin makes between "Sambo" and "us"; and the "swapping" involved in the confederation of Lucas and Chick has been the exchange of honorable human charity. Chick has learned well, for Lucas has taught him well. It is gratifying for us—as it must be for Lucas—to see that it is Lucas himself who provides Chick with the occasion to demonstrate just how well he has learned to be his brother's keeper. Chick can carry on exactly where Gavin has failed, and by assuming the obligations of human brotherhood. He has this to say to his uncle about responsibility:

> I dreamed . . . something about how maybe this was too much to ex-
> pect of us, too much for people just sixteen or going on eighty or
> ninety . . . to have to bear, and then right off I was answering what
> you told me, you remember, about the English boys not much older
> than me leading troops and flying scout aeroplanes in France in 1918?
> how you said that by 1918 all British officers seemed to be either
> subalterns of seventeen or one-eyed or one-armed or one-legged colo-
> nels of twenty-three. . . . [P. 205]

Gavin, of course, simply misses the point and continues, as though Chick had interrupted merely to agree with him, to mouth his unctuous rhetoric about refusing to bear injustice and outrage and dishonor and shame. Chick has given substance to his comment, however, by showing in his own behavior—as Aleck Sander and Miss Habersham have in theirs—that responsibility can be courageously assumed in the face of grim odds by children and old ladies. The implicit question is left hanging before us (and, hopefully, before Gavin): Can the men do any less—with honor?[5]

While *Intruder in the Dust* does seem quite obviously the story of the education of Charles Mallison, its focus seldom departs from the figure responsible for that education, Lucas Beauchamp. Passive as his role admittedly appears to be through much of the novel, he exerts a very urgent force on Chick Mallison and, of course, in various ways, on the whole community. He quite actively taught Chick the lesson of human brotherhood; he then provided Chick with the opportunity to prove what he had taught him—and this with the lightest of pressure. And restricted as Lucas's actions are in the novel, we yet know him well enough. We see that he is a problem to the white community because he refuses to accept the stereotyped role of "nigger." The community expresses the generosity of its attitude in the posture of Mr. Lilley, the willing lyncher: "He has nothing against what he calls niggers. . . . All he requires is that they act like niggers" (p. 48). Lucas is even a problem to his own kind, as young Aleck Sander explains to Chick, who has come to enlist Aleck's aid. (Chick's response, by the way, is revealing: "Then maybe you better go to the office and sit with Uncle Gavin instead of coming with me" [p. 86].) Lucas is "uppity." Or, to an unprejudiced eye, he is simply proud. And apparently that pride in himself is justified. We infer, from the fact that Cass Edmonds had deeded to him in perpetuity a house and ten acres of land to farm, that Lucas has proven himself capable, responsible, and industrious. We see, in his disdainful attitude to the trash who badger and threaten him in the store and then in his calm self-possession in the face of the mob with lynching in their eye, that Lucas is a man of courage. His distraction by grief at Molly's death must impress us as it did Chick Mallison with a sense of Lucas's capacity for love. And the evidence of his human generosity is amply supplied by the early episode of Chick's "baptismal" dunking in the creek and his subsequent treatment of the boy: Chick "knew [for example] that the food had been not just the best Lucas had to offer but all he had to offer" (p. 17). One may pause at Lucas's claim to McCaslin identity as he is confronted by the group of would-be intimidators in the store: "I aint a Edmonds. I don't belong to these new folks. I belongs to the old lot. I'm a McCaslin" (p. 19). That response sounds like vanity. But if we consider the situation Lucas is in and the audience he confronts, we might reasonably conclude that Lucas is affirming his pride in himself as someone legitimately established; no upstart, but a tried and tested member of long standing in the community, who makes that affirmation in terms he knows the redneck rowdies will at least understand. On the basis of this evidence in *Intruder in the Dust,* we can easily enough deem Lucas a rather admirable character.

When we consider *Intruder* as sequel to *Go Down, Moses*—as it clearly urges us to do—then the evidence is richly augmented and our estimation of Lucas heartily confirmed. We had ample indication in the earlier novel of Lucas's qualities of justifiable pride, courage, and responsibility, and especially of his capacity for love and generosity. We also recall from *Go Down, Moses* the opinion of those who knew him well that he was beyond vain pride of blood and

family. There is Roth Edmonds's highly figurative estimate, in "The
Fire and the Hearth," which gathers together all the varied evidence
we have had about the nature of Lucas's pride:

> He's more like old Carothers than all the rest of us put together, including old
> Carothers. He is both heir and prototype simultaneously of all the geography
> and climate and biology which sired old Carothers and all the rest of us and our
> kind, myriad, countless, faceless, even nameless now except himself . . . intact
> and complete, contemptuous, as old Carothers must have been, of all blood
> black white yellow or red, including his own. [P. 118]

We are not quite convinced of old Carothers's general contempt for
all blood, as we have accepted Isaac's explanation of the legacy left to
the offspring of Tomasina—"cheaper than saying My son to a nigger." But we can discern the significance of that puzzling initial statement that Lucas was more like old Carothers than even old Carothers
was: Lucas, surely, is the man old Carothers was meant to be and
could have been if only, as a matter of fact, he could have shared that
contempt for the argument of "blood" which Roth attributes equally
to him and Lucas. The testimony of *Go Down, Moses* does not change
the impression we get of Lucas from *Intruder;* it substantiates and
enriches that impression agreeably.

It is instructive to be aware of certain similarities between Lucas's
role in *Intruder in the Dust* (or, indeed, in both that and *Go Down, Moses*)
and the roles of certain other important characters in the Yoknapatawpha fiction. He shares the courage and self-possession and human sympathy of Dilsey in *The Sound and the Fury.* Somewhat like
Benjy Compson, in the same novel, Lucas serves to test the other
characters. According as they treat him, so do we judge them. He is
even a little like Joe Christmas of *Light in August* in that both of them
are seeking recognition of themselves simply as integral human beings, both attempting to evade the stereotype identity so easily imposed upon them by the society in which they have to function. Consequently, Lucas is also like Charles Bon in *Absalom, Absalom!,* who also
seeks that simple recognition. In this, incidentally, Faulkner anticipates Ralph Ellison, whose nameless Invisible Man tries frantically to
emerge into himself from the roles imposed upon him by a society
which sees him only as they want him to be—or rather see him not at
all. The importance in Faulkner's fiction of this quest for honest
recognition by society can hardly be overemphasized. Strongly implicit there is the idea that in such recognition lies society's hope for

redemption. It is hardly too much to suggest that in this Intruder may be found the Moses invoked in the title of the earlier novel. If only Lucas could be seen clearly and recognized for what he is, then could those necessary qualities of his be put to use, and then would "my people" be set free.

Fond Gavin Stevens is almost as right as he thinks he is about confederation. Miss Habersham has confederated with Molly Beauchamp and Chick with Aleck Sander; more important, perhaps, is the fact that Miss Habersham and Chick and Aleck Sander have confederated with Lucas. And of course, to say it again, the most significant and expressive confederation is the beautifully reciprocal alliance of Lucas and Chick. Gavin was half right, maybe; he just had the terms wrong: basic human brotherhood and mutual charity were included in the swap—both ways.

One other item in Chick Mallison's education needs mention, in part because of its importance to this novel and in part because of its implications for the Yoknapatawpha Saga as a whole. Young Chick's crucial recognition of the common humanity of Lucas Beauchamp, revealed to him through Lucas's grief over a lost loved one, has its parallel and complement in his recognition of the same quality in old Mr. Gowrie, also revealed in his grief for his dead son. Faulkner insists on the similarity: Charles "thought suddenly with amazement: *Why he's grieving:* thinking how he had seen grief twice now in two years where he had not expected it or anyway anticipated it, where in a sense a heart capable of breaking had no business being . . ." (p. 161). The revelation strikes Chick that common humanity is to be found in both camps of outsiders normally excluded from the society with which Chick once felt his only kinship—both the "niggers" and the "rednecks."

The Gowries have an added fascination in their distinct relationship with the Snopeses; they are a statement in a slightly different key of the theme which Faulkner will develop with full orchestration in the Snopes Trilogy. Here is our introduction (in *Intruder in the Dust*) to these denizens of Beat Four:

> a ramification of cousins and inlaws covering a whole corner of the county . . . it in its turn was integrated and interlocked and intermarried with other brawlers and foxhunters and whiskeymakers not even into a simple clan or tribe but a race a species. . . . [P. 35]

The current family of Gowries with which the novel is specifically concerned has six sons including the twins—Vardaman and Bilbo.

I. O. Snopes has six sons (by two different but simultaneous wives) including the twins—Vardaman and Bilbo. The Gowries are originally a frightening and hateful crew, like the common run of Snopeses; so that the grief of old Nub at Vinson's death is perhaps as shocking a revelation for us as for Chick Mallison. But it is precisely this revelation of common humanity in the Gowries that most catches our interest since it provides a forecast and preview of how Faulkner will develop the career of the Snopeses when once he resumes the trilogy begun in 1940 with *The Hamlet* (or, indeed, even some fifteen years earlier with the material of the "Father Abraham" manuscript): common humanity of the most hopeful quality will finally emerge from that erstwhile unpromising horde—as a grateful Saving Remnant. And Chick's recognition of this quality in the Gowries will serve as helpful preparation for his understanding of the Snopeses in the trilogy. *Intruder in the Dust* shares this quality of forecasting the future of the Snopeses with the short story "Barn Burning" (1939), in which Flem, the super-Snopes, finds his complement in the surprising and admirable young Sarty Snopes, his brother. Thus, if Gavin Stevens and his ilk prove disappointing failures in *Intruder in the Dust,* there are nevertheless these grateful few, the Saving Remnant, in whom we can rest our hope—Nub Gowrie, Lucas Beauchamp, and young Charles Mallison.

The confederated characters (Miss Habersham, Chick, and Aleck Sander) stand, finally, as a severely marked contrast to Uncle Gavin Stevens. His apathy and weakness render him incapable of meeting the demand presented almost tacitly by Lucas Beauchamp. The basis for that apathy and weakness would seem to be fear of change—basically the problem with Isaac McCaslin and Quentin Compson (and, of course, with his own alter ego, Horace Benbow); like those others, Gavin must cling jealously to the status quo. Although he can entertain as a theoretic proposition the notion of alteration in the organization of society—an alteration which he agrees will come "Some day," "in time," "But not next Tuesday"—he cannot face the actuality. That is Gavin's evil; and because it is like the passive and apathetic evil of Horace Benbow and of Isaac McCaslin and (most significantly) of the paradigm Quentin Compson—the actual suicide—it is a self-defeating and self-destructive evil. In *Intruder in the Dust,* at least, Gavin's position bears no fruit: it is self-incapacitating and can thus be legitimately listed with those careers in the Yoknapatawpha Saga which develop the theme of the Self-Destructiveness

of Evil. More important, however, than Gavin's resignation and
withdrawal is young Chick Mallison's active and affirmative triumph;
and in a very real sense, it is a triumph over his Uncle Gavin and
those whom he represents.

Faulkner has, furthermore, relied again on the informing theme
of the Second Chance in this novel, although with a slight modification. The two "Chances" here are not really sequential but simultaneous. Some sense of sequence is given, however, by the fact that the
two Chances are offered to successive generations, the first to Gavin
Stevens (who denies his responsibility—amid much affirmative talk)
and the second to his nephew Chick Mallison, who grasps the opportunity and (not unlike Peter, after all) turns bravely into the very
heart of prejudice and persecution to affirm the right. Chick Mallison's action is the most affirmative since that of Bayard Sartoris in
The Unvanquished. Both youths have acted against the unwritten
"laws" that bind their society; both have proven themselves "above
the law" in the familiar Pauline sense of the term. The echoes of
scripture which both novels employ reinforce the significance of the
actions of Bayard and Chick, which in turn revitalize the terms of
that old language which has moulded so much of the culture of the
Mallisons, the Sartorises, and a majority of Faulkner's readers—
whether they will or no.

Intruder in the Dust, then, leaves us hoping for a reappearance of
Charles Mallison—a reappearance in a broader arena for the exer-
cise of his talents.

> . . . leave her to heaven.
>
> Shakespeare, *Hamlet*, I. v. 86

XI

Requiem for a Nun

Two decades after the publication of *Sanctuary*, Faulkner turned again to Temple Drake to see what had become of her. *Requiem for a Nun* (1951) takes up Temple's story eight years after her escapade that began at the Old Frenchman's Place, and discovers her married to a reformed Gowan Stevens. We learn that she has borne two children, one of whom has been murdered by the black maid, Nancy Mannigoe (formerly a whore and a drug addict), as her extreme attempt to prevent Temple from running away with Pete, young brother of Alabama Red—the man whom Popeye had employed in *Sanctuary* as his vicar in fornication. *Requiem* tells Temple's story in the form of a script for a play in three acts; each act begins with a substantial prose passage which recounts the history of Jefferson from its beginning down to 1951. As the two apparently discrete parts of *Wild Palms* actually comment fruitfully upon each other, so do the two parts of *Requiem*—the play and the prose history—comment upon and illuminate each other.

First, so far as the play is concerned, *Requiem* develops the Theme of the Second Chance as the means of working out Temple's salvation—or perhaps the preparation for her salvation. The lawyer who attempted unsuccessfully to defend Lee Goodwin against the charge of murder in *Sanctuary*, Horace Benbow, has been metamorphosed into Gavin Stevens in *Requiem*. The lawyer's relation to Temple is established as Gavin proves to be the uncle of Temple's husband, Gowan Stevens. Gavin himself capsulizes the Theme of the Second Chance as he offers his explanation of Temple's accepting Pete, the young brother of Red, who was murdered in *Sanctuary*, as her lover:

204

I imagine that he (the new one, the black mailer) even looked like his brother—a younger Red, the Red of a few years even before she knew him, and—if you will permit it—less stained, so that in a way it may have seemed to her that here at last even she might slough away the six years' soilure of struggle and repentance and terror to no avail.[1]

Pete, then, is presented as being for Temple a second Red; the memory of Red, to be sure, returns clustered with all the other debris of *Sanctuary*—Popeye and Tommy and the whole escapade at the Old Frenchman's Place and later at the brothel, and also Gowan. And Gavin Stevens's explanation not only suggests Pete as a Second-Chance Red, a younger and cleaner and "private" Red, but also as a Second-Chance Gowan. He imagines the burden of having to live with a forgiving, compensating, honorable yet jealous husband—Gowan—and sees in Pete "a man so single, so hard and ruthless, so impeccable in amorality, as to have a kind of integrity, purity, who would not only never need nor intend to forgive anyone anything, he would never even realize that anyone expected him to forgive anyone anything" (p. 147).

And as we have come to expect in Faulkner's fiction, the Second Chance for Temple is expressed in terms of love—using the term in its broadest application. Our sympathy is aroused somewhat for Temple at the outset, for we learn that Pete has come to her initially as a blackmailer, threatening her with the love letters she had written to Red. They are "good letters," Temple admits; "I mean—good ones . . . Better than you would expect from a seventeen-year-old amateur" (pp. 129–30). But we learn further that the letters very soon ceased to be the reason for her consorting with Pete; he has even offered to return them to her, and more than once. So Temple quite definitely has had the opportunity to refuse the involvement with Pete, even as she had ample opportunity (as she fully acknowledges in *Requiem*) to free herself from the earlier involvement with Popeye and Red and all the crew of *Sanctuary*. She cannot take that opportunity. She confesses with laconic frankness, "Temple Drake liked evil" (p. 117).

The play concerns itself with the importance of the Past, of Evil, and of Suffering, and of the relationship among these three, insisting that the Past is never past, that it is never over and done with but, on the contrary, is always with us, especially the Evil of the Past. The point is made that we must accept the responsibility for the Evil of the Past as our inevitable heritage, not try to repudiate it or deny it, but be ready to suffer for it. Early in the second scene of the first act Gowan tells his Uncle Gavin that he has been "on the wagon" for eight years; that is, ever since the fiasco at Goodwin's which led to all the grief involving Temple with Popeye, and for which his drunkenness had apparently been responsible. Eight years without a drink, Gowan says, is "all I had to pay for immunity." Gavin replies, "There's no such thing"; and then adds a moment later, "There's no such thing as past either" (pp. 61–62). (This is in fact a reiteration of the idea expressed in both *Go Down, Moses* and *Intruder in the Dust,* where we were shown Isaac McCaslin's grievous error in refusing to accept responsibility for the Evil of his inheritance and of his own Evil in perpetuating that of his grandfather; and also young Chick Mallison's discovery of the impossibility of squaring himself with Lucas Beauchamp and thus getting rid of his responsibility to be his brother's keeper.) In the third scene Gavin makes essentially the same point to Temple: "The past is never dead. It's not even past" (p. 80). For Temple, now Mrs. Gowan Stevens, has affirmed that "Temple Drake is dead"—the girl she once was is no more—as an attempt to disavow any responsibility for whatever follies (or worse) that seventeen-year-old was guilty of. And the main effort of the play is to urge Temple to recognize that she remains responsible for past actions, especially for her evil actions of the past, and to accept the suffering for them that is the only means of redemption and salvation.

The persistence of Evil, and specifically the Evil of Temple's past, is shown quite graphically: first in the hiring of Nancy Mannigoe as nurse for her children, and second in the reappearance of Temple's love letters to Red. Nancy's qualifications, "a whore and a tramp and a dope fiend," might have seemed to reflect great credit on the young Stevens couple's broad-mindedness and generosity in employing her; it would look as though they had been working to rehabilitate an unfortunate fallen woman. Yet, the real reason for hiring Nancy was to provide Temple with a companion. "Temple Drake, the white woman, the all-Mississippi debutante, descendant of long lines of statesmen and soldiers high and proud in the high proud annals of our sovereign state, couldn't find anybody except a nigger dope-fiend whore that could speak her language" (p. 105). In case we had any doubts, or in case our impressions of *Sanctuary* had dimmed, we are reminded sharply in *Requiem* that Temple had actu-

ally enjoyed much of her experience in the Memphis brothel. (Gowan says she "loved it," p. 63.) Nancy, then, provides Temple with the
means of keeping that Past alive, of keeping its Evil hot and piquant.
In a very real sense, Nancy symbolizes for her that particular Evil of
Temple's past. Similarly, the letters written to Red—so many, and so
rich and gamey—return to speak to her of that Past, with its husky,
lusty voice of love gone lecherously awry and perverse. Temple must
be made to recognize that what she has done since the trial of Lee
Goodwin has eloquently denied her own claims that the Past is behind her and that its Evil is no more. In allowing herself that recognition, she will, in fact, be accepting the responsibility of Suffering
for the Evil of the Past.

Now the play traces the three steps in Temple's progress toward
that desired end through the means of its plot, ostensibly Gavin Stevens's attempt to gain the Governor's pardon for Nancy Mannigoe,
with Temple's help, by claiming Nancy's temporary insanity. The first
act has mainly to do with Gavin's persuading Temple to make a representation to the Governor. We have seen Gavin just recently sharpen-
ing his detective ability in the stories of *Knight's Gambit* (1949), and he
can rely on that again now. He has reason to suspect even more than
he knows about Temple's role in motivating Nancy to murder the
baby. Furthermore, Gavin also recognizes that in making the representation to the Governor, Temple would be led to disclose something
about her own past and character as she accounts for Nancy's "insanity" at the time of the murder. When he finally counters Temple's
argument that what is past is past and that "Temple Drake is dead,"
with his flat denial—"The past is never dead" (p. 80)—Gavin has
made the initial breach in Temple's defense. So she agrees to see the
Governor. She is coming; she is on her way.

Faulkner's stage directions make clear what the Governor is to
suggest to the audience: "He is symbolic too: no known person,
neither old nor young; he might be someone's idea not of God but
of Gabriel perhaps, the Gabriel not before the Crucifixion but after
it" (pp. 98–99). It is implied that Temple now has the chance for
confession and penance before a somewhat more exalted tribunal.
As she begins to unburden herself, to bare her soul, the play rises to
its dual climax. First there is her recognition of her fierce attraction
to Evil, her frightful unhindered propensity to involve herself in it,
which leads to her admission that she simply "liked evil" (p. 117).
But with this the play broadens its implications and extends the

region of guilt without at all exculpating Temple. She recalls Gavin's words about trafficking with evil—that you don't dare; but she adds the qualification—

> Uncle Gavin was only partly right. It's not that you must never even look on evil and corruption; sometimes you cant help that, you are not always warned. . . . You've got to be already prepared to resist it, say no to it, long before you see it; you must already have said no to it long before you even know what it is. [P. 117]

Nothing much is explicitly stated about where Temple's preparation to say no to evil might have come from, but the very presence of Gowan and the distinct echoes of *Sanctuary* make the implications sufficiently precise. Gowan's association of himself with the concept of the Virginia Gentleman, both in *Sanctuary* and (rather sardonically) in *Requiem,* and his distinct failure to match that ideal by wretchedly having conveyed Temple into the den of iniquity at the Old Frenchman's Place, suggest one potential source of Temple's preparation to say no to evil. We also recall the glimpse we had in *Sanctuary* of Judge Drake and his sons, and understand the better Temple's reference to her lineage: "long lines of statesmen and soldiers high and proud in the high proud annals of our sovereign state"—not of Virginia, but of Mississippi, yet participating in the same chivalrous ideals as those espoused (theoretically) by Gowan, and dedicated, surely, to that principle attributed to the heroic general and statesman after whom the county seat was named: "that honor must be defended whether it was or not since, defended, it was, whether or not . . ." (p. 94).

Temple was failed, as Caddy Compson had been, by the gentlemen of her family and near association. Where else could she have been expected to gain the preparation to withstand the allurements of Evil if her own gentlemen had failed her? One might even go so far as to say that the very social system itself failed her in failing to regard its women, its ladies, as full-fledged human beings capable of absorbing lessons of preparation for the actual world in all its earthy realities—grim and evil or not. That system and its guiding code—according to the abundant testimony of Faulkner's chronicles of Yoknapatawpha County—were fashioned precisely to protect its ladies from the touch of actuality; and the memorable gestures of the gentlemen who embody the code in Faulkner's fiction—and indeed

some of the guiding principles of the code—are cosmetic arrangements calculated to hide or disguise the blemishes caused by the
touch of reality. Those arrangements are of the order of closing the
barn door and pretending the horse is safely within. Gowan's marrying Temple is quite of that order (and how like Quentin Compson's
fond claim of having committed incest with Caddy!), as he himself
admits: "Sure. Marrying her was purest Old Virginia" (p. 63). It is a
way, after all, of defending Temple's honor "whether it was or
not"—like the paternal and fraternal care in which Temple was
engulfed at the close of Goodwin's trial, after the damage was done.
Unprepared, she discovered that she liked Evil.

The second part of the double climax of act 2 comes with the
flashback to the moment just preceding the actual murder, when
Temple was planning to run away with Pete, taking her baby with her.
Nancy then confronts her with all the means of dissuasion at her
disposal. She chides her with her inveterate evil tendency, indicating
that whatever is making Temple plan to run off with Pete has always
been there: "It was already there in whoever could write the kind of
letters that eight years afterward could still make grief and ruin. The
letters never did matter" (p. 159). And although Temple keeps to her
plan to leave, she does admit that "It wasn't even the letters. It was
me" (p. 166). Nancy takes, then, the final step. But the real break has
occurred, as this flashback rehearses it for Temple and for the audience, with the admission of guilt—the recognition of the persistence
of the Evil of the Past. It also shows us Temple about to refuse her
Second Chance. But progress has been made and, as the act ends,
Temple discusses with Gavin the means of redemption. He tells
Temple that the Governor has refused the pardon; she feels momentarily trapped, but seems to see the point of it all: "So good can come
out of evil." Gavin agrees and adds, "It not only can, it must" (p. 179).
Temple is allowed to discover that there really had never been any
hope of saving Nancy, and to prepare for her own last step in the
direction of redemption. She sees that Nancy's "journey" is not to be
interrupted, but, more important, she can see where and when it
began—and who had set her on her way: "Her journey started that
morning eight years ago when I got on the train at the University—"
(p. 180). Yet there is one last step to take. Temple has recognized
certain things about her condition yet does not fully realize what has
been achieved for her by her "fruitless" representation to the Governor. She has spent all this time and exposed her spotted soul to no

final avail; she feels "just suffering. Not for anything: just suffering" (p. 181). The final act takes up the question of Suffering.

Temple faces Nancy again and finally. Nancy knows that the representation to the Governor has changed nothing for her, and indeed did not expect it would. The point now is what it all will mean for Temple. She has come a long way; she envies Nancy her calm and—not resignation, but acceptance. Temple is able now to ask for the help she needs: "I'll do anything He wants if He'll just tell me what to do. No: how to do it. I know what to do, what I must do, what I've got to do. But how?" (p. 235). Nancy tells her simply "Trust in Him . . . Maybe that's your pay for the suffering" (p. 236). And then, at Gavin Stevens's question, Nancy affirms that the salvation of the world is in man's suffering. One hears the faint echo of St. Paul's "foolish" question, Shall we continue in sin that grace may abound? Nancy counters with the explanation that man hasn't *got* to sin but that, being human, he just can't help it. And she adds that God doesn't oblige you to suffer for your sins, "But He gives you the chance" (p. 238). It is a simple lesson, perhaps absurdly simple; yet it comes through with conviction as a recognition of the human condition and an age-old answer to its ills. Temple has been obliged to recognize her acts of evil from the past, to recognize that they can not be forgotten or repudiated, but must be accepted and acknowledged. The consequent suffering, which attends accepting responsibility for those sins of the past, is the only means of redemption. Temple seems to have taken Nancy's lesson—accepted Nancy's sacrifice—when finally she makes full confession of her guilt and admits responsibility for the evil of the present as consequent upon her evil of the past, and specifically for the death of her own baby: "I destroyed [it] myself when I slipped out the back end of that train that day eight years ago . . . " (pp. 239–40). With that, Temple has taken her ultimate step toward the salvation one hopes for. And Faulkner underlines the sense of aspiration as he achieves the dramatic resolution with the play's closing word. Offstage, Gowan has called "Temple"; she replies, significantly, "Coming."

Ms. Panthea Reid Broughton has a perceptive comment in her instructive essay, *"Requiem for a Nun:* No Part in Rationality," that is particularly relevant here:

> Faulkner, like Bergson, seems to think there are two ways by which we may get outside ourselves: we may move down to homogeneity, repeti-

tion, and materiality, or up to a "living moving eternity" [Bergson's phrase]. Apparently the vast pattern of American life represents a downward step. *Requiem for a Nun* reflects, however, Faulker's increasing faith that it is possible to transcend the homogeneous, the material, and the rational, and achieve a "living moving eternity."[2]

Apparently Nancy's sacrifice has achieved its purpose—and in something like those terms. Given her extended and painful Second Chance, Temple has accepted the opportunity and achieved her triumph over evil.

There are those who will feel, however, that the end of the play is a bit too neat, and others who will be disappointed and frustrated at Nancy's simple faith. Such frustration is visible even in Noel Polk's excellent essay "The Textual History of Faulkner's *Requiem for a Nun.*" Quite correctly, Mr. Polk insists that Gavin Stevens not be regarded as "the hero of the novel," even in observing Gavin's harshness in holding Temple to the confrontation with herself. But he errs, I believe, in his interpretation of Nancy's role. He explains—

In the published version his [Gavin's] moral idealism rigidifies, his love of truth becomes a zealous pursuit of justice "as he sees it". . .— and it is his insistence on judging a tragic human situation in terms of an absolute truth that creates and then compounds the absolutely needless suffering which Temple is made to undergo.[3]

Mr. Polk rejects the simple Christian faith at the heart of Nancy's sacrifice—and indeed behind Gavin's argument with Temple as well: Stevens' simplistic dictum, borrowed from the Governor, that good 'not only can, it must' come out of evil . . . , is, at least in the context he makes it, absolutely wrong; nothing good has come from the suffering he has caused for Temple and Gowan—in the name of love—and certainly nothing good has come from Nancy's murder of that baby" (p. 126).[4] While he is perfectly right in his claim that Temple is "directly at the moral center of *Requiem for a Nun*" (p. 127), the lustre of his argument is dulled not only by his urgent dismissal of the religious aspect of the morality involved but also by the vehement rhetoric employed in that dismissal. On the question of who is *not* at the moral center of the novel he exclaims: "Not Stevens, whose sophistry and glib romanticism have turned a crazed 'Nigger dope-fiend whore' and a murderess into a martyred saint. And certainly not Nancy, who commits the single most vicious crime in all of William

Faulkner's work, and justifies it in the name of a rote and senseless theology whose central tenet is simply to 'believe' " (p. 127).

More persuasive, in part because more faithful to the persistent religious attitude of Faulkner's fiction, is the explanation offered by Ms. Panthea Reid Broughton—precisely the explanation Mr. Polk rejects (although he makes no reference to Ms. Broughton's essay):

> Temple must . . . adopt something of the supra-rational faith of Nancy. . . . She must adopt, in short, a mythic mode of thought.
> Such a mode of thinking which transcends reason is essentially foreign to Temple. . . . That Nancy smothered Temple's baby, willingly sending herself to the gallows in order to save Temple, Gowan, and the other child, is difficult for most readers to accept. But to try to find logic in Nancy's deeds or to tally up deaths against lives is to miss the point. However difficult it is for us to comprehend, Nancy believes in an afterlife for herself and the baby. She sacrifices herself and the child, after trying everything else, in order to shock Temple out of abandoning her family for a lover, to prevent her from regressing into the Temple Drake of *Sanctuary*.[5]

One understands, then, why artists have often felt it is difficult to present satisfactorily the triumph of Good—and, in our time, especially difficult to present that triumph in religious terms. And, if we confine our attention to the play alone in *Requiem for a Nun,* many among us will feel that here is proof of the modern artist's problem, and that the play remains a mixed success at best.

But Faulkner has given a breadth of appeal to this tale of Temple's struggle with the Past, with Evil, with the burden of Suffering, by means of his three introductory prose accounts of the history of Jefferson. The History provides a background which not only affords a setting but also a meaningful commentary on the careers of Temple and Gowan and Nancy Mannigoe. We notice at once the superficial connection between the three prose pieces and the three acts of the play which they respectively introduce. First, the Courthouse, scene of Nancy's trial; second, the Golden Dome, scene of Temple's and Gavin's appeal to the Governor; third, the Jail, scene of Nancy's incarceration during her last days. Beneath and beyond that connection is the nature of the historical account itself.

The History draws together the various accounts of Yoknapatawpha County and its pertinent relations which appear in Faulkner's fiction. Not only has it gathered all this together, as though to suggest that Temple's story gains its full significance only when seen against that background, but its very means and manner of rehearsal—repetition and reiteration, from one section to another—suggest that the History is cumulative and only rightly understood as such. By that stylistic means Faulkner makes the History express tacitly the equivalent of Gavin Stevens's reiterated comment in the play, that the past isn't dead—it isn't even past.

As the History unfolds, it reenforces the familiar impression that Faulkner's other works have created. The three founders of Yoknapatawpha comprise an interesting trinity, in a way representative of Health, Education, and Welfare: Doctor Habersham, medical man; Alexander Holston, tutor to the doctor's son; and Louis Grenier, "the Huguenot younger son who brought the first slaves into the country and was granted the first big land patent and so became the first cotton planter . . ."(p. 7). Habersham and Holston, the Health and Education two-thirds of the trinity, might have been all right had they been associated with a proper third, the Welfare, but it does not fare so well here under Faulkner's pen. The brief description of Grenier (just quoted) anticipates the long passage in act 3 which helps to confirm the nature of Progress as it has been achieved by a people, a county, Jefferson, who "confound forever seething with motion and motion with progress . . ." (p. 4). Change, motion—

> That fast, that rapid: a commodity in the land now which until now had dealt first in Indians: then in acres and sections and boundaries:—an economy: Cotton: a king: omnipotent and omnipresent: a destiny of which (obvious now) the plow and the axe had been merely the tools; not plow and axe which had effaced the wilderness, but Cotton: . . . not the rifle nor the plow which drove at last the bear and deer and panther into the last jungle fastness of the river bottoms, but Cotton; . . . creating its own parasite aristocracy not only behind the columned porticoes of the plantation houses, but in the counting-rooms of merchants and bankers and the sanctums of lawyers, and not only these last, but finally nadir complete: the county offices too: of sheriff and tax-collector and bailiff and turnkey and clerk. . . . [Pp. 195–96]

And that is the legacy of the Greniers, the negative inversion of Welfare.

Here we have again the familiar Faulknerian rehearsal of evil—barter, exploitation, abuse not only of human beings but of the land as well. Slavery and short-sighted, avaricious mismanagement of agriculture. The History keeps reviewing itself, gathering itself up again, telling us more than once how Jason Compson swapped a racehorse for a huge tract of land from the Chickasaw Ikkemotubbe, telling us how the Indian caretakers of the virgin lands were otherwise replaced and the land raped, how the pioneers and hunters were in their turn dispossessed, "then the land speculators and the traders in slaves and whiskey who followed the husbandmen, and the politicians who followed the land speculators, printing deeper and deeper the dust of that dusty widening, until at last there was no mark of Chickasaw left in it any more . . ."(p. 188).

To be sure, there is a strong note of nostalgia for the unspoiled land (and how timely, after all!), but it is also evident that the regret for the lost green goodness is at least equally shared with regret over the means by which it was lost—the means which make "progress" indistinguishable from "change" and which in turn prevent honest judgment and evaluation of change. It is not so much that the golden age, the good old time, was lost, but that it was so thoughtlessly and indeed maliciously lost. That is the injustice, the evil. And what can cope with that injustice if not truth or love—and pity or courage or honor?

It is important to recognize the focus of the regret, because there is room for incautious interpretation of it as the History leads into the Civil War. For as the introduction to act 3 rehearses that breathtaking decline of progress from barter in people, to barter in land, and to the triumph of King Cotton, it leads directly to that moment when "the destiny of the land, the nation, the South, the State, the County, was already whirling into the plunge of its precipice . . .Mississippi among the first of the eleven to ratify secession . . . "(pp. 197–98). The fever of the Civil War (to borrow the terms of the metaphor used in *Absalom, Absalom!* and elsewhere) is thus closely associated with the disease—the whole thoughtless way of life based on exploitation and abuse, yet crowned and camouflaged by the cosmetic code of Southern gentility.

We ought, then, to be prepared for the final review of the History, its glimpse into the postbellum world where "only the aging unvanquished women were unreconciled, irreconcilable . . . facing irreconcilably backward toward the old lost battles, the old aborted cause . . ." (pp. 205–6); and to recognize that, while the narrative tone is gentle and indulgent, the passage still underlines the fond error of that attitude. The distinction ought then to be clear between the note of nostalgia and regret for the lost goodness and the means of its loss on the one hand, and, on the other, Faulkner's dramatic *representation* of the nostalgia and regret for a way of life based on exploitation and abuse. The unvanquished and irreconcilable old women are tacitly compared, by simple juxtaposition, with the statue of the Confederate soldier unveiled by Miss Virginia Depre: "the marble eyes . . . stared not toward the north and the enemy, but toward the south . . . his own rear—looking perhaps . . . for reinforcements . . . for deserters, or perhaps himself for a safe place to run to . . ." (pp. 206–7). The final turn of the screw, however, is applied by the information that, as the twentieth century moves on, the number of irreconcilables is increasing; i.e., the movement of retrogression is gaining momentum and bulk. In other words, the accumulating, reiterative history of those prose introductions expresses the idea that not only is the Past with them, but so is its unrecognized Evil; that the Evil is repudiated and the Suffering also. And in this, of course, the passages of prose in *Requiem for a Nun* have expressed the central themes of the three acts of the play. The two modes are thus mutually illuminating, essentially parallel. And while it is nowhere stated in the prose, we are nevertheless urged to the inference that the fruits of the Evil and the burden of the Suffering have been alike laid principally upon the shoulders of the Negro—ever since the advent of Louis Grenier. If the way to salvation and redemption is through admitting the Evil of the Past and accepting the consequent Suffering, it is necessary for the Southern "Cotton aristocracy" to recognize how the Negro has been made scapegoat, and to begin to assume full responsibility itself, and thus to overcome the accumulated injustice with truth and love and pity and courage and honor.

(At this point we can perhaps most easily see the organic unity of *Requiem for a Nun;* and there is, in addition to the evident thematic parallels between prose and drama, a definite "intrusion"of Yoknapatawpha history into the play at the moment in act 2 when Temple tells the story of the Negro man whose wife died after only two weeks of marriage and who went berserk—the story of "Pantaloon in Black" from *Go Down, Moses.*)

Nancy Mannigoe's role is quite explicitly that of willing scapegoat for Temple Drake. Nancy had resorted to the ultimate evil, taking a human life, in her attempt to prevent Temple from continuing in her headlong pursuit of sin—from running off with Red's brother and taking her baby along with her. Nancy commits the murder with full knowledge of the evil she is doing, but hopeful of achieving a good end thereby; and she is perfectly aware of what the action will mean for herself. She never hesitates to admit her guilt nor attempts to avoid what punishment will follow at man's hands. It is significant, of course, that her confession is directed to God—"Yes, Lord" (p. 45); "Yes, Lord, I done it" (p. 167). Nancy has faith that her Lord will understand her action and judge it fairly and forgive her.

If Nancy's sacrifice is to have real and lasting benefit for Temple, however, Temple must accept the sacrifice with full understanding. She must accept the burden of that gift by admitting her own responsibility for the necessity of that gift, that sacrifice—by admitting her own sin. That need is given peculiar emphasis by the fact that Temple has originally chosen Nancy quite literally because she represents Temple's own sinful past. We can easily say that Nancy symbolizes or is the emblem of Temple's evil. Temple must "accept" Nancy just as Arthur Dimmesdale must "accept" his little Pearl in *The Scarlet Letter.* And when Temple is finally brought to that point at which she can say that she was herself responsible for the death of her baby, she has in effect accepted Nancy's sacrifice. Figuratively speaking, Nancy's sacrifice for Temple is equivalent to Jesus' sacrifice for all who will *accept* Him—with all that that implies about responsibility for creating the need of such sacrifice. But also, in the more literal terms of the play, Temple's final admission of guilt and responsibility has virtually absolved Nancy from guilt—although, of course, not from the descent of legal punishment. In both senses, then, redemption has been made possible; we are made to feel that good can indeed come out of evil— as Gavin Stevens had insisted it must.[6]

The apparently religious solution of the play is accompanied by the social solution to ills tacitly offered by the prose History in *Requiem.* One such connection, as indicated by Professor Broughton in her essay on *Requiem,* is that between Cecilia Farmer and Nancy Mannigoe. Professor Broughton comments, "The image of Cecilia as a static lodestar associates her with the courthouse which as static symbol of Community drew the men out of themselves into a cooperative vision. Just as the courthouse as symbol was imperishable, so Cecilia, 'drawing the substance—the will and the hope and dream and imagination—of all men,' transcends time" (p. 758). Then she explains the specific connection of Cecilia and Nancy:

> Just as, in the prose preamble to the last act, Cecilia Farmer's just *being* burst the confines of time, space, and logic, so too in Act III, Nancy's just *believing* bursts the structure of law and reason. Her behav-

ior presents a challenge to Temple to break from the rational-empiric mode, from merely doing her "best according to [a] code" to accepting a mystical involvement with God and the whole race of men throughout all time. [P. 762]

It seems to me that the particular association between the intent of the play and the intent of the prose History is further insisted upon (again only tacitly and by subtle artistic arrangement) by the connection between Nancy Mannigoe and Louis Grenier—a connection not personal but representative or mimetic. There is, in the first scene of act 2, the odd and apparently undigested piece of dialogue concerning Nancy's name. When the Governor is reminded of it he says, "Oh yes, Manigault. The old Charleston name." Then Gavin Stevens, who would know about such things, adds: "Older than that. Maingault. Nancy's heritage—or anyway her patronym—runs Norman blood" (p. 103).[7] Norman *Huguenot* blood, doubtless. We recall the French Louis Grenier, whose name (we learn elsewhere) is eventually corrupted to Grinnup as Maingault was to Mannigoe, as the first slave-owner of Yoknapatawpha; and we recognize Nancy's heritage of French blood has come from no other source than some French-descended slave-holder. This little emblem of miscegenation—dramatic synecdoche for slavery—functions effectively here as elsewhere in Faulkner's work.

The statement of *Requiem for a Nun*, made in concert by play and History, ultimately concerns redemption and salvation: man must accept responsibility for the evil he has done, collectively and individually, and must be aware of the scapegoat he has created and upon which he has unjustly loaded his own sins. That statement expresses the theme of the Self-Destructiveness of Evil—by negation, so to speak. Temple has evidently been successful, finally, in avoiding participation in the ultimate commitment to evil which is self-destructive. By having done so, she perhaps qualifies for membership in Faulkner's Saving Remnant. If the scapegoat has fulfilled its sacrificial role, one must then acknowledge the sacrifice and admit responsibility for it—as Temple has been able to do, and as the white South must also do. In specific terms, the white South must admit responsibility for what it has done to the enslaved Negro and accept the sacrifices the Negro has suffered—willingly (like Nancy) or not. That, of course, will require courage and love and pity and honor—as Gavin Stevens insists. But the need is urgent if any temple is to be resanctified and any sanctuary truly established.

Sir, say no more.
Within me 't is as if
The green and climbing eyesight of a cat
Crawled near my mind's poor birds.

    Trumbull Stickney, "Dramatic Fragment"

XII

The Town

During the years which intervened between *The Hamlet* and the completion of the Snopes trilogy, certain changes took place in Faulkner's attitude to his material. Faulkner alludes directly to this phenomenon in his introductory note to *The Mansion:*

> This book is the final chapter of, and the summation of, a work conceived and begun in 1925. . . . the purpose of this note is simply to notify the reader that the author has already found more discrepancies and contradictions than he hopes the reader will—contradictions and discrepancies due to the fact that the author has learned, he believes, more about the human heart and its dilemma than he knew thirty-four years ago; and is sure that, having lived with them that long time, he knows the characters in this chronicle better than he did then.

It is less the "discrepancies and contradictions" and much rather the result of Faulkner's having "lived with" those characters and come to understand them (and himself) better that must concern us here. The principal change—reflecting shifted emphasis and altered focus—accounts largely for the development to be found in the story and the thematic elements already set forth in *The Hamlet.* The change is most notable in the "humanizing" of Eula Varner Snopes, in the major involvement of Gavin Stevens, and in the emergence of Chick Mallison as a distinctly "hopeful" hero.

Although critics are rather uniformly grateful for Faulkner's continuation of the Snopes story, they tend to feel that there is a falling off in quality, the last two volumes seeming thinner than the thick and rich *Hamlet.* Certainly *The Town* (1957) is less "poetic," less mythic, less metaphoric and figurative in its expression, and thus

218

correspondingly more direct, discursive, and explanatory than *The Hamlet*. But it has its virtues, including its continued consistent development of its major characters, who emerge (especially Eula) as more complex and consequently more human figures, and also the uniformly high quality of the dialogue.

The Town continues the Snopes chronicle by pursuing two of the central themes of *The Hamlet:* (1) the successful progress of Flem's career, and (2) the theme of natural, human love. The two are here intimately associated and complementary, for the second concerns Flem's wife, Eula, and Major de Spain, her lover. The focus of the novel is mainly on the Eula-Manfred affair, but Flem's secretive and shrewd progress is never far from our attention, for his ability to use Manfred's interest in Eula to further his own welfare is one of the main features of his career. De Spain is responsible for Flem's job as superintendent of the power plant, and the strength of De Spain's shares of bank stock later helps to elect Flem vice-president of the bank. Flem, in turn, is responsible for the crowd of Snopes cousins who swarm over Jefferson and Yoknapatawpha County. As he moves steadily up the ladder of success he draws with him the hierarchy of dependent "cousins,"[1] whose various roles color and qualify Flem's career as they serve to develop the general theme of love.

Most memorable and significant is the progress of Montgomery Ward Snopes in the establishment of the Atelier Monty. His apprenticeship, during the war, with the YMCA canteen service taught him (if Snopeses need to be taught such things) how to take advantage of human weakness, or human propensity for evil. The particular significance of the Atelier Monty is that it catered to the voyeuristic tastes among the citizens of Jefferson. In this Monty affirms especially his cousinship with the enterprising Lancelot ("Lump") Snopes, who obligingly removed the plank from the side of the barn in which Ike and his cow made love. And again Monty emphasizes Faulkner's point that the true Snopes apears where human evil already exists, even if only potentially. It is also significant that Monty is (like many of the Snopeses) benefitting here from a perversion of human desires for love—he is the typical Snopes pander, a pander to perversity.

Flem, of course, is patently the pander as well, as the voluntary cuckold virtually always is. Particular emphasis is given to this feature of Flem's maneuvering by his attempt to shift blame for the theft of brass onto Tom Tom and Tomey's Turl by playing them against each other. Young Chick Mallison's comment on the situation is persuasive: "Tom Tom's home [was] violated not by Tomey's Turl but by Flem Snopes; Turl's life and limbs put into frantic jeopardy not by Tom Tom but by Flem Snopes."[2] Similarly, Flem is the basic evil in the illicit union of Eula and Manfred. As Faulkner depicts that union we are able to sympathize with it (as the townspeople do, in spite of themselves), for we see the great potential for good, for the triumph of natural creative impulse, cruelly frustrated. In the opening pages of the novel Chick Mallison speaks for Jefferson:

> Nor were we really in favor of adultery, sin: we were simply in favor of De Spain and Eula Snopes, for what Uncle Gavin called the divinity of simple unadulterated uninhibited immortal lust which they represented. . . . [P. 15]

We recognize an edge of the sardonic here as part of the slightly defensive pose of young Chick. But much of the novel's effort is devoted to clarifying the essential distinction between the Eula-Manfred union (with the divinity of its simple, unadulterated, uninhibited, and immortal force) and mere "adultery, sin." We feel the presence of evil, all right, but the novel strives to define that evil carefully, to identify its sources, and to suggest the means by which it may be overcome, if only by indicating clearly the reasons for the failure of those who would oppose that evil.

Our sympathies are further awakened as we share in Chick's understanding of De Spain's startled discovery of Eula as they dance together at the ball. The sardonic edge has gone from Chick's voice as he imagines Manfred's thoughts: "Hold on here; have I maybe blundered into something not just purer than me but even braver than me, braver and tougher than me because it is purer than, cleaner than me. Because [Chick adds] that was what it was" (p. 74). Manfred's discovery, distinctly touched with terror, contrasts with Eula's freedom and naturalness:

> Mrs Snopes was dancing that way, letting Mr de Spain get her into dancing that way in public, simply because she was alive and not ashamed of it like maybe right now or even for the last two weeks Mr de Spain and Uncle Gavin had been ashamed; was what she was and looked the way she looked and wasn't ashamed of it and not afraid or ashamed of being glad of it, nor even of doing this to prove it, since this appeared to be the only way of proving it. . . . [P. 75]

That last clause is eloquent with pathos.

The unabashed, natural wholesomeness of Eula's behavior and especially its motivation stand out clearly. That quality is expressed a little later as Ratliff observes that Eula and Manfred "never no more needed to waste time understanding one another than sun and water did to make rain. They never no more needed to be drawed together than sun and water needed to be" (pp. 99–100). But Ratliff is here perhaps too generous to Manfred. Certainly Eula is in *The Town* essentially the same character she was in *The Hamlet*—a figure of great potential awaiting the advent of the appropriate partner to fulfill and realize her. She is presented less insistently as the mythic figure of the female principle (although as overwhelmingly attractive to the male as ever), and has become rather a convincingly complex woman. The pathos of her situation is hence all the more acute. Letting herself go as she dances with Manfred does indeed appear "to be the only way of proving" that "she was alive and not ashamed of it . . . of being glad of it" (as Chick observes)—until Manfred takes her to bed as his mistress. And then that divine and immortal "lust" (as Gavin must call it) turns to "adultery, sin."

The fault, too obviously, belongs to Flem—dog in the manger, willing cuckold, eager pander—but it is Manfred's fault also. Just what Manfred could have done is not easy to argue—carry her away perhaps like a young Lochinvar and redeem the adultery by finally legalizing their union, whenever and however possible. The trouble is that he willingly enough accommodates himself to Flem's arrangements, advancing the cuckold in order to continue enjoying the wife. And just how willing Manfred was to take on full responsibility for Eula remains highly dubious. So there is Eula again, victimized once more by the lack of courage and willing responsibility that true love requires. As *The Town* reminds us, Manfred is really Hoake McCarron over again.

Sadly enough, the townspeople cannot act in accordance with their natural sympathy with and attraction to the lovers; they cannot even admit their sympathy. We are encouraged to think them so much the less human, in consequence, for Faulkner depicts those observers of Eula's *élan vital* as miserable cowardly wretches:

> all the other little doomed mean cowardly married and unmarried husbands looking aghast and outraged in order to keep one another from seeing that what they really wanted to do was cry, weep because they were not that brave, each one knowing that even if there was no other man on earth, let alone in that ball room, they still could not

have survived, let alone matched or coped with, that splendor, that
splendid unshame. [P. 75]

Their best representative is Gavin Stevens, something of a complement to Manfred, who, as he fails Eula through basic cowardice, also
aids Flem's progress, thus helping to call down upon Jefferson and
Yoknapatawpha County the general plague of Snopesism. Worse, he
lends the deceptive cloak of chivalric honor to their shared cowardice.

Gavin, something of a paradox whose virtues become vicious in
their exaggeration and whose "vices" become potentially redeemable, is not an easy character to manage.[3] He is what used to be
called "well educated," an idealist, but his attention to his ideals
seems largely intended to liberate him from involvement in reality.
His "chivalric" behavior reflects that kind of idealism. With the constant prompting and covert direction of V. K. Ratliff, Gavin becomes
a chief opponent of Flem Snopes and Snopesism; he also attempts to
act as champion of Eula—against both Flem and Manfred. His action consists mainly of empty and futile gestures. Gavin is just man
enough to feel the attraction of Eula, but he cannot accept her
womanliness; instead, he must try to make her into the "ideal" of the
Southern Lady. Chick Mallison accurately diagnoses his attack on
Manfred at the ball: "Uncle Gavin wasn't trying any more to destroy
or even hurt Mr de Spain. . . . What he was doing was simply defending forever with his blood the principle that chastity and virtue
in women shall be defended whether they exist or not" (p. 76).

In view of Gavin's willingness to take a beating from Manfred and
later from young Matt Levitt, it may seem inaccurate to call Gavin
cowardly, to accuse him of lack of courage. Yet that fault is indeed
his basic failure. He could well say of himself (as Manfred does) that
Eula is "not just purer than me but even braver than me, braver and
tougher. . . ." For Gavin is afraid of life—life and human love. What
makes Gavin's failure so nearly tragic is that he knows, intellectually,
a good deal about right and justice; his head serves well, but his
heart is faint. Furthermore, he is conscious of his failings, as we see
(for example) in his response to Eula's calling him a gentleman: "So
is Manfred. . . . And that other one [Hoake McCarron]. . . . Both
alike. . . . But not like me. All three gentlemen but only two were
men" (pp. 94–95).

Gavin obviously has the full heritage of Horace Benbow—except,
significantly, his ability to take a Belle Mitchell—but also more than a

little of that of J. Alfred Prufrock. The latter heritage is instructive. Faulkner evidently understood Eliot's nonhero well. Like Prufrock, Gavin is intellectual and timid, and quite aware of his own weakness and timidity in the face of life's reality and of love. As he is fascinated but intimidated by Eula, so is he later by her daughter, Linda. And as he plays his elaborate and perverse games of flirtation with Linda, he pauses to ponder his carefully arranged meetings and near meetings: "the interminable time until a few minutes after half past three filled with a thousand indecisions which each fierce succeeding harrassment would revise" (p. 206). At times almost ridiculous; almost at times the fool. Like Prufrock, Gavin knows; so how should he presume?

But after all, Gavin Stevens is perhaps worse off than Prufrock. While Eliot's hero is moved to digress by a whiff of perfume, and notices with relish arms that are braceletted and white and bare, his fear is the rebuff that might greet his amorous overtures; Gavin's fear is of the amorous overtures that greet *him!* When Eula comes to him at night in his office to offer him in genial simplicity what poor J. Alfred yearns for—love—Gavin's reaction is the stereotypical response of the hysterical, prim virgin: "Dont touch me."

> "Because you are unhappy," she said. "I don't like unhappy people. They're a nuisance. Especially when it can—"
> "Don't touch me!" I said. . . . if I had just had sense enough to say *I am, I want, I will and so here goes. . . .* "
> "Lock the door," she said. " . . . Stop being afraid of things," she said. "Why are you afraid?" [Pp. 93–95]

To say that Gavin's virtue has triumphed as he refuses to accept this invitation to adultery is to miss the point, as he has refused for the wrong reasons. He does not hesitate to accept the compensatory delights of a simply voyeuristic Humbert Humbert. He can play his perverse game of adolescent flirtation with the young Linda so long as she is scarcely pubescent. If Gavin has failed Eula (and himself, and, by extension, all of the Jeffersonian society, for which Eula has been something like its fertility goddess) through failure of courage to love, he has the chance for compensation as Linda approaches young womanhood. She will be Gavin's Second Chance. He is evidently interested in Linda's welfare and ultimately in freeing her from Snopes's influence. Eula sees the means of achieving that end, and she urges Gavin insistently "Marry her." Gavin, of course, can not. He has failed Eula—as all the males have— and has compounded that failure in his refusal to take full and legitimate responsibility for her daughter. His observation on Eula's suicide is thus more than pathetically ironic—it is hideous:

> "She was bored. She loved, had a capacity to love, for love, to give and accept love. Only she tried twice and failed twice to find somebody not just strong enough to deserve, earn it, match it, but even brave enough to accept it. Yes," he said, sitting there crying, not even trying to hide his face from us, "of course she was bored." [p. 359]

Ipse dixit.

I want to insist on the quality of Gavin's treatment of Eula and young Linda not only because it may be mistaken for a virtuous and chaste refusal to yield to temptation but also because the quality of his behavior in this is part of the general antilove theme, which was more elaborately developed in *The Hamlet*. Like T. S. Eliot, Faulkner makes a strong claim for the importance and supreme value of love; he differs from Eliot in his habitual indication of the source of genial human love. Almost from the outset, Eliot intimates that man's dilemma in a loveless world derives from his exclusively secular, mercantile, and cosmopolitan preoccupations, which have cut him off from God—the divine source of human love. Faulkner, on the other hand, usually implies that the source of love is in nature—in the land itself or in the wilderness. It might be argued that Faulkner is something of a pantheist, but I would not wish to push the argument quite so far. It is enough to say that in his fiction proper love and respect for the natural world—the land, the wilderness—regularly accompanies proper love and respect for human beings: the natural is equated with the good, the unnatural with evil. Thus Gavin Stevens fails as Eula's champion and rejects her offer of love not for the usual virtuous reason, but out of fear—fear of love and fear of life; his adolescent flirting with Linda is part and parcel of that same timidity. His behavior is unnatural in the sense I have just been using that term; and Gavin shares in the general metaphoric culpability of that society which cannot accept Eula properly and which therefore suffers the blight which such sterility, such impotence, produces. Our sense of this perverse and unnatural quality in Gavin is heightened increasingly through *The Town* and *The Mansion* by Faulkner's use of Chick Mallison's narrative point of view. Gavin Stevens emerges finally as the literary cousin of Quentin Compson and Isaac McCaslin as well as of Horace Benbow—the loveless, the cowardly, the irresponsible.

With Gavin's inability either to accept what Eula has to offer or to extend to her the reciprocally genial aid she needs (including responsible care for Linda), the progress of Flem Snopes's success is made easier. And in watching that progress "You've got to be careful" (in Eula's words to Gavin, p. 331), or you will begin to feel some admiration for Flem. Having drawn the whole string of hopeful Snopeses up with him as he climbs the ladder—"the whole rigid hierarchy moving intact upward one step as he vacated ahead of it," as Ratliff puts it (p. 31)—Flem turns his hand to housecleaning the Snopes abode. He has already refused to hasten home from his honeymoon (in *The Hamlet*) to intervene on Mink's behalf in his trial for the murder of Jack Houston; and he will carefully prepare a lengthy extension of Mink's incarceration through the double cross in Mink's escape plan. Immediately and most dramatically Flem works for the prosecution of Montgomery Ward Snopes. He is working, apparently, for the good of Jefferson, and especially by removing its ugliest stain—a Snopes stain—the Atelier Monty. Furthermore, he is working to gain respectability. Now it is a truism that not all those who enjoy respectability merit respect, but perhaps a truism in need of repetition. Beneath that cloak of respectability Flem will continue to manipulate human beings, to capitalize on man's potential for evil, to be (in a word) as fiendish as ever—but much less visibly so. Ratliff helps us to understand the implications of Flem's behavior as he explains it to Chick:

> "Respectability," Ratliff said.
> "That's right," Ratliff said. "When it's jest money and power a man wants, there is usually some place where he will stop; . . . But when it's respectability . . . there aint nothing he wont do to get it and then keep it. . . . there aint nothing he will stop at, aint nobody or nothing within his scope and reach that may not anguish and grieve and suffer."
> "Respectability," I said.
> "That's right," Ratliff said. [P. 259]

Flem's apparent success in *The Town* culminates in the departure of Manfred de Spain after Eula's suicide. The field is left open now for him to rise to the presidency of the bank. He retains control of Linda, evidently, as Gavin proves unable and unwilling to intercede effectively and save the girl from Flem's control. The super-Snopes has arrived—or so it would seem; for that note is insisted on by Ratliff as he comments upon the removal of the last Snopes stain from the Jefferson scene—Byron's wild half-breed children: "the end of a erea . . . The last and final end of Snopes out-and-out unvarnished behavior in Jefferson, if that's what I'm trying to say" (p. 370).

It is admittedly a somewhat depressing conclusion to the novel. We have seen the progress of the plague of Snopeses which have swarmed over Jefferson "like an influx of snakes or varmints" (p. 112), and furthermore we have been made to feel that the Jeffersonians have called down the plague upon themselves, that they have earned it (whether they deserve it or not). Gavin observes—as Ratliff relates it—

> we got them now; they're ourn now; I don't know just what Jefferson could a committed back there whenever it was, to have won this punishment, gained this right, earned this privilege. But we did. [p. 102]

What Jefferson did and has continued to do is consistently evident throughout the trilogy: it has been weak and lax and cowardly and mean. In a word, Jefferson has been (if, in many instances, only latently) evil; and the sign of Jefferson's threatened decay and putrefaction is the growth of the Snopeses. They are the mold on the cheese.

Toward the end of the novel Ratliff rehearses for us once again the conditions that made it possible for Flem to gain a foothold and begin his steady climb. To some extent the evil of old Will Varner, if expressed through Jody's mistaken gambit, gave Flem his eager beginning. Of course virtually all of Jefferson and Yoknapatawpha share in the blame. But as Ratliff puts the finger on Will Varner, we clearly see the point Faulkner is making: "his son-in-law had . . . not only out-briganded him in brigandage but since then had even out-usury-ed him in sendentary usury . . ."(p. 328). The Snopeses are both the sign and the magnification of the evil that the people of Yoknapatawpha County have done.[4]

Yet in that picture of near despair, as it might seem, there are quite firmly presented those hopeful signs which Faulkner has almost always provided—the more readily visible the larger our view of the whole Yoknapatawpha Saga. The first of these is expressed in the development of the Theme of the Second Chance—The Quo Vadis Theme. In *The Town*, of course, the Quo Vadis Theme is developed to explain the failure to accept a specific Second Chance. It is principally Gavin Stevens who fails, but in various ways the whole of Jefferson and of Yoknapatawpha County—and indeed all of us—share in the failure. That failure is prompted by the lack of love and courage necessary to accept and cherish properly the good which Eula Varner Snopes embodies and represents. To begin with, the general situation in *The Town* is a rehearsal of that in *The Hamlet* insofar as both novels are concerned with Eula. Gavin Stevens becomes involved in Eula's history when he intrudes upon her union with Manfred de Spain; his intrusion persists. *The Town* insists quite sufficiently on the similarities between Manfred and Hoake McCarron, as though mankind (or at least Yoknapatawpha County) were being given a Second Chance in Manfred, a chance to compensate for Hoake's failure of courage to assume proper responsibility for Eula. We can see and appreciate in all its rich significance the Manfred-Hoake similarities if we have read the first volume of the Snopes trilogy before embarking on the second. Even within *The Town,* however, that similarity and its significance can be easily enough grasped. Gavin's association of the two may be somewhat covert when he thinks that in calling him a gentleman Eula has compared him to Manfred and to Hoake. But Ratliff's observation on the naturalness and inevitability of Manfred's attraction to Eula makes the association quite specific: "he never had jest Manfred de Spain to have to cope with, he was faced with a simple natural force repeating itself under the name of De Spain or McCarron or whatever into ever gap or vacancy in her breathing as long as she breathed . . ." (p. 101). Certainly the reference is much richer for us if we have indeed read *The Hamlet* before *The Town*.

Now Gavin is superficially right and justified in his intrusion upon the Eula-Manfred affair insofar as he is attacking the dishonorable aspect of it—the adulterous aspect, which results from Eula's being wed to Flem and the fact that the "natural force" (good though it is in itself) is embodied in the lover Manfred. But as we come quickly enough to recognize, Gavin is in effect attacking that natural force itself, and without even realizing it; although Ratliff does: "because the only thing De Spain had that he wanted, Lawyer didn't know his-self that was what he wanted until his paw told him that last afternoon" (p. 83). Thus, whatever good Gavin's chivalric attempt at being Eula's champion might have achieved must fail—through his ignorance of himself and through the fear and unnatural revulsion he shares with the other townspeople (the "little doomed mean cowardly married and unmarried husbands") at Eula's "splendor, that splendid unshame." Gavin is presented with his Second Chance—and in specific and simplified terms—by Eula's nocturnal visit to his office. His abrupt question to her—"What do you want here?"—is virtually his pathetic equivalent of Peter's "Quo vadis?" Unlike Peter, however, Gavin, unable to recognize what has appeared before him, fails a second time.

The theme is given its fullest, most expansive development as Gavin is faced with his second chance to be champion of the good, to be the virtuous antagonist to the unnatural forces of Snopesism; and that is offered in the form of Linda Snopes, Eula's daughter. This important thread of the theme of the Second Chance is continued forward strongly in *The Mansion* for its full development and ultimate denouement. And it is unmistakably the specific offer of a chance to espouse the good which Eula has embodied and represented.

Gavin's "affair" with Linda begins promisingly enough. He reasonably pursues, in his attention to her, the laudable aim of saving Linda from Flem and Snopesism generally. There can be little doubt that Gavin is genuinely interested in her welfare. He attempts to aid in her education by offering her supplementary reading and the opportunity of easy informal conversation with him, product of Harvard and Heidelberg; he gives what help and advice he can in providing for her continued education—away from Jefferson and the immediate influence of Snopesism; and he even offers the opportunity of broadening her social experience by inviting her to dinner at his home with the Mallisons. All this is in itself commendable. Yet these attentions to Linda are indelibly colored by Gavin's unmistakably prurient and adolescent fascination with the girl. Their intercourse consists of the coke and poetry dates, the arranged and carefully missed appointments and encounters, with Gavin thrilled voyeuristically—"too terrified in fact to touch" (p. 208). And of course his sister, Chick's mother (as later, with increasing perspicuity, Chick himself), is suspicious of Gavin's "real" reason for interesting himself in the adolescent Linda.

Eula hopefully encourages Gavin's interest in her daughter, seeing there the chance for Linda which she herself missed. Gavin apparently sees in the girl an acceptable—because young and unthreatening—surrogate Eula. And, by means of some distinct parallels, the novel further emphasizes this opportunity as Gavin's Second

Chance. Gavin's association with Linda earns him a brief but bloody
enough thrashing from the vigorous and lusty young Matt Levitt,
who roars about Jefferson in his yellow cut-down racer (and roars
past Gavin's home to taunt and threaten him); just as his intervention as Eula's would-be champion earns him a bloody enough
thrashing from Manfred, who roars about Jefferson and past Gavin's home in his red E. M. F. to taunt and threaten him.

Quite as explicit as these parallels is Gavin's virtual choice, at the
most crucial moments of his association with Linda, to fail Eula a
second time. This second failure is Gavin's refusal to take the full
responsibility for Linda which his interest in her welfare and his
evident attraction to her would seem to indicate. And as Eula sees
the apparent aim of Gavin's behavior, which is to rescue Linda from
the atmosphere and environment which Flem's control has created
for the girl, she is certainly in favor of that aim and does what she
can to promote Gavin's achieving of it. Linda will thus have the
advantages which her mother missed. Yet when the avowed opponent of Snopesism is confronted with the fact that Flem Snopes,
Linda's titular (legal) father, is the obstacle to Linda's going away to
college, Gavin yields immediately: "So there's nothing I can do"
(p. 226). Of course Eula contradicts him and urges him repeatedly to
marry Linda, and of course Gavin refuses.

Eula's suggestion is neither precipitant nor misdirected, but has
much to recommend it. She is surely justified in her interpretation of
Gavin's behavior to Linda. Furthermore, the reader has perhaps even
more evidence than Eula and can at the very least hope that Gavin's
actions mean that his interest in Linda is the kind that would normally
lead to marriage. For Linda's part, there is strong evidence that she
would not be averse to a proposal of marriage from Gavin, in such
scenes as that of her reaction to Matt Levitt's bloodying up of Gavin:

> "I don't want to marry anybody!" she said, cried; she was clinging
> to me again . . . [etc.] "Not anybody!" she said. "You're all I have, all I
> can trust. I love you! I love you!" [P. 193]

Certainly Linda has turned to Gavin partly as to a father figure, but
just as certainly there is more to the attachment than that. Eula's
urgently repeated exhortation—"Marry her, Gavin"—is in many
ways most reasonable. His refusal to take Linda is thus a second
denial of Eula.

Even within that second denial Gavin is given a Second Chance—a *second* Second Chance, so to speak. After the whole affair has blown up and Eula is explaining to Gavin her marriage with Flem—including the fact of Flem's impotence (which Gavin, indeed, has already guessed)—she appeals again: "Marry her, Gavin" (pp.330, 332). And yet again Gavin refuses. Eula commits suicide.

Eula's suicide is not Gavin's responsibility alone, but his role among the causative factors is major and perhaps crucial. Mr. Cleanth Brooks asks us to consider why Eula remains with Flem and suggests that she is being practical: "Why, though she loathes Flem, should she bother to leave him? He is impotent. Eula apparently is satisfied with her long-term sexual relationship with Manfred de Spain, and Flem, presumably, raises no objection and sets up no inconvenient hindrances."[5] But it surely is not difficult to accept the notion that Eula is interested in Linda's "good name"—that she accommodates herself to the status quo for the sake of her daughter (and Ratliff will comment on Eula's reasons in precisely this way later, in *The Mansion*). That Eula "apparently is satisfied with" her relationship with Manfred is debatable, at the very least; and part of the trouble in that relationship is Manfred's apparent satisfaction with it. Eula evidently can expect no viable solution to her problem to come from Manfred; Gavin's fond intrusion as the champion of virtue and honor certainly must have awakened some sort of expectation in Eula, and she is pathetically slow to give up hope. Thus she twice urges Gavin to marry Linda. Linda's good name and future thus assured, Eula would be free to leave Flem—with or without Manfred. And by the same token, Flem would be deprived of his control of the Varner inheritance.

A great opportunity missed, a wonderful Second Chance refused, Gavin's failure finds its complement in Flem's success in persuading Linda to make over her inheritance to him. And Eula is left with a single honorable option, presented retrospectively in *The Mansion* as her "having to decide . . . *If I was a eighteen-year-old gal, which would I rather have: my mother publicly notarised as a suicide, or publicly condemned as a whore?*"(p. 145). Gavin Stevens could well have prevented all this had he had the courage of his apparent convictions, had his interest in Linda been mature and wholesome, had he been strong enough to risk the sacrifice which the responsibilities of true love always present. *The Town* ends with something of a reiteration of the conclusion of *The Hamlet:* the victorious Flem Snopes has risen a good deal higher on the ladder of respectable success.

Nevertheless, even as we witness the evident triumph of Flem, the super-Snopes, aided by the repeated capitulation of such potential adversaries as Gavin Stevens, we see that the novel is not a story of despair. Gavin's failure is to some extent "tragic," and in so far as it is, his story is instructive and satisfying—and ultimately not depressing—as tragedy must be. But beyond that there are motifs at work in *The Town* to influence our feelings and guide our responses so as to mitigate against despair. One is the prevalent Faulknerian theme of the Self-Destructiveness of Evil—here given faintly, though explicitly and discursively (and it will be resumed and developed amply in *The Mansion*). While the Snopeses are presented as a plague which mankind's (or at least Jefferson's) evil tendencies have earned, a plague of evil to out-do evil, yet there is some hopeful credibility in Gavin's notion that there is inevitably an end to them—that God will not permit them to continue, to last, to endure. He notes that "all Snopeses are male":

> as if *Snopes* were some profound and incontrovertible hermaphroditic
> principle ... Or even more than a mere nature principle: a divine
> one: the unsleeping hand of God Himself, unflagging and constant,
> else before now they would have owned the whole earth, let alone just
> Jefferson, Mississippi. [P. 136]

If not quite self-destroying, Snopes may at least be finally incapable of self-perpetuation. The fact that their chief representative, Flem, is himself impotent seems to lend some credence to Gavin's hopeful idea.

If this is rather negative and passive comfort, something more positive and active is to be found in Faulkner's development of the related theme of the Saving Remnant. From within the very ranks of the evil crew of Snopeses may come—and in *The Town* has already come—that kind of individual whose virtuous behavior may redeem finally the evil that the Snopeses have done. Obviously it is to the sons of Eckrum Snopes, and especially to Wallstreet Panic, that we can turn to find the basis for optimism. Ratliff underlines the point emphatically enough as he explains Wall's gingery wife: "She's got to purify Snopes itself. She's got to beat Snopes from the inside ..." (pp. 149–50). We might recall briefly Wall's qualifications (in addition to his having won a wife like that). He is from the outset obviously a favored being, Nature's darling, as we saw in the Spotted Horses section of *The Hamlet*: the ponies' miraculous concern for little Wall is recalled for us by Ratliff near the opening of *The Town*—"That horse boy . . . anything but Snopes boy" (pp. 34–35). Wall has successfully withstood Flem's attempt to get at him by offering him money when he has overbought and needs a loan. Significantly enough, Wall accepts a loan from Ratliff, who explains, "All I wanted was jest a note for it. But he insisted on making me a partner" (p. 149). A most hopeful partnership, to be sure—even though it has achieved little in the way of contravening Flem's efforts by the end of the second volume of the trilogy. Wall continues to flourish honestly and creatively, however, and we are justified in feeling that he will increase in wisdom and moral stature—a redeemed item of the Snopes plague, one of the Saving Remnant.

For they have been dipped in Time
And Time is only beginnings
Time is only and always beginnings
And is the redemption of our crime

Robert Penn Warren, "The Ballad of Billie Potts"

XIII

The Mansion

We must turn to the third volume, *The Mansion* (1959), for the completion of the statement made by the Snopes trilogy, and also, indeed, for the final shaping of the statement of the whole Yoknapatawpha Saga. *The Mansion* appropriately and eloquently concludes the Saga. Not only does it carefully draw together the various strands of the Snopes fabric, it also ties up various important "loose ends" (as they are now made to seem) from the major strands of the pattern of Yoknapatawpha's history.

Subdivided according to its three main headings—MINK, LINDA, FLEM—the novel tells the story of Mink's release from prison and his subsequent odyssey, of Linda's adulthood and return to Jefferson, of Flem Snopes's establishment as bank president and of his death. The three stories are obviously connected. They gain in significance through two other "stories" which the novel develops: the reestablishment of the Eula cult, and the political career of Clarence Snopes. Since the novel is concerned basically with the converging of these stories as they lead to the death of Flem—an event which is the result of the forces of vengeance and retribution, and which apparently rids the community of its principal evil figure—we can begin by considering the roles of the major characters in achieving that terminal event. Our feeling at the end of *The Mansion* is, inescapably, that justice has finally been done; because the plague called down on Jefferson and its environs in Yoknapatawpha by man's evil propensities—especially his failure of love and courage—has been lifted, the opportunities for men of good will to function successfully have been increased. The agents of that justice in *The Mansion* are well qualified and their choice is particularly significant.

First of all Mink. In spite of his "meanness," his killing of Jack Houston, his threatening behavior toward his wife, and his almost insane obsession with revenge, Mink is possessed of unmistakable virtues. And as we recall what we have known of him from the beginning of the trilogy, the virtues emerge impressively and the "meanness," if not explained away, becomes pathetically understandable. Most immediately apparent as we read *The Mansion* is Mink's unshakable commitment to and belief in honor and justice. He knows in the depths of his being that life is controlled by those forces; it matters little whether Mink calls the force Old Moster or "them-they-it," for he knows it is divine and, furthermore, ultimately reliable. Mink will "help" that force of justice to see that fair play is done when he feels the necessity, hence his killing of Houston and finally his killing of Flem. But those killings are not done for any mean personal gain or for any cheap advantage. Mink is proud and fierce and he kills for pride and manhood, as John Longley well says.[1] With Mink it is a matter of honor: he expects justice—or "fairness," as he sometimes calls it to distinguish it from what the Law can do to a person—and he expects from others the honorableness he tries to live by himself.

As we recall, Mink is also fiercely monogamous. *The Hamlet* has given us the touching history of Mink's romance, and it is important to remember both his strict commitment to his wife and also her reciprocation. Our first view of the couple is misleading in the way that our first view of Thomas Sutpen in *Absalom, Absalom!* is misleading—not false, just seriously incomplete. When Ratliff arrives at Mink Snopes's to employ his ruse about the order for a sewing machine, Mink's wife's insistent curiosity drives Mink to seize a stick of stove wood and, in his reptilian way, drive her back into the house. And later, after Mink returns from killing Houston, his wife calls him a "little murdering bastard"; he strikes her repeatedly and drives her away. It is hardly surprising that Ratliff will sum up Mink as "mean . . . the only out-and-out mean Snopes we ever experienced," for that was what he had seen; but Ratliff is seldom deceived, and we can detect the faint irony in his explanation that Mink was "just mean without no profit consideration or hope atall" (*Town*, p. 79). We recall his cousin Lump's astonishment that Mink has not robbed the dead Houston: "Do you mean to tell me you never even looked? *never even looked?* . . . By God, he had at least fifty dollars. I know. I seen it . . . " (*Hamlet*, pp. 233–34). The motive was pride and honor, "no profit . . . atall."

It is especially important to recall the salient features of Mink's depiction in *The Hamlet* to correct our impression of his relation with his wife, Yettie, to counterbalance the claim that he is simply mean. Their romance is characterized by Mink's intensely monogamous commitment to Yettie, and that commitment is clearly reciprocated. Indeed it was Yettie, widely experienced in amorous affairs, who initially chose Mink—because of his fervent and spunky sexual performance; but their subsequent marriage is evidently sustained by more than that. Mink's recurrent image of her as a figure in a lighted doorway suggests that his attitude is very like adoration (see my discussion of this image above, in the *Hamlet* chapter). Yettie's devotion to him, in turn, is expressed by the eagerness with which she offered her premature alibi for Mink to protect him from being taken for the murder of Houston, and even by her pardonable means of earning money for Mink's defense—selling the only commodity she had, following the lead of Ruby Goodwin in *Sanctuary*. Mink is an odd, warped, and Snopesey lover, but pathetically capable of love (what else dare we call it?) nevertheless.

Faulkner has withheld until *The Mansion* his development of another aspect of Mink's character—calculated to increase our sympathetic involvement with him—and that is his strong religious faith, which has evolved during his years in prison but which is quite of a piece with his character as we have come to know it in the earlier books of the trilogy. *The Mansion* virtually begins with a statement about Mink's belief in "a simple fundamental justice and equity in human affairs," embodied in the vague "them-they-it" later identified as Old Moster, the folk Domine. Furthermore, the novel proves his faith and implies that he is in some way or other one of the elect. Mink's suggestion that the vengeful criminal Shuford H. Stillwell may be prevented by divine intervention from killing him—"Still Mexico, I notice. . . . Maybe He will kill him there"[2]—is proven true. The symbolism is a bit heavy-handed: a church falls down and crushes Stillwell (p. 101). A more elaborate and satisfactory development of the same idea occurs in the Goodyhay episode, book 12 of the novel. Here Mink is cared for and his lost ten dollars replaced through Goodyhay's efforts.

Goodyhay himself deserves a word of comment, for his part in the novel gives impressive statement to the Quo Vadis theme which recurs so frequently in Faulkner's work. Goodyhay is something of a latter-day Saint Peter, and his religious experience in the midst of war a reenactment of the Quo Vadis myth. He thought he was already safely dead "when all of a sudden Jesus Himself was standing over him saying Fall in" (p. 268); and then he is given the chance to repeat Peter's three-fold denial of Christ, which he does. But like Peter fleeing from his onerous responsibilities in Rome by escaping along the Appian Way only to be confronted there by Christ and given another chance, Goodyhay is given his Second Chance.

> "I cant . . . ," I says.
> "Fine," He said. "That's three and finished. You wont ever have to say cant again. Because you're a special case; they gave you three times. But there's a general order coming down today that after this nobody has but one. Pick him up." So I did. "Dismiss," He said. . . . [P. 281]

And there is Goodyhay, looking after Mink, doing the Lord's work (as he understands it), like a regular Christian soldier—like what the Spartans would have called a brick, and others a rock.

The narrative voice assumes a choral function. Commenting on Goodyhay's work in the world of Yoknapatawpha, it reaches explicitly beyond the proscenium into the world of actuality to make its specific contemporary reference—and to extend most urgently the application and relevance and import of its statement. The ironic veil of the narrative tone is perfectly transparent:

> . . . be damned if here aint a passel of free-loading government-subsidised ex-drafted sons of bitches acting like whatever had caused the war not only actually happened but was still going on, and was going to keep on going on until somebody did something about it. A passel of mostly non-taxpaying folks that like as not would have voted for Norman Thomas even ahead of Roosevelt, let alone Truman, trying to bring Jesus Christ back alive in the middle of 1946. [P. 272]

Mr. Cleanth Brooks has well observed that if Mink Snopes feels weirdly out of place in the world into which he has been freed, he feels perfectly at home among Goodyhay's congregation.[3]

The final test of Mink's faith occurs, of course, at the moment he confronts Flem. The pistol misfires once, but Mink knows it will fire on his second attempt because Old Moster just punishes; He doesn't play jokes. It is as though Mink is God's chosen instrument to effect the act of retributive justice that brings the evil career of Flem Snopes to a close. That impression is strengthened by various exchanges between Gavin Stevens and Ratliff through book 16 of *The*

Mansion. As Ratliff contemplates Mink's impending liberation from Parchman, he tells Gavin that they all (Linda, Flem, Mink, and the two of them) are involved in whatever it is—fate, destiny, luck or hope (pp. 373–74). When Gavin affirms that God is not going to permit Mink to come all the way to Jefferson and shoot another man, Ratliff replies, "Dont that maybe depend on who God wants shot this time?" (p. 389). And finally Gavin thinks frantically, "*We cant stop him . . . Maybe even a rattlesnake with destiny on his side dont even need luck, let alone friends*" (p. 394). It had to be Mink.

Once the deed is done, Mink goes to his reward, lapsing into the gentle embrace of Mother Earth. Sometimes that last scene is misunderstood as expressing Mink's final defeat, his succumbing to his enemy. There is some basis for that misconception, best represented by the long passage in book 5 where the earth is defined as the natural enemy of men like Mink: "the ground, the dirt which any and every tenant farmer and sharecropper knew to be his sworn foe and mortal enemy—the hard implacable land which wore out his youth and his tools and then his body itself"(p. 90); and more specifically, Mink realizes that "People of his kind never had owned even temporarily the land which they believed they had rented . . . It was the land itself which owned them . . . not the owner, the landlord . . . but the land, the earth itself passing their doomed indigence and poverty from holding to holding of its thralldom as a family or a clan does a hopelessly bankrupt tenth cousin" (p. 91). And it is while working in the prison cotton fields that Mink feels that the earth has called a truce. But even though the passage asserts that the thralldom comes not from owner or landlord but from the land itself, the very language tacitly insists that the wracked tenants and croppers in their indigence and poverty are victims of the very social and economic organization that condemns them to that role of peasant serf. In prison, Mink is, ironically, free of that system and enjoys that odd freedom to be found in strict institutionalization that is so appealing to the tall convict of "Old Man" (*The Wild Palms*), and to a certain number of those who elect to serve in the permanent armed forces.

Faulkner has not inverted his typical theme of the importance of man's real estate—that theme which indicates that proper respect for and treatment of the land and of human beings go hand in hand, that the misuse of the one is regularly accompanied by misuse of the other. The land, the wilderness, nature are one, and at once the source and the test of human goodness. We think readily of good

men like the MacCallums (*Sartoris*) and Uncles Buck and Buddy
McCaslin (*The Unvanquished* and *Go Down, Moses*), who express that
goodness. We recall the frequent association of the Negro with the
land (or sometimes with the wilderness), which is also seen to account for his virtue. But he is very much in the situation of Mink in
the prison cotton fields: the land he works is in no sense his; he has
no reason to regard it as an adversary, an opponent, over which he
must try to be victorious if he is to *gain,* to get ahead. Only the
poorest and most unfortunate poor-white sharecroppers, who must
work as if they were free to earn their own way—even though all
cards are stacked against them (as the passages last quoted, above,
make amply clear)—regard the hard land as their enemy; it is a kind
of transference. Faulkner's attitude has not changed in this regard in
The Mansion. And thus, when Mink has finally completed the pageant in which the virtuous victim rises to slay the figure of dominant evil, part of our feeling that wrongs have been righted results
from the pacific effect of the land's gentle embrace of the tired
Mink: he is on his way home, much as Sam Fathers and Ben and
Lion (in "The Bear" of *Go Down, Moses*) are at home in the earth,
"not held fast in earth but free in earth and not in earth but of
earth, myriad yet undiffused."[4]

Mink, then, has the necessary qualifications to serve as the instrument of divine, natural justice. But his killing of Flem is nonetheless
an act of murder, just as his killing of Houston was. If an instrument
of divine justice, Mink is nevertheless a Snopes instrument. His virtues are real virtues but somewhat odd, as though reflected in a
distorting mirror—as the "virtues" of a real Snopes are bound to be.
The Snopeses generally, after all, are the mold, not the cheese itself!
And thus the righting of the wrongs which concludes the Snopes
trilogy is worked out in terms of the Self-Destructiveness of Evil—
Snopes eliminates itself. It is furthermore appropriate that Mink—
the Snopes who embodies the virtues of love and honor (though
warped)—be the principal active agent.

Of course he has help, and mainly from Linda, Eula's daughter.
And in the union of Linda and Mink for the purpose of exterminat-
ing Flem, we have the conjunction of two of Faulkner's major dominant themes. To the theme of the Self-Destructiveness of Evil is now
added the theme of the Second Chance (the *Quo Vadis* theme,
which we have already seen stated briefly in the story of the Reverend J. C. Goodyhay).

At first glance, Linda's role in the killing of Flem is somewhat puzzling. She has enjoyed whatever benefit there was in having Eula as a mother; she has been the object of the generally well-intentioned avuncular consideration of Gavin Stevens; and she has known the apparently fulfilling love of Barton Kohl and of taking her place with him beside other humanitarian idealists to strive against forces of fascist oppression. But her right to figure as an agent of vengeance against Flem is as legitimate as Mink's. Flem has simply poisoned her life. Linda shares in whatever misfortune befell Eula in becoming Flem's wife; he has used both of them as means to his own financial security, his economic and social progress. He has stood squarely in the way of Linda's opportunity to broaden her experience by going to school well away from Jefferson and to meet eligible young men. And he finally secures her Communist Party card as his last weapon against her. Flem's influence as a representative (and embodiment) of the forces against nature and against love is reflected also in Linda's brief and tragic association with Barton Kohl. War has destroyed her love—almost a cliché in Faulkner's fiction from *Soldiers Pay* onward. As a figure of active, destructive sterility, Flem combines all those features which qualify him supremely as the legitimate target of Linda's vengeance. And while Linda is the main operative force in the arrangement of Flem's murder, she has much of our understanding and sympathy and almost (perhaps) our forgiveness.

For Linda, on her side, has been generously assisted to that end— the killing of Flem—by Gavin Stevens. To put it bluntly, Gavin has failed her roundly and perhaps more fundamentally even than he failed her mother; and it is the kind of failure which gives particular emphasis to the significance of Flem's death and Linda's contributive role in that event. Faulkner resumes in *The Mansion* the thread of Gavin's inadequate response as a man to Linda as a young woman. She is no longer the little teen-aged virgin who titillated his prurience in *The Town*, but a mature widow who is as fond of Gavin as ever. He now takes shelter behind what he calls the twenty-year difference in their ages (actually only eighteen years separate them); but as usual Gavin simply lacks the courage of his desires. Linda offers herself to him even more explicitly than her mother had done, for she knows as well as Eula did what Gavin wants and presumably needs—and further, she apparently wants Gavin. The significance of that offer and refusal is augmented by the resumption, in *The Mansion*, of some of the mythic quality of Eula, so that our sense of Gavin's refusal of Linda as a repetition of his refusal of her mother and of all that that amounts to is considerably heightened.

That resumption begins as early as book 6 with Ratliff's rehearsal of Eula's qualities and experience—Hoake McCarron's coming "like a wild buck from the woods" straight to where Eula was waiting, not especially for him, but for "any wild strong buck that was wild and strong enough to deserve and match her" (p.118). Ratliff explains that he is not talking about love but about "Natural phenomenons." His description is faintly reminiscent of Emily Bronte's of Cathy and Heathcliff, but McCarron is of course a Heathcliff *manqué*, who will not accept the responsibility of his tremendous and wild feeling for his paramour. Ratliff continues, reminding us of Eula's discovery by De Spain—hopefully "the McCarron that wouldn't start or break up when they collided together" (p. 127)—but Manfred is after all not a great improvement over Hoake: Eula remains Mrs. Snopes. And then Ratliff observes that poor Gavin is not even a Hoake McCarron. Finally, in book 8, Chick Mallison rehearses his commentary on the Eula-Manfred union and the townspeople's secret and grudging sympathy with them, and pays Eula another compliment in reenforcing Ratliff's interpretation:

> We would all be on hers and De Spain's side; . . . only the preachers would hate her because they would be afraid of her since the god she represented without even trying to, for the men to pant after and even the women to be proud that at least one of their sex was its ambassador, was a stronger one than the pale and desperate Galilean who was all they had to challenge with. [P. 212][5]

Just enough of the rich and fecund mythic ambience given Eula in *The Hamlet* is recalled in the third volume of the trilogy to remind us succinctly of what had passed through Yoknapatawpha half-appreciated, what opportunity that community had failed properly to grasp. And with that, we are likewise distinctly reminded that Linda is her mother's daughter—that she makes available some kind of adequate compensation, a little like that offered by the second-generation Cathy and Hareton in *Wuthering Heights*. But Gavin cannot bring himself to seize courageously the opportunity extended to him. And against the immediate background of Ratliff's and Chick's recalling what Eula had been and meant, Gavin's reiterated refusal gains more bitter (and tragic) poignancy. The language of the lengthy dialogue between Linda and Gavin in book 10 helps establish the theme of the Second Chance, recalling specifically the scene in *The Town* which follows Gavin's altercation with Matt Levitt— Linda clinging to Gavin and repeating "I love you," and Gavin assuring her (ironically!) that she need not marry anybody—and generally, Gavin's rejection of Eula's repeated suggestion that *he* marry Linda; and it is thus his second denial of Linda:

> *. . . I Refuse to marry you . . .*
> "But you can   me," she said. That's right. She used the explicit word. . . .
> "You're blushing," she said.
> I wrote *that word . . .*
> I wrote *. . . thats wrong too what shocks is that all that magic passion excitement be summed up & dismissed in that one bald unlovely sound*
> "All right," she said. "Dont use any word then."
> I wrote *Do you mean you want to*
> "Of course you can," she said. "Always. You know that."
> I wrote *Thats not what I asked you . . .*
> *because we are the 2 in all the world who can love each other without having to . . .* as she clasped me, clinging to me, quite hard, the dry clapping voice saying,
> "Gavin. Gavin. I love you. I love you, . . . " [Pp. 238–39]

Furthermore, Linda quite specifically likens this refused offer of herself to Gavin without marriage to her mother's refused offer of herself to Gavin in his office (in *The Town*):

> "Why didn't you?"
> I wrote *because she felt sorry for me . . .*
> "I dont feel sorry for you. You know that. Dont you know it will be important to me?"
> I wrote *Then maybe it was because I wasnt worthy of her & we both knew it but I thought if we didnt maybe she might always think maybe I might have been. . . .* [P. 241]

Here we see Gavin Stevens—combining features of J. Alfred Prufrock and (as Mr. Cleanth Brooks impressively contends) of Tristan[6]—at one of his best moments; here he takes an honest view of himself, which he is not always capable of doing: *maybe . . . I wasnt worthy of her.* Our anguish derives from the fact that Gavin in this so much resembles Horace Benbow, Quentin Compson, and Isaac McCaslin: he *will not* take the responsibility and simply claims that he *can not* do so. Like theirs, Gavin's is a willed impotence.[7] And thus the reiteration of Gavin's refusal of Linda as his Second Chance missed, occurring in the closing pages of the novel, drives home that tragic theme and exposes again Gavin's cowardice. Linda has again declared her love; Gavin has embraced her, and she laments, "You have had nothing." Gavin "knew exactly what she meant: her mother first, then her; that he had offered the devotion twice and got back for it nothing but the privilege of being obsessed, bewitched, besotted if you like" (pp. 424–25). Her mother first, then her. Gavin hugs his rectitude and relishes the condition he has chosen in eagerly calling to his pale and desperate Galilean, "Thou hast conquered!"

Ratliff is given the last statement, in comic terms, of the tragic features of Gavin's refusal of the proffered Second Chance. As the novel closes he expresses to Gavin the hope that no daughter of Linda's will ever show up in Jefferson: "You done already been through two Eula Varners and I dont think you can stand another one."

Mink, Linda, and poor Gavin have all contributed to the murder of Flem Snopes. Now although Ratliff definitely states—and we are from one point of view tempted to agree—that Flem was actually the only real Snopes left in Jefferson, *The Mansion* is full of references to the whole clan. It is absolutely necessary to the successful rounding off, to the full development of the significance, of the Snopes trilogy (and of the Yoknapatawpha Saga as a whole) that the clan be reviewed and disposed of. Before that can be done, the last spreading of the Snopes stain—this into the political arena—has to be noted. The brief story of Clarence Snopes not only accomplishes that, but adds greatly to the significance of Snopesism in the total pattern of the trilogy. We have seen Senator Clarence before, of course, playing his active and nefarious role in *Sanctuary*. But more attention is given in *The Mansion* to his specifically political activity, attention which affords Faulkner the occasion to make further topical references to the Klan, WPA, NRA, Senator Bilbo, Huey Long, etc., and to suggest that people get what they "deserve" in the way of political representatives and programs—unless something beneficient is done to prevent it (see pp. 160–61). Faulkner makes the point throughout the trilogy and elsewhere in the Saga, that Yoknapatawpha has earned the dessert of Snopesism and the Snopeses. Quite as memorable as the political aspect of Clarence's story and more important in terms of the narrative's thematic expression is his association with his cousin Virgil. Virgil's somewhat extraordinary sexual prowess (he is a sort of Snopesian Maupassant) underlines his relationship to cousins Mink and Ike, and especially the latter, for Clarence cashes in on Virgil by betting on his sexual staying powers as Lump had turned Ike and his cow into a peep show. In the case of all three—Virgil, Mink, and Ike—we see not only a normal human virtue become somewhat unusual when embodied in a Snopes but also another Snopes (in the cases of Virgil and Ike) making that somewhat skewed virtue more completely bizarre and more fully demeaned by avid exploitation of it. This aspect of Clarence Snopes's career gives additional, and comic, emphasis to the pervasive idea of Snopesism as an antinatural force, helping to make the defeat of Snopesism all the more urgently desirable. Ratliff's role in the destruction of Clarence Snopes as a political force in Jefferson—his clever employment of the dogs on three legs to express the notion that as a public figure Clarence is all wet—earns him our gratitude and admiration; it also prepares us to accept his role in the ultimate destruction of Flem, the super-Snopes.

That the end of Flem be taken seriously as the end of nefarious Snopesism in Jefferson and Yoknapatawpha, it is appropriate that the early sections of the novel remind us of the various guises under which that plague has manifested itself in the county. In book 4, Montgomery Ward Snopes gives a brief but fairly complete résumé of the Snopes clan. Especially noteworthy is the persistence with which sexual malfeasance attaches to each figure in the list (and Monty himself, we recall, gained his distinction by the showing of "dirty pictures"). He speaks of

> the free Snopes world where Flem was parlaying his wife into the presidency of a bank and Clarence even drawing per diem as a state senator between Jackson and Gayoso Street to take the wraps off Virgil whenever he could find another Arkansas sport who refused to believe what he was looking at, and Byron in Mexico or wherever he was with whatever was still left of the bank's money, and mine and Clarence's father I. O. and all of our Uncle Wesley leading a hymn with one hand and fumbling the skirt of an eleven-year-old infant with the other. . . . [P. 83]

(Byron in this company looks a little like the exception that proves the rule. He deserves his place, however, beside Clarence or rather beside Virgil by dint of his semiliterate love letters to Narcissa Benbow, whose combination of snobbishness and prurience fanned the amorous aspirations of romantic Byron with no intention of providing their satisfaction—in *Sartoris*. Narcissa must bear much of the blame for Byron's theft and frantic departure from Jefferson.)

There they all are. Some comfort is given in Ratliff's somewhat later review of the family, for his purpose is to indicate how success-fully Flem has eliminated his embarrassing cousins in order to estab-lish his own respectability in Jefferson. And the balance of the novel is devoted to accounting for the rest of the Snopeses and chiefly Flem himself. Virtually all the Snopesian loose ends are tucked in by the conclusion of the trilogy.

But *The Mansion* picks up and defines as loose ends, to be further tucked in, various threads from earlier pieces of the Yoknapatawpha Saga, particularly from the Sartoris and Compson stories (as we have seen them developed in *Sartoris* and *The Unvanquished,* and in *The Sound and the Fury* and *Absalom, Absalom!,* and elsewhere). Most atten-tion is given to Flem's besting Jason Compson in the latter's attempt to outmaneuver him in the real estate deal and the establishment of the Eula Acres development—the last use made (and how appropri-ate!) of Benjy's pasture: "Snopes's title to the entire old Compson place stood, so that even Jason gave up at last" (p. 328). Benjy (we are told) had already set himself and the Compson house on fire and burned up in it. The nature of the references to the Sartoris story confirms the translation of Horace Benbow into Gavin Stevens, which we had seen as early as Faulkner's completion of the Temple Drake story in *Requiem for a Nun.*

By drawing together these various strands from his other stories into the fabric of the Snopes trilogy, Faulkner has done more than tie up loose ends: he has thus extended the significance of his persistent themes by setting them together for reciprocal emphasis in the final book of the Yoknapatawpha Saga. Furthermore, the phenomena of parallels between the several stories, and of virtual identification among several heroes (the Horace Benbow-Gavin Stevens merging is merely the most salient) urge upon us a view of Faulkner's Yokna-patawpha Saga as something like T. S. Eliot's view of western history, especially as expressed in *The Waste Land*—that all wars, for example, are the same war, a perpetually recurring metaphor for man's failure of love. This is focussed in the character of Gavin Stevens, Faulkner's most nearly ubiquitous hero. Gavin's assumption of Horace Benbow's identity, his background, his education abroad, his war experience as a YMCA director, even his odd but significant hobby of translating the Old Testament back into the classical Greek, becomes a feature of

The Town and *The Mansion,* and is specifically rehearsed in *The Mansion.* Gavin only lacks, we are liable to recall, a sister Narcissa and a mistress and wife Belle Mitchell. Melisandre Backus Harris is scarcely comparable to Belle, but she does marry Gavin. And as for an equivalent of the serene Narcissa, the still unravished bride, etc., of Horace's glass-blown Platonic and incestuous dreams, the language of *The Mansion* seems to offer at least tentatively the figure of Linda Snopes Kohl. Chick Mallison's impression of the widowed Linda, influenced by her deafness, is first of a woman "immured, inviolate in silence, invulnerable, serene"; then a bit more specifically, "the inviolate bride of silence, inviolable in maidenhead, fixed, forever safe from change and alteration"(p. 203). And the repeated Keatsian echo is strengthened as Chick thinks again of her as "the bride of quietude and silence striding inviolate in the isolation of unhearing, immune . . ." (p. 230). This characterization of Linda expresses Gavin's attitude to her in quite the way that the same characterization of Narcissa Benbow expresses Horace's attitude to her. The taboo of incest, which kept the Horace-Narcissa relationship just within the bounds of chastity, has been replaced in the Gavin-Linda relationship by the odd and perversely Puritan prurience we have seen in its two stages in *The Town* and then in *The Mansion.* Chick sees the widow Kohl as serene and inviolable in her deafness, and is, of course, reflecting his uncle's attitude to her; Chick has quite normal speculations otherwise about what (to put it with his own bluntness) Linda is like with her clothes off. (Gavin has a sister, to be sure, but Mrs. Mallison is signally different from Narcissa; and this perhaps "saves" him from the peculiar anguish of Horace.)

A brief reference to Gavin's Harvard days has the effect of urging a comparison between him and Quentin Compson. Chick refers to his being invited to Charleston by his friend Spoade and adds, by way of explanation, that Spoade's "father had been at Harvard back in 1909 with Uncle Gavin" (p. 206). The association of Spoade and Harvard, augmented by the rehearsal of the Compson history, and then by the addition of the specific date, almost inevitably encourages our imaginative juxtaposition of Gavin and Quentin Compson. Consequently, we are made sharply aware of the startling similarities between the two. Quentin, Gavin, and Horace Benbow have thus been closely associated in our minds as three of a kind—or perhaps as three views of the Faulknerian "good, weak hero," the one who says "This is rotten, I don't like it, I can't do anything about it. . . ."

There is only the most minor of references to Isaac McCaslin in *The Mansion:* we learn that while still in high school Jason Compson started clerking in Uncle Ike McCaslin's hardware store, and that "for all practical purposes Jason Compson was now the McCaslin Hardware Company" (p. 323). Yet, since Gavin Stevens has taken over from Ike McCaslin in the two-part story of Lucas Beauchamp— i.e., in the last section of *Go Down, Moses* and then throughout *Intruder in the Dust*—the similarity between the two emerges distinctly. We recognize easily enough that Horace, Quentin, Isaac, and Gavin are really the composite hero with whom Faulkner had principally been occupied throughout his long career. And to a considerable extent the Yoknapatawpha Saga has been devoted to tracing out and making understandable the tragic failure of this hero—the man of ideals and intelligence who simply lacks the courage of his convictions, especially in the important area of love. Not that the Yoknapatawpha Saga is mainly a long love story (except perhaps in the sense the Eliot's *Waste Land* is mainly a love story), but that the hero's general failure is expressed with the most compelling dramatic immediacy by his specific and willful failure at love. In Faulkner's fiction love, and especially in its sexual manifestation, is a useful and eloquent synecdoche.

Yet the Yoknapatawpha Saga and the Snopes trilogy itself are neither of them simply tragic and certainly, as I have been insisting, not pessimistic. If the weak hero's failure and man's weakness generally have earned the descent of the Snopes plague, Faulkner's fiction has quite consistently shown that the agents of evil bring on their own destruction. We see this in his earliest fiction, and the trilogy concludes with the expressive pageant of Snopes destroying Snopes. He has realized in the trilogy with supreme effectiveness his response to a question put to him at the University of Virginia (May 15, 1958): "The Snopeses will destroy themselves."[8] The theme of the Self-Destructiveness of Evil does much to allay any pessimistic note that may seem to creep into the Yoknapatawpha Saga. Beyond that, however, there is the additionally hopeful phenomenon of what I have called the Faulknerian Saving Remnant. In the center of the Snopes plague itself Faulkner has discovered for us a positive, redeemable, and indeed already redeemed force—a Snopes rising up from the midst of his clan like a rose on a dung hill. The sons of Eckrum Snopes and even old Eck himself afford us the opportunity for admiration and optimism. Wallstreet Panic Snopes in particular (aided of course by his gingery little wife, who wants to beat Snopes from the inside, as Ratliff points out) is the man of virtue and courage and responsibility—the new salt of the earth.

In his sardonic review of his relatives, Montgomery Ward Snopes draws our attention to this Snopesian Saving Remnant (and his irony is intentional): "I dont count Wallstreet and Admiral Dewey and their father Eck, because they dont belong to us: they are only our shame" (p. 83). And Ratliff confirms the truth of Monty's observation in his review of the family, asserting that "Eck's boys, Wallstreet Panic and Admiral Dewey, they hadn't never been Snopeses to begin with" (p. 153). To take Ratliff literally is, of course, to miss Faulkner's point entirely. The honest and industrious Eck and his sons might well have had another name (Tull, Bookwright, Workitt, even Armstid) if Faulkner's purpose had been only to portray some good, simple Yoknapatawpha folks. But they are Snopeses, un-Snopesey Snopes if you like, but the point is thus emphasized that from the very dregs of modern society (as Faulkner presents them) can come—if given the chance—those simple, admirable qualities in which we can safely rest our hope for the success of mankind. Again Faulkner has foretold this development: "Snopes will evolve into you might say an accepted type of Snopes."[9] Furthermore, the idea of finding this Saving Remnant within the very ranks of the plague of rats and termites was evidently in Faulkner's mind from the outset, from that moment at which (he said) he "thought of the whole [Snopes] story at once like a bolt of lightning lights up a landscape."[10] And there is still somewhere, perhaps just beyond the boundaries of Yoknapatawpha County, the original un-Snopesey Snopes—Flem's young brother, Colonel Sartoris Snopes, who chose honesty and justice over loyalty to family.[11]

In addition to the redeemed Snopeses we are left with two more traditional champions of the enduring virtues in the persons of V. K. Ratliff and young Charles Mallison. Ratliff is a kind of folksy and comic version of T. S. Eliot's Tiresias, a figure of great understanding and broad sympathy. His opinion of things is usually proven to be the most reliable; his breadth of sympathy extends at last even to embrace Flem Snopes, his arch-enemy. As the best of Faulkner's readers have noticed, Ratliff is the first and most consistent and most effective opponent of Snopesism—and especially, of course, of Flem. Good as Ratliff is in many ways, he is nevertheless shown to be human and fallible. Like another eminently admirable hero of Faulkner's fiction, Lucas Beauchamp, Ratliff is capable of arrant folly. In his first campaign against Flem, he tries to combat him on Flem's own terms, and the first third of the trilogy ends with Ratliff's momentary defeat. And it is interesting to note that in this piece of folly, Ratliff digging for gold in the ground of the Old Frenchman's Place is quite similar to Lucas seeking the buried coins in his land; and both Ratliff and Lucas have resorted to corruptions of the old lore of the divining rod used to find nature's true wealth, water: Ratliff has employed old Dick and his souped-up peachfork as Lucas employed the gold-divining machine. Beyond that, Ratliff's anti-Snopes career is steady and sensible and successful.

Ratliff is a good counter to Flem Snopes. Their backgrounds are similar, as V. K. relates. The impotent Flem is sexually neuter, and there is something faintly androgynous about Ratliff—another subtle reflection of his Tiresias identity, perhaps. He is calm and unflappable. Their very similarity, indeed, facilitates Faulkner's expression of their crucial differences. Ratliff is much closer in character to Wallstreet Panic than to Flem, and it is significant that Wall refuses Flem's offer of financial aid at an embarrassing moment in his young business life and accepts that offered by Ratliff; and it is appropriate that Ratliff be Wall's partner in the business as a consequence.

We recognize that Ratliff is, by his own admission, intimately involved in the final pageant of Snopes self-destruction; but his involvement is mainly that of commentator, the voice of cautious advice and interpretation. His "guilt" in Flem's murder is that he did nothing to prevent it other than to comment upon what Gavin and Linda were in fact preparing in their efforts to free Mink from prison. Ratliff stands by, steadily commenting, and watches as Fate or Divine Justice uses the available instruments to achieve Its ends. His goodness, as we have seen it throughout the trilogy, is a cause for optimism; and Ratliff holds an important and rather distinct place beside Dilsey, Byron Bunch, Gail Hightower, the MacCallums, Lucas Beauchamp, Uncle Buck and Uncle Buddy, and finally Chick Mallison.

Chick Mallison has been well prepared for his role in the Snopes trilogy (and we have been well prepared to accept and understand that role) by his experience at the side of Aleck Sander (to form a later equivalent of the Bayard-Ringo pair of *The Unvanquished*) in *Intruder in the Dust*. Lucas Beauchamp has been more successful with young Chick Mallison than Sam Fathers was with young Isaac

McCaslin. Chick could well say—altering Isaac's empty claim about Sam's influence—"Lucas Beauchamp set me free." He has also had the advantage of listening to the cerebral wisdom of his Uncle Gavin and to the vital common sense (the visceral wisdom) of V. K. Ratliff. Only quietly and almost covertly does Faulkner establish Chick's claim to be the final hopeful hero, at least in clear potential, of the Yoknapatawpha Saga, as though Chick were that man of the future who will not only endure but prevail. Increasingly, as the trilogy moves toward its close, Chick assumes a critical attitude toward his Uncle Gavin. He never really moves beyond the boundary of respect, but Chick is a man now, in *The Mansion;* that baptism we witnessed in the presence of Lucas Beauchamp early in *Intruder* has been confirmed by Chick's passing through the alembic of his war experience. And his judgment of Gavin, often only tacit and implicit, focusses on the most crucial and significant aspect of his uncle's failure. He ponders the possibility of Gavin's having made love to Linda Snopes Kohl, wonders why not, and offers the persuasive explanation of Gavin's lacking the fire of a Paris or of a Manfred de Spain. But a more telling and more comprehensive judgment of Gavin as the good, weak hero—the Faulknerian tragic failure—is eloquently implicit at every pause in his explanation of man's responsibility: "We are too old, too tired, have lost the capacity to believe in ourselves—"

> "Damn it," his uncle said. "I said good day."
> "Yes sir," Charles said. "In just a moment. Because quote the United States, America: the greatest country in the world if we can just keep on affording it unquote. Only let 'afford' read 'depend on God.' Because He saved you this time, using V. K. Ratliff of course as His instrument. Only next time Ratliff may be off somewhere selling somebody a sewing machine or a radio . . . and God may not be able to put His hand on him in time. So what you need is to learn how to trust in God without depending on Him. In fact, we need to fix things so He can depend on us for a while. Then He wont need to waste Himself being everywhere at once."[P. 321]

Chick Mallison is the healthy Horatio who will remain after the band of angels have carried off the ailing Gavin-Hamlet. In such as Chick we can put our hope.

Envoi

Though he is captive
his mighty singing
says, satisfaction is a lowly
thing, how pure a thing is joy.
This is mortality,
this is eternity.

Marianne Moore, "What Are Years?"

mediate descendants, and that of the rise and threatened success of the traditionless, vulgar, and grossly immoral rednecks.[11]

It is the case with Faulkner, as with Balzac, Zola, and perhaps Proust, that each individual novel is satisfactory as a discrete item; yet the whole of the Saga is impressively more than the sum of its parts. In that respect the Saga resembles certain works of Faulkner's contemporaries which are made up of satisfactorily separable pieces but which are far richer in their totality—Sherwood Anderson's *Winesburg, Ohio,* Joyce's *Dubliners,* Hemingway's *In Our Time.* And Faulkner's *The Unvanquished* and *Go Down, Moses* are themselves interesting examples of the same composite form.

The unity of the Saga is due, in part, to the consistent geographic setting of the novels, Faulkner's postage stamp of native soil—Yoknapatawpha County with its capital in Jefferson. In this, the Yoknapatawpha Saga resembles *Dubliners* and *Winesburg, Ohio* in the consistent reliance on specific setting as unifying device. The unity of Faulkner's Saga is due also to the regular reappearance of various Yoknapatawpha inhabitants—generations of them, indeed: the old pseudoaristocratic families of Sartorises, Compsons, and De Spains; the solid white peasantry of MacCallums, Bookwrights, and Tulls; the black families of Dilsey and Roskus, Molly and Lucas, Ringo, and Aleck Sander; and the poor whites and rednecks like the Gowries, the Armstids, the Bundrens, and of course the Snopeses. It is not simply that the novels resume and further develop the careers of these families as the main concerns of their plots—as *The Unvanquished* completes *Sartoris* by flashback and *Absalom, Absalom!* similarly completes *The Sound and the Fury, Requiem for a Nun* completes *Sanctuary,* and *The Town* and *The Mansion* complete the trilogy begun with *The Hamlet;* it is, further, that we find passing references in a given novel to other characters and events than those with which that particular novel is concerned—characters, events, and careers which belong to other parts of the Saga, and not even always to parts already published. Sometimes, indeed, these passing references seem almost like little loose ends that simply don't "belong"—until one has read the whole of the Saga, finished the chronicle, and sees the ultimate connections.

The Saga, then, does not develop as a steady chronological progression. It has a significant informing structure. It divides readily into two parts, what I have called two "movements": the first (from *Sartoris* through *The Unvanquished*) is defined by the two accounts of

[margin annotations: "misspelled McCallum", "see Patawa"]

But he must read it again. He could not remember the whole shape of the thing.

> Virginia Woolf, *To the Lighthouse,*
> "The Window," XIX

XIV

The Yoknapatawpha Comedy

The Yoknapatawpha novels, taken together, express a fundamental faith in mankind—that faith which Faulkner uttered in his Nobel Prize acceptance speech: "I decline to accept the end of man. . . . I believe that man will not merely endure: he will prevail."[1] As we have seen, the richly realistic "record of man" as it appears in these novels also gives expression to the persistent themes responsible for the sense of affirmation and optimism arising from the fiction—the theme of the Self-Destructiveness of Evil and the theme of the Second Chance (or the Quo Vadis theme). We have seen that those characters who act in the service of evil are regularly frustrated and ultimately provoke their own defeat—both those who actively pursue evil ends and those who passively serve evil ends by failing to do what they know is good. These latter are often the intelligent and perhaps even well-intentioned characters, principally Horace Benbow, Quentin Compson, Isaac McCaslin, and Gavin Stevens—men whose failure of courage and, hence, of love prevents them from acting on their good ideals. They are Faulkner's quasi-tragic heroes; they are tragically self-destructive. And while we have seen that many of Faulkner's characters fail to grasp the Second Chance when it is presented to them, we have also seen that not all fail. The blessed few, the Saving Remnant,[2] emphatically exhibit "a soul, a spirit capable of compassion and sacrifice and endurance." Not only do they discount, finally, the inevitability of the tragic careers of Faulkner's "good, weak heroes," they also complement effectively those self-destructive characters who flourish briefly in the service of evil.

better here

I would by no means suggest that Faulkner was always quite clear about and consciously aware of his intentions. Like most artists he tended to discover his proper themes in the process of developing his stories, to recognize his intentions during the task of revision—and especially revision of short story material for inclusion in his novels. Yet the very persistence of these themes suggests that a singleness of purpose—whenever, and however consciously, recognized by the author—did indeed motivate the creation of the Yoknapatawpha novels. The consistency of expression in the development of these themes yields a unity of impression; and it is perhaps for that reason that the Yoknapatawpha fiction has come commonly to be called a Saga.

It is well over a quarter of a century since Malcolm Cowley quietly observed that Faulkner's Yoknapatawpha fiction comprises a single unified work. "It sometimes seems to me," he wrote, ". . . that all the people of the imaginary county, black and white, townsmen, farmers, and housewives, have played their parts in one connected story."[3] Other critics since then have at times briefly assented to that observation, but I think no one has seriously examined the implications of Mr. Cowley's perceptive remark and thus grasped its profundity.[4] *NO!* It is frequently noted that the work of a major novelist does exhibit a peculiar unity; but the unity to be found (and which I believe Mr. Cowley observed) in Faulkner's Yoknapatawpha fiction is the kind of unity one might expect in a single novel—not only persistence of theme, setting, and characters but also the progress and development, the effect of cumulation from *Sartoris* to *The Mansion*, that convey the sense of organic unity and focussed significance that one gets from a single novel. The baker's dozen of Faulkner's Yoknapatawpha novels are indeed very much a single opus. In this respect the Yoknapatawpha Saga resembles Zola's fictional history of the Rougon-Macquart family, or Proust's extended chronicle, *A la recherche du temps perdu*, or, best of all, Balzac's *Comédie humaine*.

We have biographer Joseph Blotner's word for it that "As for prose fiction, there was no doubt in Faulkner's mind, or Phil Stone's, about who was the greatest artist in the field. It was Balzac."[5] And it is interesting to consider what in that writer's work particularly appealed to Faulkner. He told Cynthia Grenier (in September 1955), "I like the fact that in Balzac there is an intact world of his own. His people don't just move from page one to page 320 of one book. There is continuity between them all like a blood-stream which flows from

page one on through page 20,000 of one book. The same blood, muscle and tissue binds the characters together."[6] He said essentially the same thing to Jean Stein vanden Heuvel, and later in the interview gave the familiar account of his discovery of Yoknapatawpha.

> Q: What happened to you between *Soldiers Pay* and *Sartoris*—that is what caused you to begin the Yoknapatawpha Saga?
> Faulkner: With *Soldiers Pay* I found out that writing was fun. But I found out after that not only each book had to have a design but the whole output or sum of an artist's work had to have a design. . . . Beginning with *Sartoris* I discovered that my own little postage stamp of native soil was worth writing about. . . . [7]

One feels that the informing design of the whole Saga had existed in Faulkner's imagination from the outset of his career—or from the middle twenties, at least—and was constantly available to him, and that for any given story he had merely to reach in and break off a convenient piece from the rich basic stock. Or, to borrow from Malcolm Cowley's apt metaphor, to cut another plank from the living tree:

> All his books in the Yoknapatawpha saga are part of the same living pattern. It is this pattern, and not the printed volumes in which part of it is recorded, that is Faulkner's real achievement. . . . All the separate works are . . . like wooden planks that were cut, not from a log, but from a still living tree.[8]

The available evidence proves the soundness of Mr. Cowley's observation and the aptness of his metaphor. Faulkner frequently explained, during the middle fifties, that he had conceived the whole story of the swarming Snopeses instantaneously—"like a bolt of lightning lights up a landscape and you see everything but it takes time to write it, and this story I had in my mind for about thirty years. . . ."[9] And the testimony of the "Father Abraham" story indicates clearly enough that he had at least the broad, general scheme of the Snopes plague in his mind in the middle twenties. (It was further fleshed out, tentatively, in Faulkner's letter to Robert Haas in 1930.)[10] Furthermore, at about the same time he wrote the extensive *Flags in the Dust* (out of which *Sartoris* was carved by Ben Wasson for publication). Before 1929, then, Faulkner had set down the two complementary stories that would be his principal literary concerns for the next thirty years—that of the decadent Southern pseudoaristocracy and its im-

Sartoris history which bracket it, and the second (from *The Hamlet* through *The Mansion*) by the initial and the final volumes of the Snopes trilogy which bracket it. Two additional unifying threads which help bind the two parts are: (1) the metamorphosis of Horace Benbow into Gavin Stevens, and (2) the return of the sewing-machine salesman, whom we first met as V. K. Suratt in *Sartoris,* as V. K. Ratliff in *The Hamlet,* where he begins his anti-Snopes campaign which burgeons through the trilogy. And the final volume, as I have indicated in the preceding chapter, successfully concludes both the Snopes trilogy and the Yoknapatawpha Saga as a whole. If Faulkner did not "break the pencil" after completing *The Mansion,* he abandoned it in favor of an instrument of softer lead to set down *The Reivers.*

The mode of nostalgia dominates the first movement of the Saga; its concern is with the past, its view "back-looking," and its progress generally retrogressive. The stories of the first two novels (*Sartoris* and *The Sound and the Fury*) find their completion respectively in the last novel of this movement (*The Unvanquished*), which is a flashback to a time two generations earlier, and in the second last (*Absalom, Absalom!*), which is a flashback to a much more recent past but contains within it material contemporary with that of *The Unvanquished*—the Civil War. This first movement seems concerned with answering such questions as Why did the South fall? Why did God let the South lose the Civil War? What legacy has been left from antebellum days? The action of this movement serves to discover the evil that was gnawing at the base of the glorious antebellum Southern structure and caused it to topple, to identify the consequent evil that poisons the modern postbellum world, and to recognize the virtue of the unspoiled, simple people who have remained in touch with and so been nourished by the source of Good. The mode of anticipation dominates the second movement of the Saga—and it is increasingly hopeful anticipation; its concern is with the present and the future, its view forward looking, and its progress advancement. If the first movement has seemed to emphasize human failure—of courage, of love, of responsibility—the second even more clearly emphasizes success. The second movement as a whole may, indeed, be seen as predominantly a successful grasping of the Second Chance, even as the first movement predominantly expresses the Self-Destructiveness of failure, that failure which results from the evil of man's inhumanity. The second movement seems to pose the

single question: How can the fallen South be redeemed?—i.e., given
the failure of the pseudoaristocratic way and the subsequent destructive dominance of the plague of Snopesism and redneckism, where
can be found the heroic qualities needed to redeem fallen society?
The coin of evil here shows its "democratic" face—the obverse of the
"aristocratic," with which the first movement principally dealt.

Questionable

These two movements of the Saga—the two acts of this drama—are
further united by the persistent development of the career of the
familiar Faulknerian "good, weak hero." In reading through the
whole opus of the Yoknapatawpha Saga, one has the same sense of
following the career of a definite protagonist as in reading Hemingway's *In Our Time* or, indeed, Eliot's *The Waste Land*. And the Yoknapatawpha protagonist is strikingly consistent. He is intelligent, full of
rhetoric and exalted moral principles, but afraid of life's actuality; he
is thus fundamentally an escapist and consequently a figure of impotence. He is romantically chivalrous yet loveless, despite his characteristic incestuousness or nympholepsy. His love (or lust) is merely cerebral; his virtue mainly theoretic. He is wise and sensitive enough to
define most of the threatening evils of his world, but lacks the courage
to oppose those evils effectively. He represents the antebellum, white,
psuedoaristocratic establishment, and he usually defines the principal
evil as the political, social, and moral threat posed by the rising rednecks—focussed in the Snopeses and chiefly in Flem. He presents
himself as the principal opponent to that threat, but his opposition is
verbal merely, like that of a member of a debating team. He is usually,
of course, singularly ineffectual. His name is Horace Benbow or
Quentin Compson or Isaac McCaslin or Gavin Stevens.

He yearns to slough off the legacy of responsibility he has inherited as a burden from his predecessors, and the legacy involves responsibility for the condition of the Negroes—the transmitted curse
of slavery—and for the very rise of the rednecks. And while the
redneck threat is not quite so clearly defined in the first movement
of the Saga as it will be in the second, it is evident enough. The
spreading stain of Snopesism is already detectable and even its ultimate achievement distinctly anticipated there. *Sartoris* retains, from
both the "Father Abraham" manuscript and *Flags in the Dust,* the
prophetic thumbnail sketch of Flem Snopes's success.

> Flem, the first Snopes, had appeared unheralded one day behind the
> counter of a small restaurant on a side street, patronized by country
> folk. With this foothold and like Abraham of old, he brought his blood

and legal kin household by household, individual by individual, into town, and established them where they could gain money. Flem himself was presently manager of the city light and water plant, and for the following few years he was a sort of handy man to the municipal government; and three years ago, to old Bayard's profane astonishment and unconcealed annoyance, he became vice president of the Sartoris bank, where already a relation of his was a bookkeeper.[12]

The protagonist's unwillingness to accept real responsibility for the world he has created—or at least for the conditions his predecessors created and willed to him—is expressed in his fundamental exclusiveness. He can be friendly and protectively avuncular with the Negroes and his white inferiors, but he will involve himself seriously only with his own kind. His exclusiveness is given dramatic expression in the protagonist's typical incestuous tendencies. We find this in Horace Benbow's attitude toward Narcissa, in Quentin's toward Caddy, in Henry Sutpen's toward Judith (which Quentin sees as a startling reflection of his own situation), and even in the enforced relationship of Colonel John Sartoris and Drusilla Hawk. But this incestuous love remains theoretic, cerebral, for it never achieves physical consummation. The protagonist moves through a world which is (certainly for him, at least) largely loveless—for he has made it so; and he moves relentlessly to his own defeat, for his bent is fundamentally suicidal.

The significance of the weakness, of the impotence and futility of the protagonist is augmented in the first movement of the Saga by the added dimension of the specific evil of racial discrimination, of slavery and its legacy, which is a central concern of *Light in August* and *Absalom, Absalom!* The last phase of this movment, however, presents the strong implicit statement of *The Unvanquished*—that each generation, each cycle of the wheel, needs and may indeed effect the return of a truly heroic champion who embodies the redeeming and sustaining virtues, and who will act on them; that is Bayard Sartoris.

In the second movement of the Saga the career of the protagonist (now consistently Gavin Stevens) shows a steady decline, in spite of his helpful discussions with Temple Drake in *Requiem for a Nun;* and that decline persists precipitously into the terminal phase, *The Mansion.* Yet as we proceed through the second movement we find that *Intruder in the Dust* has begun the development of what will become a most encouraging figure, properly part of the Saving Remnant, who

will increase in wisdom as in stature through the balance of the
second movement of the Saga to emerge finally (in *The Mansion*) as a
proper hero—the man the protagonist is never able to become, in
fact something very close to the modern equivalent of Bayard Sartoris as he is developed in *The Unvanquished*, a Second-Chance Bayard:
Charles "Chick" Mallison, nephew of Gavin Stevens.

The important idea discussed at length by Gavin and Temple in
Requiem—that good not only can but must come out of evil—is realized in the emergence and progress of Wallstreet Panic Snopes. In his
review of the clan, Montgomery Ward Snopes has explained with
pleasant irony that Eck and Wall are "our shame": for they are atypi-
cal Snopeses. I would reemphasize my opposition to the frequent
suggestion (even apparently supported by some of Faulkner's subsequent comments) that Wall and his father are not really Snopeses at
all. In a sense they are not, of course, for they do not behave like
typical Snopeses. But Faulkner made them part of the clan as though
to insist on the idea that from the heart of this most despicable and
threatening group could arise a useful and admirable human character. Wall has the necessary virtues of courage and industry and
compassion and responsibility, and he has the wit to rely, in time of
financial difficulty, upon the aid of Ratliff while refusing the aid of
Flem. [13] And in those two, Wall and Ratliff, we have two more members of the Saving Remnant who have emerged clearly and hopefully
again at the end of the trilogy; with them, of course, is the figure of
the young man Charles Mallison, who is the potential hero of the new
era.

The central *agon* of the Saga has been resolved; yet it has in a
sense ended in what seems to be a stalemate. The theme of the Self-
Destructiveness of Evil has closely embraced both protagonist and
antagonist: both are figures of impotence. Nevertheless, the basic
conflict sustained throughout the Saga has involved two impotent
forces; and it has been a conflict between two sorts of evil, either of
which, if triumphant, would prevent true progress in the modern
world—neither could effectively "redeem the time." By cancelling
each other out in impotent stalemate they leave the field open to the
enduring Saving Remnant and to the emergence of the potentially
redemptive figure of the true hero. Chick Mallison has been well
prepared by his early association with the powerful Lucas Beauchamp and also with Aleck Sander, and by the precepts of his uncle
Gavin and the common sense of V. K. Ratliff. He has furthermore

been tested in the recent war—and a war, it is worth noting in this context, that is not quite of his own making, in contrast to the crucial war which involved his Sartoris and Compson predecessors in the 1860s. If Chick in all this is reminiscent of Bayard Sartoris, he is yet something of a modern, democratic equivalent of Bayard. The young Sartoris did, after all, belong to the pseudoaristocracy of the antebellum world, and it is precisely the absence of such as he in the modern, postbellum world that has been the motive force through much of the Saga's searching concern.

With the establishing of the potential of Chick Mallison at the close of *The Mansion* the Saga has really completed its cycle, which began with the figure of the superannuated Bayard and his incapacitated heir—grandson of the same name—and ends with a capable and figurative heir, a "new Bayard" named Charles, who participates in the final and distinctly hopeful expression of the theme of the Second Chance. The Saga, then, comes to a successful resolution, a complete and satisfying denouement. The sense of completeness derives in part from the brief resumption of several narrative motifs from earlier pieces of the Saga in order to bring them to conclusion, in part from the impression of unity focussed by the composite protagonist engaged in a persistent *agon,* in part from the culmination of that *agon* with the cancelling out of impotent protagonist and antagonist and thus the fruitful resolution of the Saga's consistent dominant themes. The resolution is not only successful but inescapably hopeful as it leaves us with the distinct emergence of a new and legitimate hero, the young representative of the constant Saving Remnant.

> Question: Sir, it means that your basic conception of life is optimistic?
> [Faulkner]: Yes.[14]

The Yoknapatawpha Saga is our modern American divine comedy.

Notes

Introduction

1. William Faulkner, *Essays, Speeches and Public Letters by William Faulkner,* ed. James B. Meriwether (New York: Random House, 1965), p. 120 (hereafter cited as *Essays, Speeches*).

2. Walter Brylowski, *Faulkner's Olympian Laugh: Myth in the Novels* (Detroit: Wayne State University Press, 1968), p. 15. Mr. Brylowski has perceived, although given rather incidental notice to, an idea which Faulkner consistently develops and which I consider a dominant theme: "The function of his mythic analogues becomes an exploration of evil beyond the bounds of morality. It is a mode allowing him to treat in narrative form his vision of a world permeated with evil and yet to balance this with his faith that evil will, in the long run, consume itself while the 'verities'—courage, honor, love—will maintain their static nobility and allow men to 'endure.' "

3. Quoted from Frederick L. Gwynn and Joseph L. Blotner, eds., *Faulkner in the University* (New York: Random House, Vintage Books, 1959), p. 27. I am further encouraged to call this the "Quo Vadis Theme" since that is the title of one of the novels of Henryk Sienkiewicz (another Nobel laureate), whom Faulkner much admired. See Joseph L. Blotner, *Faulkner: A Biography,* 2 vols. (New York: Random House, 1974), pp. 1271, 1351, and 1474 for mention of Sienkiewicz.

4. Matthew Arnold, "Numbers; or the Majority and the Remnant," in *Philistinism in England and America,* The Complete Prose Works of Matthew Arnold, vol. 10, ed. Robert H. Super (Ann Arbor: University of Michigan Press, 1974), pp. 147, 150, 151.

5. In his recent book, *William Faulkner: Toward Yoknapatawpha and Beyond* (New Haven: Yale University Press, 1978) (hereafter cited as *Toward Yoknapatawpha*), Mr. Cleanth Brooks offers this comment: "Whatever . . . the merits of the somewhat simplified novel that [Ben Wasson] managed to produce, the reader of the 1970's will probably prefer *Flags in the Dust* over *Sartoris.* For his decision will scarcely be based on consid-

erations of literary accomplishment alone, or even primarily" (pp. 390–91). The implications there are most pertinent: I have based my choice of *Sartoris* over *Flags* on my sense of "literary accomplishment," although I share the gratitude of Mr. Brooks and others that *Flags* is now easily available for the interested student.

6. Edmond L. Volpe, *A Reader's Guide to William Faulkner* (New York: Noonday Press, 1965), pp. 344, 345, 348; and Blotner, *Faulkner: A Biography*, p. 1793.

7. Blotner, *Faulkner: A Biography*, p. 1794.

8. Michael Millgate, *The Achievement of William Faulkner* (New York: Random House, 1966), p. 292 (hereafter cited as *Achievement*).

Chapter I

1. *Faulkner in the University*, p. 27.

2. *Sartoris* (New York: New American Library, Signet Books, 1961), p. 103; subsequent references will be to this edition and will be given parenthetically in the text.

3. Mr. Cleanth Brooks claims that "Narcissa, in her fear and distrust of men, is also epicene in the sense of 'sexless.' The adjective is accurate in this instance, for though she is to bear Bayard Sartoris a son, her marriage to him is a disaster" (*Toward Yoknapatawpha*, p. 166). But both *Flags* and *Sartoris* make it clear that marriage for Bayard is always a disaster because of his bereft grief, and not because either of his wives is sexless. Mr. Brooks later observes (and quite convincingly), on the matter of Byron Snopes's letters to her, that "Narcissa was ashamed . . . but at the same time she was titillated and vaguely excited" (p. 173). That is hardly the response of a "sexless" woman.

4. At the University of Virginia, Faulkner gave this response to a question about young Bayard: " . . . that one of the twins really wasn't brave and knew it. His dead brother was the braver . . . the one that survived not only had suffered the psychotic injury of having lost a twin, but also he would have to say to himself, The best one of us died, the brave one died, and he no longer wanted to live, actually. He came back home but he probably had no good reason to live . . . " (*Faulkner in the University*, p. 250). *Flags in the Dust* offers much more explicit evidence of the superiority of Johnny and of Bayard's reaction to the loss of his brother. *Sartoris* is able to make its point with greater economy and subtlety.

5. Earlier evidence can be found in such passages as these: " 'I'm glad I have you instead of one of those Sartorises, Horry.' She laid her hand quickly and lightly on his thin knee" (p. 144). "Narcissa reached her hand beneath the table and touched her brother's knee again. 'I *am* glad you're home, Horry' " (p. 149). And later, on learning that Horace plans to marry Belle, Narcissa makes an instructive decision (temporarily): " 'I shall never marry,' she told herself. Men . . . that was where unhappiness lay, getting men into your life. 'And if I couldn't keep Horace, loving him as I did. . . .' She read on, lost from mutable things"

(p. 212). *Flags*, again, offers much more, and more explicit, evidence. Rather surprisingly, then, Mr. Brooks insists that Horace harbors no incestuous thoughts concerning Narcissa: "For him, her virginity is quite literally inviolable, for although he dotes on Narcissa, she *is* his sister, and Horace has not the slightest intention of committing incest. He is content to hold her hand occasionally and to tell her she is 'the bride of quietude,' as if she were a kind of animated Grecian urn" (*Toward Yoknapatawpha*, p. 166). While he may have no intention of actually committing incest, the desire is distinctly and manifestly expressed—and even to some extent mutually shared. See specifically my further comments, pp. 17–18 of this volume.

6. See above, p. 13.

Chapter II

1. Faulkner's term. See *Faulkner in the University*, p. 6.
2. Robert A. Jelliffe, ed., *Faulkner at Nagano* (Tokyo: Kenyusha, 1962), pp. 103 ll. 24–27, 104 ll. 1–6, 9–10.
3. *The Sound and the Fury* (New York: Random House, Vintage Books, 1954), p. 411; subsequent references will be to this edition and will be given parenthetically in the text.
4. Mark Spilka, "Quentin Compson's Universal Grief," *Contemporary Literature* 11 (1970): 456–57.
5. T. S. Eliot, "Baudelaire," *Selected Essays*, new ed. (New York: Harcourt, Brace and World, 1950), p. 380.
6. In his illuminating study of the novel, André Bleikasten makes this helpful comparison of the attitudes of Quentin and Dilsey: "While for Quentin there is an unbridgeable gap between the temporal and the timeless, Dilsey's eternity, instead of being an immobile splendor *above* the flux of time, is already present and at work *in* time, embodied in it just as the word was made flesh. Time, then, is no longer felt as endless and senseless repetition, nor is it experienced as an inexorable process of decay. It does have a pattern, since history has been informed from its beginnings by God's design. And it can be redeemed and vanquished, but, as T. S. Eliot puts it in the *Four Quartets:* 'Only through time time is conquered.' Which is to say that the hour of its final defeat will be the hour of its fulfillment and reabsorption into eternity." See *The Most Splendid Failure: Faulkner's "The Sound and the Fury"* (Bloomington, Ind.: Indiana University Press, 1976), p. 193 (hereafter cited as *Splendid Failure*).
7. M. Bleikasten has made a similar observation: "Firmly rooted in the eschatalogical doctrine of Christianity, Dilsey's concept of time is theological, not chrono-logical. . . . Given the religious context of Easter where they occur, her words obviously refer to the beginning and end of time, to the Alpha and Omega of Christ" (*Splendid Failure*, p. 194).
8. *Faulkner in the University*, p. 18.
9. Carvel Collins, "The Pairing of *The Sound and the Fury* and *As I Lay Dying*," *Princeton University Library Chronicle* 18 (1957): 116,118. James

Dean Young, in "Quentin's Maundy Thursday," *Tulane Studies in English* 10 (1960): 143–51, rehearses Collins's argument insofar as it covers Quentin, and adds some further illustration of the parallel with Maundy Thursday; he also comes to a similar conclusion, and his comment on Ben (essentially a reiteration of Collins's position) is to be noted: "Benjy . . . is an ineffectual Christ since he cannot intervene for others and cannot become a savior. . . . Benjy is . . . statically being harrowed himself on that Saturday between the Crucifixion and the Resurrection" (p. 151). I discuss the role of Benjy as "savior" later in this chapter. See also my article, "Hawthorne, Faulkner and the Pearl of Great Price," *Papers of the Michigan Academy of Science, Arts, and Letters* 52 (1967): 391–401 (hereafter cited as Michigan Academy Papers).

10. Hyatt Waggoner, *William Faulkner: From Jefferson to the World* (Lexington, Ky.: University of Kentucky Press, 1959), p. 70.

11. The term is the late Frederick J. Hoffman's. See his *William Faulkner,* Twayne Series vol. 1 (New York: College and University Press, 1961), pp. 33 ff., especially p. 36: "the 'good weak hero' . . . is 'good' because he *intends* to act positively and with merit; but his weaknesses, whatever they are, quite definitely prevent his success in having a moral effect." Hoffman's categorization of characters under this heading, however, differs somewhat from mine.

12. *Faulkner in the University,* pp. 245–46.

13. Cf. Collins and Young; see note 9 above.

14. André Bleikasten's *Splendid Failure* offers a thoroughly detailed and convincing refutation of the argument that *The Sound and the Fury* is ultimately a pessimistic novel. M. Bleikasten has also assembled an impressive array of data (similar in many instances to mine) that would support the argument that the novel is, on the contrary, clearly optimistic in expression; yet he refuses to reach that obvious (to me) conclusion and satisfies himself (and perhaps others) by observing that Faulkner makes neither pessimistic nor optimistic reading inevitable, but leaves that choice to the reader.

Chapter III

1. *Faulkner in the University,* pp. 87, 207; cf. pp. 113, 115.

2. *The Mansion* (New York: Random House, Vintage Books, 1959), p. 271.

3. *As I Lay Dying* (New York: Random House, Vintage Books, 1964), p. 98; subsequent references will be to this edition and will be given parenthetically in the text.

4. In his useful *A Reader's Guide to William Faulkner* Edmond L. Volpe does well to associate Bundrens and Snopeses; yet, in emphasizing the shared viciousness, he seems to me unfair to the Bundrens: "The doings of the Bundren family are of a piece with the avaricious enterprises of Flem and his relatives in the Snopes stories and novels" (p. 127).

5. Millgate tells us that this information came from an interview with Mr. Tate; see *Achievement,* p. 111.

6. The motif of paths and roads to be followed—the horizontal weft of the novel's patterned fabric—is introduced in the opening sentence of the novel: "Jewel and I [Darl] come up from the field, following the path in single file." And the three initial paragraphs begin the characterization of these two brothers. The path "turns and circles the cotton-house at four soft right angles and goes on across the field again," and Darl follows the path. Jewel, however, here early demonstrates his rigidity and inflexibility by going right through the cotton-house via its windows: "Jewel, . . . looking straight ahead, steps in a single stride through the window. Still staring straight ahead, his pale eyes like wood set into his wooden face, he crosses the floor in four strides with the rigid gravity of a cigar store Indian dressed in patched overalls and endued with life from the hips down, and steps in a single stride through the opposite window and into the path again just as I come around the corner" (pp. 3–4).

7. *The Sound and the Fury*, pp. 34–35. Dilsey is the paradigm of the mentally and morally healthy in Faulkner's fiction, a health regularly associated with recognition of the fact of death as the crucial moment in human life. It is a bit surprising, then, to find David Williams proposing "the premise on which the whole story [of *As I Lay Dying*] might well be constructed: that in death there lies neither end nor beginning"—in his scholarly and provocative *Faulkner's Women: the Myth and the Muse* (Montreal and London: McGill-Queens University Press, 1977), p. 102 (hereafter cited as *Faulkner's Women*). That attitude would seem to blur the distinction Faulkner would constantly have his characters bear in mind. Cf. Bleikasten, note 8 below.

8. In an excellent study of the novel, André Bleikasten points to the importance of the attitude to Addie's death which various members of the family share—an attitude that suggests that most of them (Darl is always the exception) feel she is still alive:

> L'attitude des Bundren devant le cadavre d'Addie . . . nous retient surtout à cause de ce qu'elle révèle de leur attitude devant la mort. Attitude des plus ambiguës: la familiarité qui se noue entre les vivants et la morte. . . . Les Bundren . . . parlent d'Addie comme si elle était encore en vie. . . .
>
> Pour ces primitifs, il n'y a donc pas de séparation réelle entre la vie et la mort.

See his *As I Lay Dying* (Paris: Librairie Armand Colin, 1970), p. 137 (hereafter cited as *Dying*); and cf. Williams, note 7 above.

9. Judith Sutpen makes the distinction between "something that *was* once for the reason that it can die some day" and something that "cant be *is* because it never can become *was* because it cant ever die or perish . . ." (*Absalom, Absalom!*, [New York: Random House, Modern Library, 1951], pp. 127–28). In his carefully argued essay, "Enigmas of Being in *As I Lay Dying*," *Modern Fiction Studies* 16 (1970): 133–46 (hereafter cited as "Enigmas"), Robert Hemenway observes that Darl's musings on time

and being provide "an unequivocal identification of existence: time is life, the only measure of being, and this identification is the thematic center of *As I Lay Dying.* . . . Man is not immortal; he must face an eventual oblivion, the 'is-not' of human death, characterized by the loss of time" (pp. 141–42).

10. Bleikasten agrees that Cash's work on the coffin is a distraction, but suggests that the coffin may be, on the other hand, a mother surrogate like Jewel's horse and Vardaman's fish: "A voir Cash à ce point obnubilé par la fabrication et le transport du cercueil, l'on se demande s'il n'en a pas oublié le contenu. A moins que le cercueil soit pour lui ce que le cheval est pour Jewel, le poisson pour Vardaman: un objet transfert" (*Dying*, pp. 101–2).

11. The effect of this whole passage, heavy with the sense of animal vitality in the close dark, is to suggest that the yearning Dewey Dell is resorting to a surrogate for the absent Lafe by masturbating.

12. Cf. a briefer version of this image: as the wagon load passes Tull's, Darl observes, "We go on, with a motion so soporific, so dreamlike as to be uninferant of progress, as though time and not space were decreasing between us and it" (p. 101).

13. The most satisfying commentary on this matter specifically and on Darl's mixed musings on *being* generally, is Robert Hemenway's essay "Enigmas." Mr. Hemenway explains that "When Darl concludes . . . 'I am is,' he has unknowingly defined existence as consciousness itself, a definition that limits man's essence to the 'is' of present tense reality." Then, on Darl's persistent questioning of his knowledge of his own being, Hemenway adds: "A compulsion to ask such questions is critical, for it exhibits an awareness that living is not necessarily knowing. Darl is conscious of the uncertainty of existence . . . but Jewel is unaware, . . . his lack of consciousness confirms a virtual dehumanization, a condition suggested by his substitution of a horse for his mother" (p. 136).

14. See Iago's words to Brabantio (*Othello*, I. i. 17–18): "your daughter and the Moor are now making the beast with two backs."

15. *Faulkner in the University*, p. 111; my italics. And just here we might recall Faulkner's characterization of Jason Compson IV as "The first sane Compson since before Culloden and (a childless bachelor) hence the last," in the Appendix to *The Sound and the Fury*.

16. *Faulkner in the University*, p. 113.

17. See André Bleikasten's similar comment on Darl (*Dying*, p. 106): "Mais la folie de Darl est à vrai dire autre chose qu'un cas de pathologie mentale. Elle est détresse et désordre, mais elle est aussi savoir et poésie. De tous les personnages de *As I Lay Dying*, c'est sans doute ce Hamlet rustique qui entretien les rapports les plus étroits avec le romancier. Faulkner en fait son principal narrateur et, dans une certaine mesure, son délégué: si Cash est une image du romancier-artisan, Darl représente le romancier-poète." Later, M. Bleikasten augments this observation with an almost lyric comment, departing from Addie's statement on "words":

Pour tenu qu'en soit le fil, le langage possède donc ainsi le pouvoir de lier. Si le plus souvent il n'est que dissimulation et duperie, il n'exclut pas la possibilité d'une communication, fragile et éphémère sans doute, mais réelle. La création faulknérienne est un pari sur cette possibilité, avec toute l'inquiétude et toutes les incertitudes du pari. Elle est l'effort opiniâtre et jamais achevé du romancier pour construire la réalité dans son oeuvre à partir de l'irréalité des mots, et "l'échec splendide" qui couronne parfois cet effort. [P. 154]

Cf. Williams, *Faulkner's Women*, pp. 116–17.

18. *William Faulkner: the Abstract and the Actual* (Baton Rouge, La.: Louisiana State University Press, 1974), p. 176.
19. Broughton, p. 177.
20. "Enigmas," p. 144.

Chapter IV

1. Robert Penn Warren makes this most pertinent observation: " . . . the violation of nature will, we are told, be revenged by the violators on themselves. . . . In other words, for all their victories, the Popeyes and Jasons and Snopeses, have missed the only thing worth having: life." He adds, "further, if these violators and exploiters have no proper relation to nature, neither do they have a proper relation to the human community." See "Faulkner: The South, the Negro, and Time," in *Faulkner: a Collection of Critical Essays*, ed. Robert Penn Warren (Englewood Cliffs, N.J.: Prentice-Hall, 1966), pp. 255, 256 (hereafter cited as *Faulkner*).
2. *Sanctuary* (New York: Random House, Vintage Books, 1967), p. 4; subsequent references will be to this edition and will be given parenthetically in the text.

   The description of Popeye, especially the "stamped tin" metaphor, is obviously a distinct anticipation of the description of Flem Snopes as he appears in *The Hamlet* (1940). In fact, his general characterization and behavior in *Sanctuary* anticipate Faulkner's development of Flem in the Snopes trilogy: his unnaturalness or antinaturalness, his impotence, his sang-froid, even the peculiar circumstances of his death at the end of his maleficent career are all reminiscent of Popeye.
3. In a most perceptive essay of 1934 ("William Faulkner's *Sanctuary,*" *Saturday Review of Literature*, October 20), Dr. Lawrence S. Kubie observed: "one feels the incessant struggle of Benbow against his own impotence and powerlessness. . . . Far deeper than that lay his incestuous yearnings for his step-daughter. . . . He is stirred to a dim recognition of his own impulses when her picture is described 'as leaving upon his eye a soft and fading aftermath of invitation and voluptuous promise.' At this point he becomes nauseated. . . . In other words, as he becomes conscious of his intolerable and unacceptable impulses, he experiences a direct revulsion of feeling which causes him to be sick. . . ." See *Faulkner*, ed. Robert Penn Warren, p. 143.

4. Henry James, "Turgenieff," *French Poets and Novelists,* ed. Leon Edel (New York: Grosset and Dunlap, The Universal Library, 1964), p. 231.

5. The distinction made here anticipates that made by Horace's alter ego, Gavin Stevens, in *The Town* (New York: Random House, Vintage Books, 1957): Gavin groups himself momentarily with the lusty and masculine Hoake McCarron and Manfred de Spain (the two lovers of Eula Varner) as three gentlemen, but adds that "only two [of them] were men" (pp. 94–95).

6. *Requiem for a Nun* (1951), of course, clears up most of the problems which *Sanctuary* raises to plague Horace Benbow. We learn that Popeye Vitelli kept Temple to provide his alibi in the murder of Tommy, and that he "produced" her when the time came. We also learn that Red was a bouncer in the nightclub which Popeye owned and which was Popeye's headquarters. We are told by Temple herself what we can easily deduce from *Sanctuary* alone—i.e., that she rather liked the brothel and even the fascinating experience of living with Popeye. But while it is legitimate to resort to *Requiem* to seek answers to the puzzles in *Sanctuary,* one ought not use them as editorial supplements. *Sanctuary* is to be read intact in its place in the Saga and allowed to exert upon us the rather frightening influence of its mysterious and awful evil. After that influence has had its effect, *Requiem*'s answers to our questions can be taken up in their turn.

7. Aubrey Williams, "William Faulkner's 'Temple' of Innocence," *Rice Institute Pamphlets* 47 (1960): 51–67; quoted in Cleanth Brooks, *William Faulkner: The Yoknapatawpha Country* (New Haven: Yale University Press, 1963), p. 394 (hereafter cited as *Yoknapatawpha Country*).

8. See Dr. Kubie's apt comment that "it is Popeye's very figure which is concretely described in the story in words which make it a graphic representation of the phallus whose impotence is the root of the whole tragedy" (*Faulkner,* ed. Robert Penn Warren, p. 145).

9. Cf. Brooks, *Yoknapatawpha Country,* pp. 130–31, for a rather different and, I think, mistaken interpretation of Horace's character and observation on spring.

Chapter V

1. *Light in August* (New York: Random House, Vintage Books, 1972), p. 91. Subsequent references will be to this edition and will be given parenthetically in the text.

2. Although Mr. Cleanth Brooks is justified in objecting to a too facile comparison of Joe Christmas and Jesus Christ, we must not be blinded to certain patent similarities between the two. There has been little reason to miss those similarities since the publication of Hugh Holman's instructive essay, "The Unity of Faulkner's *Light in August*," *PMLA* 73 (1958): 155–66. And on the shared Christ-likeness of Benjy Compson and Joe Christmas, see my essay, "Hawthorne, Faulkner, and the Pearl of Great Price," Michigan Academy Papers.

3. The apt term comes from Alfred Kazin, "The Stillness of *Light in August*," in *Three Decades of Faulkner Criticism*, ed. Frederick J. Hoffman and Olga Vickery (East Lansing: Michigan State University Press, 1960), p. 248.

Chapter VI

1. It is difficult to understand Mr. Albert Guerard's vigorous denial that Quentin Compson of *Absalom, Absalom!* is the same Quentin Compson we met in *The Sound and the Fury* in his *The Triumph of the Novel: Dickens, Dostoevsky, Faulkner* (New York: Oxford University Press, 1976), especially p. 311. Yet a reason for it may be inferred from his contention that those two novels are "great autonomous novels, not two fragments of a *roman-fleuve* or Balzacian series, and our feelings for one Quentin should not control our feelings for the other" (p. 311). Certainly the two novels are not "fragments," for each is satisfactorily whole; but the connections Mr. Guerard would deny do not make the novels less whole (nor do similar feelings for the "two" Quentins): they merely enrich the two books. A more satisfactory comment is in Cleanth Brooks's "The Narrative Structure of *Absalom, Absalom!*," Appendix B of *Toward Yoknapatawpha*, p. 310. (I address this general question more fully in my concluding chapter.)

2. *Absalom, Absalom!* (New York: Random House, Modern Library, 1951), p. 378; subsequent references will be to this edition and will be given parenthetically in the text.

3. See also Sutpen's words to Quentin's grandfather: "that little boy who approached that door fifty years ago and was turned away, for whose vindication the whole plan was conceived and carried forward . . ." (p. 274). Cleanth Brooks casts some helpful light on Sutpen in Appendix A of his *Toward Yoknapatawpha*, "Thomas Sutpen: A Representative Southern Planter?": "Psychologically, Sutpen is the convert. Like Paul on the road to Damascus, he has been struck down by a blinding revelation. . . . Sutpen is held in the grasp of a cold dream. Like the convert, he outdoes in his vehement orthodoxy those generations old in the faith" (p. 293). He concludes with this interesting distinction: "the irony of Sutpen's life is (in part at least) that he was fixated on his image of the image of the plantation which for him was an abstract idea—since he had had scant participation in it as a lived experience—and that . . . Sutpen pursued an ideal of gracious ease and leisure, with a breathless ferocity" (p. 296).

4. See, for example, Ralph Behrens, "Collapse of Dynasty: the Thematic Center of *Absalom, Absalom!*," *PMLA* 8 (1974): 24–33. Mr. Behrens correctly finds the passages from 2 Samuel to provide the source for a central idea in the novel—that such an attempt to found a dynasty is hubristic and hence doomed to fail.

5. I was first alerted to the significance of Faulkner's use of the Cadmus myth in *Absalom* by an unpublished seminar paper by my former student, the late Grace Blakey.

6. An additional similarity between Sutpen and David may be seen dimly in Faulkner's faintly associating Bon with Christ: Charles Bon dies at age thirty-three!—at least according to his gravestone, "*Aged 33 years and 5 months*" (p. 190).

7. In attempting to expose Sutpen's error of believing that his recognition of Bon would be disastrous for him, Cleanth Brooks enquires, "What, in view of the laws and customs of the time, could Bon have done?" Brooks explains that "Sutpen could probably have outfaced any charge of bigamy, and by letting the community know that Bon was part Negro, could have disposed of any notion that Henry was not his legitimate heir" (*Toward Yoknapatawpha*, p. 298). And in a note to this passage, Brooks compares Sutpen to Carothers McCaslin (*Go Down, Moses*) and Col. John Sartoris (*The Unvanquished*), "planters who sired mulatto children." One can agree that Sutpen may have been mistaken; but the crucial item which Brooks does not confront is the matter of legitimatized miscegenation: Sutpen put aside his wife Eulalia because of her black blood. Similarly, Henry's objection to Bon's marrying Judith is, quite specifically, the threat not of incest but of miscegenation; and his objection to Bon's liaison with the New Orleans woman was that it was a morganatic *marriage*—a legitimatized union. We shall see another parallel to this attitude in Isaac McCaslin's reaction to Roth Edmonds's "doe" in "Delta Autumn" of *Go Down, Moses*.

Chapter VII

1. *The Unvanquished* (New York: Random House, Vintage Books, 1938), pp. 3–4; subsequent references will be to this edition and will be given parenthetically in the text.

2. John Lewis Longley, Jr., *The Tragic Mask: A Study of Faulkner's Heroes* (Chapel Hill: University of North Carolina Press, 1963), p. 182 (hereafter cited as *The Tragic Mask*).

3. In the prose introduction to part 3 of *Requiem for a Nun* Faulkner develops the attitude of such women as these, calling them, with significant irony, the "unvanquished." The passage follows a review of the immediately postwar years of Jefferson history, which emphasizes (appropriately, since it distinctly indicates the definite association in Faulkner's mind) the end of the career of Colonel John Sartoris:

> . . . only the aging unvanquished women were unreconciled, unreconcilable, reversed and irrevocably reverted against the whole moving unanimity of panorama until . . . they themselves had an illusion of motion, facing irreconcilably backward toward the old lost battles, the old aborted cause, the old four ruined years whose very physical scars ten and twenty and twenty-five changes of season had annealed back into the earth; . . . not only a century and an age, but a way of thinking died; . . . except [for] the women, the ladies, the unsurrendered, the irreconcilable. . . .

See *Requiem for a Nun* (New York: Random House, Vintage Books, 1975), pp. 205–7.

4. See the informative essay by my former student Gorman Beauchamp, "*The Unvanquished:* Faulkner's Oresteia," *Mississippi Quarterly* 23 (1970): 273–77.

5. Of course the ambiguity remains, but it is interesting to have Faulkner's comment (the memory of his intention, perhaps) in response to a question at the University of Virginia: "why is that sprig of verbena left on Bayard's pillow?" Faulkner replied, "although [Bayard] had violated Drusilla's traditions of an eye for an eye, she—the sprig of verbena meant that she realized that that [Bayard's confrontation with Redmond] took courage too and maybe more moral courage than to have drawn blood, or to have taken another step in a endless feud of an eye for an eye" (*Faulkner in the University,* p. 42).

Chapter VIII

1. *Faulkner in the University,* p. 193.
2. *The Hamlet* (New York: Random House, Vintage Books, 1959), p. 182; subsequent references will be to this edition and will be given parenthetically in the text.
3. James G. Watson, in *The Snopes Dilemma: Faulkner's Trilogy* (Coral Gables, Fla.: University of Miami Press, 1970), p. 44, blurs the distinction between Houston, on the one hand, and Ike and Mink Snopes, on the other: "No matter how grotesque their situations or how self-centered their motives, Ike, Houston, and Mink exhibit the same fundamental passion that Eula . . . inspires. Each, in varying degrees, is a responsive, generous, and dedicated lover possessed of an innate sense of honor." There is some similarity among the three, but the differences seem to me much more instructive. What Watson says about the three applies very well to Ike and Mink, but hardly at all (as I argue) to Houston. See my further discussion of Houston's case, pp. 149–50 herein, and of Mink's, pp. 158–60.
4. Professor Panthea Reid Broughton makes the same point briefly in her perceptive *William Faulkner: The Abstract and the Actual* (Baton Rouge, La.: Louisiana State University Press, 1976), p. 56.
5. *Go Down, Moses* (New York: Random House, Vintage Books, 1973), p. 102.

Chapter IX

1. *The Yoknapatawpha Country,* p. 244.
2. *Go Down, Moses* (New York: Random House, Vintage Books, 1973), p. 102. Subsequent references will be to this edition and will be given parenthetically in the text.
3. It is interesting to speculate on this error of Ike's—not that he recalled the sum as something less than fifty dollars, but that he recalled it as

thirty. It is more than likely that Ike's mind, full enough of the story of the Nazarene, made the association between his payment and the thirty pieces of silver paid to Judas for his notorious betrayal. The betrayal is for both, of course, typically reflexive: in each case the act is also a betrayal of the betrayor himself—is ultimately self-destructive. (I am grateful to my wife, Loretta, for drawing to my attention the significance of the specific figure of Ike's error.)

4. In this connection, see Christof Wegelin, " 'Endure' and 'Prevail': Faulkner's Modification of Conrad," *Notes and Queries* 219 (1974): 375–76.

5. If one is tempted to agree with Faulkner's later comment that Ike's wife had the ethics of a prostitute (see *Faulkner in the University*, pp. 275–76), one might consider that Ike has driven her to this extreme—that the responsibility for it rests squarely on the unwilling and evasive shoulders of Ike McCaslin.

6. One of the earliest critics to object firmly and intelligently to the overpraise of Ike and to see him as a frightened failure is David H. Stewart in his "The Purpose of Faulkner's Ike," *Criticism* 3 (1961): 333–42. My own early doubts about Ike were given distinct impetus by this essay.

7. *The Yoknapatawpha Country*, p. 268.

8. The last item in our knowledge of Roth Edmonds is provided by *Intruder in the Dust*; it is the final note of his general failure of responsibility, as we can hardly help but feel. Chick Mallison has learned of Lucas's arrest for murder and in spite of himself is concerned for Lucas's safety—and the threat of a lynch mob. He takes some comfort from the reasonable thought that "the constable had taken Lucas . . . and was now sitting over him with a shotgun (and Edmonds too of course by now; even a fool country constable would have had sense enough to send for Edmonds only four miles away even before hollering for the sheriff) . . . Edmonds (again something nagged for a second's flash at his attention) and the constable—would be two. . ." (Vintage Books, p. 28). Chick is then propelled into reluctant action by recalling that Edmonds was after all not available to assume responsibility for Lucas:

> . . . suddenly he remembered from nowhere what it was that had been nagging at his attention: Edmonds was not at home nor even in Mississippi; he was in a hospital in New Orleans being operated on for gallstones. . . . [P. 30]

Of course Roth has not intentionally made himself unavailable; it is just typical of his behavior to be absent when most needed. And it is significant, furthermore, that Faulkner should have made the point, almost gratuitously (it would appear), that Roth was away—"not at home nor even in Mississippi"—when his aid might have been especially invoked. (I am grateful to my wife for urging this recognition upon me.)

9. In an unpublished essay, "Gavin Stevens: Faulkner's Modern Quixote," my former student Michael J. McRee has seized upon the essence of Gavin: "The effects of this spiritual impotence are expressed by Gavin's

actions in *Light in August, Go Down, Moses,* and *Intruder in the Dust.* In all three novels, Gavin assumes the mantle of caretaker for the antebellum South. Instead of actively seeking the betterment of the Negro, the outward manifestation of the moral decay of the South, Gavin attempts to dispose of the evidence of that decay. . . ."

Chapter X

1. Because of his role in this and all subsequent novels of the Yokna- patawpha Saga, Gavin Stevens requires a special comment. The character of Gavin is in its inception closely contemporary with the creation of Horace Benbow and Quentin Compson, and is developed contempora- neously with the development of those two and of Isaac McCaslin. The stories gathered into *Knight's Gambit* were published during the same period as the novels in which those other three characters appeared, and in those stories the character of Gavin is sketched out. According to Meriwether, *The Literary Career of William Faulkner: A Bibliographical Study* (Princeton, N.J.: Princeton University Press, 1961), p. 175 (hereafter cited as Meriwether, *The Literary Career*), the writing of the earliest story dates from 1930, and the last two from 1946 and 1949. As we have seen, Gavin also appears briefly (but prophetically) in *Light in August* (1932) and more substantially in *Go Down, Moses* (1942) before emerging as a principal character in *Intruder in the Dust* (1948). Professor Millgate offers the cogent suggestion that "the stories in *Knight's Gambit* must be seen primarily as a series of more or less deliberate exercises on the way to his final conception and characterization of Gavin Stevens" as he appears in *Intruder* and subsequent novels (see *Achievement,* p. 267, and also pp. 268– 70). I would argue, rather, that the Gavin of *Knight's Gambit* is not the "real" Gavin Stevens but only one facet of the complete character—that facet we see reflected in his mild sleuthing skills in *Intruder.* In his reply to a question about the difference between Gavin in *Knight's Gambit* and Gavin in *The Town,* Faulkner made this observation (after explaining that the action of *The Town* precedes that of *Intruder*): "Well, he had got out of his depth. He had got into the real world. While he was—could be—a county attorney, an amateur Sherlock Holmes, then he was at home, but he got out of that. He got into a real world in which people anguished and suffered. . . . That is, he knew a good deal less about people than he knew about the law. . . . When he had to deal with people, he was an amateur, he was—at times he had a good deal less judgment than his nephew did" (*Faulkner in the University,* p. 140). I believe we can see that distinction already in *Intruder.*

As the Saga moves through the subsequent novels to its conclusion Gavin seems to be ubiquitous and to become in a sense dominant: he "absorbs" the character and function of Horace Benbow, Quentin Comp- son, and Isaac McCaslin—becomes in effect the paradigm of Faulkner's conception of the white Southern intellectual, inheritor of the antebel- lum Southern pseudoaristocrats. (I develop this argument and explain its significance for the Saga's unity and meaning in my concluding chapter, "The Yoknapatawpha Comedy.") And while the early depiction of this type (especially in Quentin) enjoys a good deal of his creator's sympathy, from *Intruder* onward (*Requiem for a Nun* is a slight exception) the treatment becomes increasingly antipathetic. Indeed, it seems almost as if in gathering together the *Knight's Gambit* stories Faulkner had wanted to bestow a last kindness on that version of Gavin Stevens before pursuing the depiction of his abysmal decline through the concluding volumes of the Saga.

2. *Intruder in the Dust* (New York: Random House, Vintage Books, 1972), p. 3; subsequent references will be to this edition and will be given parenthetically in the text.

3. Chick's reluctance to get involved in Lucas's dilemma has already been challenged by his recalling that Roth Edmonds, who ought to have been summoned immediately to assume responsibility by interceding on Lucas's behalf, is (significantly and symbolically) absent—not at home nor even in Mississippi, but in New Orleans. No matter for what reason, Roth's absence marks definitely enough the end of the McCaslin-Edmonds responsibility. Chick finally assumes that burden himself. (See chapter 9, note 9.)

4. *The Yoknapatawpha Country*, p. 421.

5. A friend of mine, a professor of English who knew William Faulkner for a number of years, expressed amazement and consternation at what he felt was my harsh treatment of Gavin Stevens (and of Quentin Compson); he explained that "Mr. Faulkner was himself very like Gavin Stevens." It is an embarrassing fact, further, that much of what Gavin says about "Sambo" in *Intruder* closely resembles what the *citizen* William Faulkner had to say in his defensive letters to editors and in some of his essays. Yet it is surely quite clear that the *novelist* William Faulkner has chastized characters like Gavin Stevens and exposed their regrettable sentiments and behavior. Not an entirely unfamiliar phenomenon, of course. In his most meaningful work, an artist may often project an aspect of himself, with which he is embarrassingly familiar and finds regrettable, into a fictional character to "punish" or "exorcize" it. Such behavior may even be therapeutic for a writer—may provide him with more satisfactory relief even than alcohol. It is certainly arguable that this was exactly the case with Faulkner. One recalls, in this connection, the late Edmund Wilson's comment that *Intruder* was Faulkner's reply to Northern critics of the South. The novel does offer Gavin Stevens's reply—and it is perhaps an echo of citizen-Faulkner's; but that is not at all the response of novelist-Faulkner, who is the person in whom we must be most interested and to whom we must feel most indebted.

Chapter XI

1. *Requiem for a Nun* (New York: Random House, Vintage Books, 1975), p. 147; subsequent references will be to this edition and will be given parenthetically in the text.

2. Panthea Reid Broughton, "*Requiem for a Nun:* No Part in Rationality," *The Southern Review* 8 (1972): 757. See also Hyatt Waggoner, "William Faulkner's Passion Week of the Heart," in *The Tragic Vision and the Christian Faith,* ed. Nathan A. Scott, Jr. (New York: Association Press, 1957), p. 314: "*Requiem for a Nun,* in short, seems to me to have for its *achieved* meaning a powerful statement of the need for redemption from sin, of the necessity for the acknowledgement and confession of sin, and of the redemptive power resident in Christ."

3. Noel Polk, "The Textual History of Faulkner's *Requiem for a Nun*," *Proof* 4 (1975): 125 (hereafter cited as "Textual History"). In an earlier essay ("Alec Holston's Lock and the Founding of Jefferson," *Mississippi Quarterly* 24 [1971]: 247–69), Polk had anticipated this stern dismissal of the religious element in *Requiem.* His apt characterization of Pettigrew is followed by an arresting comparison: Pettigrew, he says,

> is, in short, an abstractionist, a man who, like Gavin Stevens and Nancy Mannigoe, in the dramatic portions of *Requiem* . . . , has allowed an abstract code (no matter how theoretically good) to rigidify and take over a life situation. He is simply not morally able to handle the very kind of freedom [which the U.S. stands for] . . . since it would require of him moral deliberation, moral choice, and moral responsibility. [P. 259]

But regularly the abstractionists in Faulkner's fiction—Horace Benbow, Quentin Compson, Isaac McCaslin, Gavin Stevens—fail because they are in the grip of the dream of antebellum chivalry, which rigidifies and takes precedence over actual life. This is the dream shared by the "unvanquished" old ladies of Jefferson (as described in the prose History of *Requiem*), to whom Polk refers in another of his essays—"Faulkner's 'The Jail' and the Meaning of Cecilia Farmer," *Mississippi Quarterly* 25 (1972): 305–25:

> Their indomitability is . . . an unwillingness to admit the defeat of their antebellum ideals and ways of life. Their subsequent attempts to maintain, in the face of progress and the modern world, the old ways, the old standards, is in fact, then, an attempt to impose an abstraction, a code of behavior which is no longer viable, upon a life situation which will not allow it. They are thus negative, life-denying [P. 318].

Quentin, Gavin, et al. may at times also appeal to the Christian code, but their failure is not so much the result of their rigidifying that code as it is their lack of courage to act as that code bids. Characters who can act faithfully as that code bids—Dilsey, for example, or here Nancy—do not fail because of adherence to that code. It is when the Christian code is rigidified and perverted, warped and misapplied (as in the case of Mr. McEachern, Joanna Burden, Doc Hines, in *Light in August*) that the real mischief occurs.

4. Mr. Polk's essay on "Holston's Lock" seems also to offer a corrective contradiction to this view that Gavin's dictum is wrong:

> So only the man who is not afraid of evil—that is, reality—can hope to foster progress. Thomas Jefferson clearly broke the law which he himself had helped to frame . . . in order to purchase Louisiana . . . an act which [had the most positive effects]. Jefferson, then, broke the law in order to preserve it. In this sense evil is necessary to society; civilization rests upon man's rapacity. [Pp. 265–66]

That sounds rather similar to the dictum about good coming out of evil; if the abrogation of the Constitution was a means to a greater end, it does seem to share something with Nancy's murder of Temple's baby.

5. Broughton, *"Requiem for a Nun:* No Part in Rationality," pp. 761–62.

6. Mr. Polk points out that in Faulkner's various revisions of *Requiem*, Gavin Stevens becomes less and less attractive as his driving Temple into a corner becomes increasingly unsympathetic. If Gavin's moral rigidity and uncharitableness constitute an evil, one might yet argue that Faulkner is also making Gavin act out his own claim that good can and must come out of evil: that *evil* of Gavin's harshness has undeniably contributed to the *good* of Temple's development as she learns to accept responsibility for Nancy's sacrifice. (See "Textual History," pp. 120 ff.)

7. There is obviously significance in Faulkner's choice of the name itself, as it suggests the illegitimate descent of Nancy—from the left hand, *la main gauche*.

Chapter XII

1. This is not to be misconstrued as a sign of generosity in Flem; it is rather a typically selfish act, a means of creating indebtedness that will bolster and secure his own position.

2. *The Town* (New York: Random House, Vintage Books, 1957), p. 28; subsequent references will be to this edition and will be given parenthetically in the text.

3. See for example herein, Chapter 10, note 1.

4. Elizabeth M. Kerr touches on this idea in her *Yoknapatawpha: Faulkner's Little Postage Stamp of Native Soil* (New York: Fordham University Press, 1969), p. 151, but gives it a somewhat different turn: "When Flem Snopes got control and took over handling the finances [of Varner's general store in Frenchman's Bend], there was no change from honest to dishonest . . . but merely a change from a careless but amiable dishonesty on the part of Will and Jody Varner, with a genial way of exacting interest on what was sold on credit, to a strict but inhuman accuracy in all money matters on the part of Flem." Cf. my discussion herein, pp. 154–56, of Flem's takeover of Varner's store, etc.

5. Brooks, *The Yoknapatawpha Country*, p. 212.

Chapter XIII

1. *The Tragic Mask,* p. 72.
2. *The Mansion* (New York: Random House, Vintage Books, 1959), p. 99;
   subsequent references will be to this edition and will be given parenthetically in the text.
3. *Yoknapatawpha Country,* p. 17.
4. Cf. *Yoknapatawpha Country,* p. 242: "Mink . . . at last can come to terms
   with the earth, and now, as fully spent as any salmon that has fought
   its way up over the falls and back into its native stream, Mink lies at
   ease—lies on the earth itself, content to see what the earth will do
   with him."
5. Chick's un-Swinburnian modification helps recall Ratliff's remark on
   Gavin's not being born "into one of them McCarron separate covers"
   but rather "into that fragile and what you might call gossamer-sinewed
   envelope of boundless and hopeless aspiration Old Moster give him"
   (*Mansion,* p. 128); like the fearful preachers, Gavin must confess "Thou
   hast conquered."
6. *Yoknapatawpha Country,* pp. 197–204.
7. Chick's version of Gavin's "case" is more poetic and kinder to Gavin
   usually, but its import is essentially the same. He wonders if his uncle
   had ever got Linda's clothes off, "and if he didn't, what happened,
   what was wrong" (*Mansion,* p. 352); and then proposes that "maybe his
   uncle's luck and fate was simply to be cursed with less of fire and heat
   than Paris and Manfred de Spain; to simply have taken simple fear
   from that first one time (if his uncle really had got them off that first
   one time) and fled while he still had life. You know: the spider lover
   wise enough with age or cagey enough to . . . fling himself free . . .
   keeping his husk, his sac, his life [only]" (p. 360).
8. *Faulkner in the University,* p. 282.
9. *Faulkner in the University,* p. 283.
10. *Faulkner in the University,* p. 90.
11. And we know that Faulkner at one time intended to begin the Snopes
    trilogy with the material of this story, published in 1939 as "Barn
    Burning." See Meriwether, *The Literary Career,* pp. 61–62, and Mill-
    gate, *Achievement,* p. 185.

Chapter XIV

1. *Essays, Speeches,* p. 120. Cf. the comment Faulkner made to Loïc Bouvard in 1952: "I have tremendous faith in man, in spite of all his faults,
   his limitations." The interview, translated, is reprinted in James B.
   Meriwether and Michael Millgate, eds., *The Lion in the Garden: Interviews
   with William Faulkner, 1926–1962* (New York: Random House, 1968)
   (hereafter cited as *Lion in the Garden*); see p. 71 for the quotation.
2. While Faulkner seems to have explicitly rejected the term, he obviously
   accepted the concept in his answers to a questioner at the University of

Virginia. Faulkner began by explaining his idea of the type of man who will prevail:

> A. . . . there's always someone . . . that will never stop trying to get rid of Snopes.
> Q. . . . A remnant?
> A. No, the impulse to eradicate Snopes is in my opinion so strong that it selects its champions when the crisis comes. When the battle comes it always produces a Roland. It doesn't mean that they will get rid of Snopes or the impulse which produces Snopes, but always there's something in man that don't like Snopes and objects to Snopes and if necessary will step in to keep Snopes from doing some irreparable harm.

See *Faulkner in the University*, p. 34.

3. Introduction, Malcolm Cowley, ed., *The Portable Faulkner* (New York: Viking Press, 1946), p. 5. Cowley had written to Faulkner, August 9, 1945: "The chief thing is that your Mississippi work hangs together beautifully as a whole—as an entire creation there is nothing like it in American literature"; see Malcolm Cowley, ed., *The Faulkner-Cowley File: Letters and Memories 1944-1962* (New York: Viking Press, 1966), p. 24 (hereafter cited as *File*). Cowley there makes quite clear his intention in putting together the *Portable Faulkner:* "I still feel . . . that Faulkner's genius was not primarily novelistic, in the usual sense of that word, but rather epic or bardic. My purpose in 1945 was to reveal that epic quality by emphasizing what others had overlooked: the scope and force and interdependence of his work as a whole" (*File*, p. 31). Faulkner's re-markable response of April 23, 1946, to Cowley's achievement is reveal-ing: "The job is splendid. Damn you to hell anyway. . . . By God, I didn't know myself what I had tried to do, and how much I had suc-ceeded" (*File*, pp. 90–91).

4. A notable exception is my former student, Mrs. Joanne Vanish Creigh-ton, whose *William Faulkner's Craft of Revision* (Detroit: Wayne State University Press, 1977), is an excellent study of Faulkner's revision of short pieces for incorporation into the novels. There, Mrs. Creighton offers this acute perception: "the Yoknapatawpha County fiction be-comes a kind of 'meta-novel' that exists above and beyond the individual stories and novels which inform it. . ." (p. 12).

5. *Faulkner: A Biography*, p. 301. In the interview with Loïc Bouvard, Faulkner coupled Balzac significantly with two others: "I was influenced by Flaubert and by Balzac. . . . And I feel very close to Proust. After I had read *A la Recherche du Temps Perdu* I said 'This is it!'—and I wished I had written it myself." See *Lion in the Garden*, p. 72.

6. Interview with Cynthia Grenier, *Lion in the Garden*, p. 217. It is encour-aging also to recall that the late Edmund Wilson was moved to make the association with Balzac in his review of *Intruder in the Dust:* "the book . . . sustains, like its predecessors, the polymorphous, polychromatic vitality, the poetic truth to experience, of Faulkner's Balzacian chronicle of Yok-

napatawpha County." From *Classics and Commercials* (1950), reprinted in Robert Penn Warren, ed., *Faulkner*, p. 225.

7. Interview with Jean Stein vanden Heuvel, *Lion in the Garden*, pp. 251, 255.
8. Introduction, *Portable Faulkner*, p. 8.
9. *Faulkner in the University*, p. 90 (April 25, 1957); see also p. 201 (June 5, 1957): "I thought of these people [the Snopeses] thirty years ago. . . ."
10. Quoted in Blotner, *Biography*, pp. 1006–8.
11. Consider the perceptive observation of George Marion O'Donnell, one of the earliest serious critics of Faulkner: "In Mr. Faulkner's mythology there are two kinds of characters; they are Sartorises or Snopeses, whatever the family names may be. And in the spiritual geography of Mr. Faulkner's work there are two worlds: the Sartoris world and the Snopes world. In all of his successful books, he is exploring the two worlds in detail, dramatizing the inevitable conflict between them." From *The Kenyon Review*, Summer 1939, reprinted in Linda Wagner, ed., *Four Decades of Faulkner Criticism* (East Lansing: Michigan State University Press, 1973), p. 84.
12. *Sartoris*, p. 147.
13. At the University of Virginia Faulkner promised that the completion of the Snopes trilogy would involve the emergence of "an accepted type of Snopes" (*Faulkner in the University*, p. 283); that is fulfilled in the development of Wall Snopes. He also promised that "Snopeses will destroy themselves" (*Faulkner in the University*, p. 282); that is graphically realized in Mink's slaying of Flem.
14. *Faulkner in the University*, p. 286.

Index